— THIRD EDITION —

NEW YORK CITY'S
BEST
PUBLIC MIDDLE SCHOOLS

A PARENTS' GUIDE

D1188356

— THIRD EDITION —

NEW YORK CITY'S BEST PUBLIC MIDDLE SCHOOLS

A PARENTS' GUIDE

Clara Hemphill

and the staff of Insideschools.org

TEACHERS COLLEGE PRESS

TEACHERS COLLEGE
COLUMBIA UNIVERSITY
NEW YORK AND LONDON

Published by Teachers College Press, 1234 Amsterdam Avenue, New York, NY 10027

Library of Congress Cataloging-in-Publication Data

Hemphill, Clara, 1953–
    New York City's best public middle schools : a parents' guide / Clara Hemphill. — 3rd ed.
    p. cm.
Includes bibliographical references and index.
ISBN 978-0-8077-4910-4 (pbk. : alk. paper)
    1. Middle schools—New York (State)—New York—Directories.
    2. Middle school education—New York (State)—New York.
    3. School choice—New York (State)—New York. I. Title.
    L903.N7H46 2008
    373.747'1—dc22   2008020071

ISBN 978-0-8077-4910-4 (paper)

Printed on acid-free paper
Manufactured in the United States of America

15 14 13 12 11 10 09 08   8 7 6 5 4 3 2 1

**To Allison,
as she completes middle school,
and to Max**

CONTENTS

Contents

Contents

PREFACE TO THE THIRD EDITION

When I wrote the last edition of this book, my son was just about to enter middle school. Now that he's in high school and my daughter is entering 8th grade, I can report with confidence that it *is* possible to get a superior education in a New York City public middle school.

Sadly, the city still has many bad middle schools. Only a few neighborhoods have good zoned middle schools; in most of the city, children must apply to special programs, "option schools," or "schools of choice" to be ensured a first-rate education. The admissions process is an exercise in aggravation and can be a frightening gauntlet for 10-year-olds and their parents. But with research and a good dose of luck, you may feel, as I do, that you've hit the jackpot in your children's schooling.

This third edition offers completely revised profiles of 74 schools, including 10 all-new entries. In Manhattan, Columbia University has opened a new secondary school specializing in math, science, and engineering (p. 101). In the Bronx, the Urban Assembly School for Applied Math and Science is off to a promising start (p. 125).

In Brooklyn, the Urban Assembly Academy of Arts and Letters (p. 144) and KIPP AMP Charter School (p. 166) are new since the last edition of this book was published. A long-beleaguered school, MS 88 (p.157), has made such as dramatic turnaround that I decided to include it. Middle College High School at Medgar Evers College has added a middle school and changed its name to Medgar Evers Preparatory School; it, too, is included here for the first time (p. 163).

In Queens, children have traditionally gone to their zoned neighborhood middle schools. However, a number of "schools of choice" have opened in the past few years. Included here are the Scholars Academy (p. 224) on the Rockaway Peninsula and three new schools in Flushing: World Journalism, East-West School of International Studies, and Queens School of Inquiry (pp. 206, 208, 210). I also added a profile of a nice zoned neighborhood school, JHS 194 (p. 214), because many Queens parents are choosing between their zoned school and the new schools. (I removed a few schools that were in the second edition either because they didn't live up to their initial promise or because other, newer schools seemed stronger.)

The Department of Education has been creating new middle school programs with dizzying speed. There are now some 533 programs that serve children in the middle school years—up from about 300 in 2004, when the second edition was published. Some of these have been created by breaking large schools into small ones as part of an attempt to make large, unruly schools safer and more intimate. Some are elementary schools to which middle school grades have been added, making them into K–8 schools. Others are combined middle and high schools serving grades 6–12.

Alas, many of these new schools are only marginally better than the ones they replace. But a few represent a real opportunity for children. This book will help you navigate a complex and constantly changing landscape to find a school that's right for your child.

—Clara Hemphill

ACKNOWLEDGMENTS

The book was a collaborative effort. It could not have been completed without the staff of Insideschools.org—the free online guide to New York City's public schools sponsored by Advocates for Children of New York. Insideschools.org staffers have visited nearly all of the city's 533 middle school programs, including the ones we decided not to include in this book. I visited nearly all of the Manhattan schools and about half of the Brooklyn schools listed here; the Insideschools.org staff visited the rest and shared their notes with me. Thanks to Insideschools.org director Pamela Wheaton and to reporters Judith Baum, Philissa Cramer, Nicole LaRosa, Catherine Man, Jacquie Wayans, Vanessa Witenko, Helen Zelon, and Laura Zingmond. Special thanks to Laura Zingmond, who fact-checked the manuscript and compiled the index.

My editor at Teachers College Press, Brian Ellerbeck, and publisher Carole Saltz, both public school parents, were enthusiastic backers of the project. The TC Press production staff, particularly Karl Nyberg, put the book out in record time, while the marketing and publicity staff worked hard to promote it.

The generosity of the Department of Education officials, principals, and teachers cannot be overstated. They opened their doors to us, allowed us to sit in on classes and to write candidly about everything we saw, the good and the bad.

My husband, Robert Snyder, and children, Max and Allison, tolerated months of my distracted attention as I struggled to complete the project, which has come to be known in our house as the Book That Never Ends. They are, as always, my greatest love and inspiration.

—Clara Hemphill

New York City Department of Education
Map of Instructional Divisions

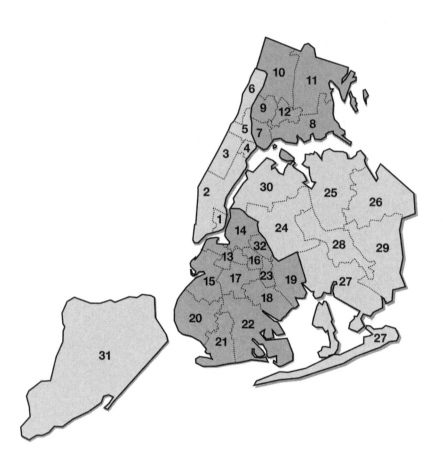

INTRODUCTION

If you're looking for a good public middle school anywhere in New York City's five boroughs, this book will help you make an informed choice. New York City middle schools get a lot of bad press—much of it justified. Far too many middle schools are chaotic, gloomy places where both the teachers and the pupils are demoralized and alienated. There are some gems, however, and in a city as big as New York, even a small percentage of gems add up to enough good schools to fill this book. New York City's best public schools offer unusual opportunities and programs that are simply unavailable anywhere else.

Where else but in a New York City public middle school could your child hold his or her 8th-grade science fair at the American Museum of Natural History? (Salk School of Science.) Or study drama with a Broadway actor? (The Professional Performing Arts School.) Or play chamber music at Lincoln Center? (Mark Twain School for the Gifted and Talented.)

It's true that even the best schools face formidable obstacles: Many buildings are in a poor state of repair; class sizes often top 32; budgets are tight. But the quality of teaching—at least at the best schools—is comparable to that of the best suburban or private schools.

The city's public schools attract teachers who are committed to urban education as a profession, who believe that equal educational opportunity is the cornerstone of democracy. The best teachers have thought carefully about how to bring children of different races and social classes together and about how to tailor instruction for children with different talents and different ways of seeing things. Those who are successful are real masters of their craft—as good as the best you can find anywhere.

The best teachers have kept up with new research on adolescent development and have continued their own training with graduate courses at local schools, such as Bank Street College of Education in Manhattan. In a city that changes as rapidly as New York does, teachers can't afford to be complacent. If they're good, they're always adjusting and readjusting their strategies.

The best middle school teachers have a special affinity and affection for kids this age. Rather than roll their eyes and moan about raging hormones, these teachers will tell you why they'd rather teach 7th-graders than anyone else on earth.

"They're crossing that bridge between childhood and adulthood, and there's this great chasm and there's a rickety little bridge like in *Raiders of the Lost Ark*," said Ira Gurkin, who was principal of MS 141 in the Riverdale section of the Bronx for many years. "And I'm standing over on the other side of the bridge, like in *The Catcher in the Rye*, saying, 'Come on over.' It takes them 3 years to cross that bridge, and we're here to catch them. They call me certifiable, but I love it."

Early adolescence is a time of tremendous physical and emotional change. Children from age 11 to 14 grow faster than at any other time except infancy. The onset of puberty brings with it exciting and confusing sensations and emotions. Friendships become more important than ever. Children begin to turn away from adults and rely more on their peers. These can be difficult years, even for a child in a good school. In a bad school these years can be disastrous—both socially and academically.

Most traditional junior high schools, with enrollments of 1,200 or more and class changes every 43 minutes, have not served children well—in New York City or anywhere else. Children in early adolescence—perhaps even more than younger children—need a school that offers them a sense of community, a feeling of belonging, and a few adults who know them well. Most traditional junior high schools offer none of these.

The notion that children this age are merely miniature high school students—as the name "junior high school" implies—can lead to inappropriate teaching practices and potentially dangerous social situations. Many young adolescents are incapable of switching gears five times a day, from English to math to social studies. Teachers who have five classes of 30 pupils each—150 pupils in all—are unable to take more than a passing interest in any one child. The results, too often, are low levels of academic achievement and high levels of bad behavior: truancy, playground fistfights, or precocious sexual activity.

Luckily, research into adolescent development over the past 2 decades has sparked a revolution in how schools teach 6th-, 7th-, and 8th-graders. New York City has been in the forefront of a national reform movement to transform traditional junior high schools into what are called "middle schools." This movement is based on the research of the Carnegie Council on Adolescent Development, which published a 1989 report called *Turning Points: Preparing American Youth for the 21st Century*. In New York, the Middle School Initiative spurred the creation of dozens of new, small schools in the 1990s and helped reorganize dozens of existing larger schools in ways that made them safer and more humane.

In schools organized according to the "middle school philosophy," kids may stay with one teacher for 1½ hours or more, instead of changing classes every 43 minutes. A teacher may have two classes of 30 pupils—60 students in all, rather than 150. A teacher may help children with study skills, such as taking notes and organizing homework, instead of concentrating exclusively on the subject matter to be taught. Teachers are encouraged to speak to children about personal or social problems and not to focus exclusively on academic performance. These schools organize the day in ways to give teachers blocks of time to talk to one another and to individual students. Teachers work in teams, organizing their lessons together. Children stay in one wing or on one floor for most of the day—effectively creating a small school within a large building.

The most obvious and immediate advantage to the middle school model is safety. When the anonymity of a large school is replaced with the intimacy of a small school, and when everyone knows everyone and children have close contact with a few attentive adults, children behave better. Schools that have adopted the Middle School Initiative have shown, almost universally, improved safety records and attendance rates. Race relations—often fractious in traditional junior high schools—seem to improve when small groups of kids learn to work out their differences with the help of a few adults who know them well.

The research on early adolescence has offered new ideas about teaching methods, as well as new ways of organizing the day. A good middle school looks more like an elementary school than a traditional junior high school, with colorful bulletin boards instead of bare walls, tables in groups instead of desks in rows, and kids working on group projects instead of listening to lectures. The curriculum isn't watered down—if anything, the subject matter is more advanced than what most of today's parents learned at this age—but material is presented in ways that are sensitive to the kids' level of maturity.

Rather than struggle through pencil-and-paper exercises on similar triangles in math class, for example, kids might be out on the playground estimating the height of a skyscraper from the length of the shadow it casts. Programs organized according to the "middle school philosophy" emphasize projects kids can touch and feel, in addition to readings from textbooks. Perhaps most important, they use approaches that can satisfy children's yearning to be grown-up in ways that are more appropriate than wearing makeup or doing drugs. Middle schools organize community service projects, in which children volunteer at centers for the elderly, tutor younger children, or clean up their neighborhood—projects that build a sense of belonging, both within the school and within the community.

Good middle schools accommodate young adolescents the way they *are*, rather than battling to get children to conform to some idealized norm. If kids this age have trouble sitting still, good schools organize the day so that they can move around a bit in class. If kids like to talk to their friends, good schools get them to work together in small groups rather than asking them to listen passively to their teacher. Good schools make sure that each kid has at least one adult who will be alert to signs of trouble with schoolwork, family, or friends. Some schools go so far as to organize weekend camping trips for their pupils—supervised by teachers—to help develop what they call "positive peer groups."

Good middle school teachers manage to get on children's wavelengths. One science teacher told me that she knows kids this age love disasters, so she spends lots of time talking about earthquakes and tidal waves. A history teacher, knowing that kids this age love descriptions of blood and gore, gave a memorable description of the guillotine in the French Revolution. Good middle school teachers have the warmth of an elementary teacher and the specialized knowledge of a high school teacher. Find a school with such teachers and the rollercoaster ride of adolescence can be manageable—and maybe even fun—for both you and your child.

Getting Started

In many parts of the city, children are assigned to a **zoned** or **neighborhood middle school** based on their address. To find out the name of your zoned school, call the City of New York at 311 or (212) NEW-YORK, or check the Department of Education website (http://schools.nyc.gov). If the school for which your child is zoned is satisfactory, you may begin and end your search there. Your child will automatically be admitted.

For many parents, however, choosing a middle school isn't that easy. In large swaths of Manhattan and Brooklyn, students are not assigned to zoned middle schools and *must* fill out applications listing their choices. In many neighborhoods, moreover, the zoned schools are dreary, or even dangerous.

If you want to investigate all your options, you'll need to look further. New York City has an extensive—if convoluted—system of middle school choice. Dozens of schools accept children from outside their immediate neighborhood, and some accept children from all five boroughs.

This system of school choice is both a curse and a blessing. The application process is time-consuming and agonizing for both parents and children. But there is also a surprising array of possibilities: schools that specialize in music, drama, dance, or science; small schools where the principal knows every child and large schools with impressive orchestras or athletics programs; accelerated schools that allow children to get a head-start on high school and nurturing schools that engage kids who are alienated by academics.

Navigating the system is a major headache, and it doesn't look as though it's going to get better any time soon. The New York City Department of Education has been shaken up by a series of radical changes that began when Mayor Michael Bloomberg wrested control of the schools from the discredited Board of Education in 2002. At first, the mayor combined (or attempted to combine) the 32 semiautonomous school districts into 10 regions and centralized the bureaucracy under his schools chancellor. Then, in 2007, he reorganized the system yet again, dismantling the offices that he had set up in 2003, granting each principal autonomy in areas such as budget and curriculum while centralizing control of admissions and placement. He set up 15 "borough enrollment offices," which are supposed to answer questions about middle school choice (see http://schools.nyc.gov/enrollment). In most cases, the central offices of the Department of Education—not the districts or the individual principals—now decide where children are assigned.

The changes may ultimately make for a more rational and equitable school system, but the transition has been frustrating. Parents don't know whom they are supposed to call to get information. Phones ring unanswered, voice mailboxes are full, and the live humans who do answer the telephones are often uninformed about basic procedures. Ask four people the same question and you may get four different answers. If you're lucky, your elementary school guidance counselor will keep you informed about the admissions process. But here are some basics to get you started.

Despite the mayor's reorganization, the city is still divided into 32 districts. Your child is entitled to a seat in the district in which you live. (If your child attends an elementary school in a different district from the one in which you live, you may choose to send your child to a middle school in either district.) So your first step is to find out what district you live in and what your options are there. (See the map on page xiv, or call 311 or 212-

5

NEW-YORK.) A number of districts—including District 3 on the West Side of Manhattan and District 15 in Brooklyn—have abolished zoned middle schools entirely. In these districts, all children must choose a middle school from a range of special programs and schools organized around a theme. Children are guaranteed a spot somewhere in the district—but not necessarily at their first-choice school. Most districts publish directories of middle school options, available from your child's elementary school guidance counselor or from a borough enrollment center.

Most districts have middle school fairs in January. These offer an opportunity to meet principals and students at the schools in your district. The fairs tend to be very crowded, but they are a good place to ask questions and get a feel for the philosophy of a school. It's also reassuring to see how nice, presentable, and articulate middle school kids can be.

In addition to any options in your district, you may want to consider schools that accept applications from all five boroughs. For example, Hunter College High School, the Institute for Collaborative Education, and the Professional Performing Arts School, all in Manhattan, admit children who live anywhere in the city. Charter schools (publicly funded, tuition-free schools that operate independently of the Department of Education) also admit children who live anywhere in the city, though they give priority to students residing in the same district as the school.

For most children, the search for a middle school begins in the fall of their 5th-grade year because most middle schools start in 6th grade. Tours for prospective parents may start in October and continue through January. Applications are due by the beginning of February.

Call each school directly to book a tour. Each school has a "parent coordinator" charged with outreach to parents and the community. The parent coordinator is usually the best person to call to arrange a tour.

Some schools will tell you they don't offer tours and that parents aren't allowed to visit classrooms. For these, consider attending a PTA meeting or a school event such as a concert or play. If all else fails, you can always chat with kids outside the school at dismissal time.

What Are Your Options?

There are different kinds of schools serving kids in 6th, 7th, and 8th grades. An old-fashioned formula that's recently become popular again is the school that houses children in kindergarten through the 8th grade. Proponents of these **K–8 schools** say it's easier to adjust to early adolescence when you're with kids you've known your whole life. K–8 schools provide continuity and stability at a time when kids need it the most. Proponents also say young adolescents tend to behave better when they can act as big brothers and sisters to little kids in the school.

Many of the K–8 schools feel like small towns in the city. They may not have the fancy equipment of a large junior high school, such as science labs or woodworking shops. The teachers tend to be licensed as "common branch" (elementary) rather than as specialists (high school). This may mean that they are less likely to have, say, a high-level science class. But many parents happily trade the fancy equipment and degrees of specialization for the safety and coziness of a K–8 school. These tend to be neighborhood schools, and it's often difficult for children from outside the school's zone to be admitted. But if you simply love a particular school, it's worth a try.

Most common in the city today are the **large middle schools** for grades 6, 7, and 8. These tend to be in buildings originally constructed for 1,000 children or more. Many have been divided into minischools, teams, or "houses" that give children and teachers the feeling of a smaller school. Rather than go from the 1st floor for English to the 3rd floor for math and back to the 2nd floor for science (as is typical in a traditional junior high school), children stay within their house or team for most of the day.

The big buildings tend to have good facilities—science labs, a large library, a gym—and a wide array of special programs, such as a band, an orchestra, organized sports. Some children at this age feel claustrophobic in a K–8 school, or in a very small middle school, and are ready to test their wings in the larger world. For them, a larger school offers many opportunities. These tend to be neighborhood schools, although many have room for children from outside their zone.

There are a growing number of **small middle schools**, with 200 to 400 pupils. These are often located on the top floor of an elementary school or in a separate wing of a larger middle school building. They share a cafeteria and a gym with the main school but have their own administration, their own admissions process, and their own distinct personality. They tend to be even more intimate and cozy than K–8 schools. Every teacher knows every child's name; no one gets lost. The staff, by and large, has chosen to teach middle school, and many have a particular affinity for this age group. There is one possible disadvantage of a very small school: The loss of one teacher can decimate a whole department. If the biology teacher takes a maternity leave, the school may have to do without biology for a few months. They may not have a sports or music department. But many parents happily trade the extras for the intimacy and personal attention that a small school provides. These tend to be unzoned schools rather than neighborhood schools. Children must fill out an application to be admitted. Some are open only to children living in their districts; others accept children citywide.

Secondary schools, with grades 6–12 or 7–12, offer continuity as well as the opportunity to use high school facilities. The more years a child spends in one building, the easier it is to build a sense of community. A high school student can pay a visit to an old 7th-grade teacher for moral support or advice. A 7th-grader can easily see how the lessons he or she is learning now will be useful in later years. Parents say it's easier to build a PTA in a school where children spend 6 or 7 years, and a strong PTA can help the administration build an effective school. Benefits include the facilities—such as a sophisticated library and an advanced science lab—and the ability for advanced pupils to take high school courses.

One possible drawback: There is a tendency for secondary school teachers to treat all children as if they were in high school, rather than tailoring their classes to the maturity of middle school kids.

The exposure to older high school students can be both an advantage and a disadvantage. Middle school children can be inspired and motivated by seeing high school students hard at work. Or, if the high school is disorganized, the rowdiness of the big kids can be threatening. (In my experience, the size of the school determines safety more than the age of the kids does. Small schools tend to be safer—however old or young the kids may be.)

There are also a handful of **K–12 schools**, where children spend their entire pre-university education in one building. Talk about continuity!

If your child has had high scores on standardized tests in elementary school (generally, the 85th percentile or better in reading), he or she may be offered a spot in a **Special Progress (SP)** or an accelerated program at your neighborhood school. You may also want to investigate the SP track at schools outside your neighborhood, as well as at various schools for the gifted. Years ago, the SP tracks were set up to speed able children through junior high school in 2 years rather than 3. (The rationale was never clear to me, but one SP alumna explained: "Why would you spend 5 minutes more in junior high school than absolutely necessary?") Now, SP refers simply to the top track in a school in which children are grouped by ability. All children stay in middle school for 3 years. However, many SP students take high school–level math and science courses, called Regents, in 8th grade. Some districts also have a track that's even more accelerated, called "gifted" or Special Progress Enrichment (SPE). Some have "honors" classes within SP.

For years, public schools functioned as a fierce sorting mechanism, separating the top students from everyone else. The top students, in SP, were offered college-prep courses. Everyone else was offered an education that often amounted to second-rate vocational training. In some districts, that's still the case. If you live in one of these, your choice is simple: Get your child into SP, or get out of the district.

Happily, some educators are now committed to educating all children, not just the top 15%. Some schools have eliminated tracking altogether, and others have found ways to make the effects of tracking less pernicious for those in the lower tracks. If you're fortunate enough to live in a district where this is the case, you may want to consider a school that refuses to group children by ability—even if your child is a high-achiever. Some parents are glad to avoid the competition that's often found in SP classes. Some feel that the social and emotional issues that young adolescents face are such that it's better not to pile on the academic work at this stage. SP classes are often gigantic—with 35 pupils or more—and some parents feel it's a worthwhile trade-off to have a smaller class with children of various abilities. And some are attracted by a nonacademic program—such as a first-rate drama department—in a school that refuses to group children by ability.

Children in SP classes need to maintain a certain average in order to stay in the track, and sometimes the pressure to keep up with classmates can be stressful. I spoke to one mother who was thrilled with her son's middle school—until his grades dropped and he was bumped into a non-SP class. He was so demoralized by the experience that he transferred to another school.

That said, there are some advantages to grouping children by ability in the middle school years. A good teacher can reach children with various abilities in any class, but the wider the range the more difficult it becomes. As children become older, the gap between the top kids and those who are struggling becomes larger, and it's very difficult for even an experienced teacher to bridge it. Some children are ready for high school–level work in 8th grade, and it seems to be a mistake not to let them take the courses that interest them. Some very high-achieving children who have been bored in their neighborhood elementary school are thrilled to finally have classmates who are as bright as they are. Even if the teachers are standard-issue, having very smart classmates can offer the stimulation that bright kids crave.

In addition to SP classes within a neighborhood middle school, the city offers a number of **selective schools** devoted entirely to children who are high-achievers. Some of these have a special entrance exam. Others don't have an exam but do have a minimum requirement in terms of scores on standardized tests. Selective schools accept children on the basis of a written application and an interview. Some schools accept children on the basis of **artistic or musical talent**, or a combination of academic achievement and artistic talent.

Theme schools offer a concentration in a particular subject area, such as performing arts, journalism, or science. Admissions may be by lottery, by exam, or by audition. The best of these offer first-rate instruction in all subject areas, while offering a little extra in the area of the school's concentration. In general, I believe middle school is too early for children to specialize. If you're considering a theme school for your child, make sure all subject areas are strong. A school that has a particular emphasis on art, for example, should also offer solid instruction in science.

Magnet schools receive special federal grants to encourage racial integration. These schools use the extra money to provide special classes around a theme—such as journalism or law. The hope is that the extra programs will attract children of different races from outside the neighborhood, like a magnet.

If Your Child Needs Extra Help: Special Education

Special education is available for children who have disabilities that keep them from functioning in a regular classroom without extra help. At each school we visited for this book, we asked about accommodations for children with special needs. Some such children are completely integrated into general education classes and receive special services from extra teachers assigned to help them; some are segregated in "self-contained" classrooms. Many schools have introduced Collaborative Team Teaching (CTT), in which two teachers, one of whom is certified in special education, work together in a class that mixes special needs and general education students. These classes typically have 8 to 10 special needs students and 20 general education students. When these are successful, both the general education students and those with special needs benefit from more individual attention. Particularly good special education programs are listed in the Quick-Reference Guide. For details on your child's legal rights and tips on how to navigate the special education bureaucracy, look at Insideschools.org.

Even if your child functions well in a general education class, it's worth taking a look at special education in any school you're considering. How a school treats kids with special needs is a good indication of how it treats any child who is struggling, or who doesn't fit the mold. Schools that value students with special needs, that identify and encourage their strengths and include them whenever possible in activities with general education pupils, are likely to be schools that are gentle and accommodating places for all children. Schools that keep special education children in the basement and exclude them from activities with other kids may be punitive and disagreeable places for other children as well.

Many of the city's very old school buildings don't have wheelchair access, but those that do are listed in the index.

Things to Think About Before You Visit

You'll need to visit schools before you decide on your first choice—and on what you consider adequate if your child isn't admitted to his or her first choice. But before you visit, you should arm yourself with as much information as you can. Check out www. Insideschools.org, a website written and edited by the same staff who wrote this book. This website, a project of Advocates for Children of New York, has profiles of every school in the city, based on our visits, as well as comments from parents, students, and teachers. (The website has short profiles of every school, whereas this book has longer entries on the best schools).

The Department of Education website (http://schools.nyc. gov) has voluminous statistical information about each school. Find data for each school by typing in a school name under "Find a School" and clicking "Statistics." The **school report card** has information such as reading and math scores, safety records, attendance, and the free-lunch rate. The **learning environment survey** will tell you if parents complain that their kids are being bullied, or if teachers say they are unhappy with the administration. The **quality review** assesses the quality of teaching and the principal's leadership, while the **progress report** gives a school a letter grade from A to F based on whether test scores are rising or falling. Warning: These reports are confusing and often contradictory, so take them with a grain of salt. If all you want is raw test scores, check out the Department of Education's division of assessment and accountability at http://schools.nyc.gov/daa.

The districts that offer **school choice** also have directories of their middle school programs; ask your elementary school guidance counselor to give you a copy or pick one up at one of the city's 15 borough enrollment centers. For addresses, call the office of student enrollment at (212) 374-2363 or check out http://schools.nyc.gov/enrollment. I've also listed the addresses in the introduction to each borough. Most districts have school fairs in January.

Location is your first consideration. If your child's school is close to home, he or she can make friends who live nearby. You can (maybe) volunteer in the school. Your child won't be tired out by a long commute. But if the local school isn't great, you'll probably consider schools in other neighborhoods. Middle school kids can handle the commute better than younger children can. Children will receive a free Metrocard for the subway or bus if they live beyond walking distance to their school.

Each entry in this book offers information on **admissions**. Zoned neighborhood schools accept all children who live in the zone, as designated by the district. Other schools may accept applications only from children who live in a particular district. A few schools accept applications from all five boroughs. Some accept children by lottery. Others interview children and ask them to write an essay explaining why they want to attend a particular school. Others require a formal entrance exam.

Each entry here also lists a school's **enrollment** and **typical class size**. Enrollment is the number of kids registered at the school. Typical class size is the size of an average academic class.

Overcrowding has been very serious in New York City public schools since the late 1980s, when large numbers of immigrants moved to the city and the children of the postwar baby boomers started to enter school. Some of the most successful schools are also the most overcrowded. Parents will fight to get their children into them, even if it means placing them in a class of 35 kids. The SP or advanced classes tend to be the most crowded. One way to get your child out of a giant class may be to investigate smaller schools that refuse to group children by ability. Some of these schools have kept their class size to 20 or 25.

Each entry also lists the percentage of children eligible for **free lunch**, a very rough indication of the poverty level of the pupils' families. The entries include the percentage of children in various **ethnic** and **racial groups** too. Citywide, middle schools are 39% Hispanic, 33% Black, 15% White, and 13% Asian.

I've given schools one to five stars based on their **reading and math scores** on 2007 standardized tests. Schools with one star (*) have 0% to 19% of children who score at or above the state standard. Those with two stars (**) have 20% to 39% at or above the state standard. Three stars (***) means 40% to 59% scored above the standard. Four stars (****) means 60% to 79% scored above the standard. Five stars (*****) means 80% to 100% scored above the standard. Some new schools don't have test data available. They are listed here as "NA" for not available.

These stars *don't* reflect how much I like a school, or how competent I found the teaching staff. They only reflect how well kids do on standardized tests. Some high-scoring schools are boring places where rote learning and memorization are the rule. Some low-scoring schools accept kids who are struggling and—with lots of work and inspired teaching—get them into college. Still, reading and math scores are at least one indication of how well a school is doing.

When you compare scores, be sure you're looking at schools with similar populations. It's not fair to compare a zoned school that accepts everyone in the neighborhood with a specialized school that requires children to pass an admissions test. A first-rate neighborhood school with three or four stars might challenge children of all academic abilities, whereas a "gifted" program with five stars might offer uninspired classes to children who are so motivated that they essentially teach themselves.

Another way to judge a school's achievement is by the quality of the **high schools** its graduates attend. Each school entry in this book lists the top three high schools chosen by its graduates, as reported by the Department of Education. (This information isn't applicable for secondary schools serving grades 6–12 or 7–12. You may want to ask how many children stay for grades 9–12. And it doesn't hurt to ask where their graduates go to college.)

Once you've looked at the statistics and drawn up a list of schools that interest you, it's time to look at them firsthand.

What to Look for on a Tour

Touring schools can be stressful and irritating or a lot of fun—depending on the school, your schedule, and the luck of the draw. If you can possibly arrange it, try to take a couple of mornings off work to visit schools—preferably with your child in tow. Children see things you don't see and ask good questions that won't occur to you.

Although some schools offer both daytime and evening tours, it's more interesting—and illuminating—to visit when classes are in session. If the schools you're interested in don't offer tours, you may have to improvise. Call the Parent Teacher Association and ask if you can attend a meeting. Say you want to be active in the PTA. (You might leave a message in the school's main office for someone in the PTA to telephone you. Middle school PTA presidents are so desperate for help they'll probably call you promptly.) Offer to volunteer in the school library, or to tutor kids through the Learning Leaders program (212-213-3370). Attend a concert or a dramatic production at the school. If all else fails, hang around the school at dismissal and talk to the kids.

Some schools offer "open houses" where hundreds of parents are jammed into an auditorium to watch a slide show and to listen to a presentation by the principal. This isn't really a tour, but it's better than nothing. Other schools offer tours with 40, 50, or even more parents. You'll have to stay with the pack and move rather briskly through classrooms. The more schools you visit, the more you'll learn, and the easier it will be for you to judge what's right for your child.

A word of caution: I went on tours for prospective parents when my son and daughter were in 5th grade. In every case, the school looked worse on the group tour than it did when I visited solo as part of my research for this book. There's something about having 50 extra people in your classroom that makes it hard for even the best teacher to teach. Moreover, public school budgets are stretched to the max, and the schools simply don't have the resources to offer small, individualized tours (or even, it seems, to answer telephone calls by prospective parents). So don't judge schools too harshly on these group tours. A disciplined school may look rigid and a relaxed school may look chaotic. If a school manages to impress you even on a group tour, it's probably very good indeed.

That said, tours are indispensable. The first thing you'll notice is the quality of the physical plant. A few schools are bright and cheery, but many are gloomy. Try to look beyond the peeling paint to the **quality of teaching**. Look at the kids' faces. Are they interested and engaged? Bored? Staring off vacantly into space? Are *you* interested in what the teacher is saying? Middle school kids tend to be squirmier than younger children, but a good teacher will hold their attention most of the time.

Do the kids' books look interesting? It's okay to have some textbooks, but I much prefer schools with **rich classroom libraries** —novels and biographies, science discovery books, colorful atlases, and original source materials such as diaries and historical documents. The more books, the better—in the classroom as well as in the school library. Schools that rely too heavily on textbooks are dull.

Are the walls bare, or are there lots of **bulletin boards with kids' work**? Look for examples of children's writing. Is the quality of work good? Are the art projects imaginative? Are the **bathrooms** unlocked? Are children allowed off school grounds for lunch? If so, it shows that the administration is confident of children's safety.

What's the noise level in the school? Chaos, of course, is bad news, but so is total silence. Kids should be talking to other kids and to grown-ups. Desks pushed together in small groups, or in a circle, encourage discussion among kids. If you see desks in rows, it often means the teacher tends to stand at the front and lecture to kids. That's not a bad method of instruction for part of the day, but you don't want it all day every day.

Even more important, grown-ups should be talking to one another. In a good middle school, teachers meet regularly to discuss everything from curriculum to individual students' progress and problems. If every teacher is locked in his or her classroom and never has scheduled time to meet with others, that's a bad sign.

Generally, there's time for questions after the tour. This is a good time to ask the principal or director to describe the school's **philosophy of education**. Like elementary schools, middle schools are divided into two camps: traditional and progressive. Some fall neatly into one camp or the other. Many are a blend of the two.

Traditional schools see their goal as transmitting a body of knowledge to children. They believe that children must learn certain dates in history, facts in geography, grammar, spelling rules, mathematical formulas, and scientific concepts. Traditional schools emphasize content—that is, the notion that certain material must be mastered. Traditional schools often emphasize preparation for standardized tests. If you see desks in rows, that's usually a sign of a traditional school.

Progressive schools, on the other hand, see their role as providing children with the tools they need to explore a new topic, to solve problems, and to conduct original research. Progressive schools emphasize process, that is, the method by which children learn to find the answers to a question. Rather than focusing on dates in history, a progressive school might encourage children to debate a topic such as "Was the arrival of Columbus in America a good thing or a bad thing?"—and require them to do research to support their case. Children might work out the Pythagorean theorem themselves—rather than having it presented to them by the teacher. Progressive schools try to transmit what they call "habits of mind"—the ability to think well and to work independently—rather than specific subject matter. Desks in groups or in a circle are often a sign of a progressive school.

Progressive and *traditional* are tricky words and different people use them to mean different things. If you ask a principal, "In what ways do you consider your school progressive, and in what ways is it traditional?" you might elicit an interesting answer. Some schools have embraced the "middle school philosophy"—a progressive idea—for the organization of a school, but have retained traditional teaching methods. Others have a traditional organization to the school day, but have introduced interdisciplinary teaching—a progressive idea. Many of the best schools mix elements of progressive and traditional teaching techniques.

The question-and-answer period after your tour is a good time to get a feel for **safety and security** at the school. You'll get a more revealing answer if you ask open-ended questions such as "How do you handle discipline?" rather than "Is your school safe?" Ask whether parents may visit the school and classes during the year. A school that welcomes parents is not afraid of what you might see on an impromptu visit.

Even at the best schools, you may hear about an occasional fistfight or a child selling drugs. No school is immune to these problems—not even the most exclusive private school or the fanciest suburban school. However, it is possible to find a school where such problems are rare and where those that do occur are dealt with promptly and effectively. Look for a school that confronts safety issues head-on rather than one that pretends nothing bad ever happens. Look for a principal who is respected and liked by the kids, who nips problems in the bud. For example, Jennifer Rehn, principal of the Robert F. Wagner Middle School (MS 167) on Manhattan's Upper East Side, and her senior staff are outside the school at dismissal every day, ensuring the kids leave safely. She even goes down to the platform of the nearest subway station to make sure children get on the train without any mishaps.

The kids I interviewed were more interested in the grown-ups' response to violence than in the violence itself. A school with a low suspension rate can feel very threatening if the principal is holed up in the office and the teachers are locked in their classrooms all day. A school with a somewhat higher suspension rate, on the other hand, can feel quite safe if the teachers and the administrators are highly visible during class changes and after school—and the kids feel the grown-ups care about what happens to them.

Small schools are generally safer than big schools. Schools that have wholesome ways for kids to have fun together—supervised school dances or camping trips—are less likely to have problems than schools that leave kids to organize their own social lives. Schools in which the principal spends lots of time talking to kids informally, in the halls or in the cafeteria, are generally safer than those in which the principal spends the day pushing papers in the office. One measure of school safety: Check out the school suspension rate at Insideschools.org (you can find the information on each school's profile).

Some parents are wowed by the beautiful facilities and equipment that they see on the tour and then are disappointed to find out that their child isn't allowed to use them. Be sure to ask. May everyone play in the orchestra, or only those who pass an audition? Is that beautiful botany lab for everyone, or only for the "gifted" students?

If classes are tracked (grouped by ability), ask how the school keeps the kids in the bottom tracks from feeling like second-class citizens. If classes are not tracked, how do they challenge the kids at the top? How does the school deal with kids who are strong in one subject but weak in another?

Perhaps the most difficult challenge for parents is **evaluating a new school**. Dozens of new programs have opened in the past decade, and parents are dizzy with the changes. How is it possible to judge a school with no track record, no test scores, not even a group of parents of whom one can ask advice? Is it better to send your child to a tried-and-true—but boring—junior high school, or to a new and exciting—but untested—minischool? There's no easy answer. But my advice is to look at the quality of the teaching and to listen carefully to the director's or principal's spiel. A principal with a vision he or she can articulate—and a plan to carry out that vision—has a chance of creating a good school. One who can only tell you he or she believes that punctuality is important, or one who parrots incomprehensible educational jargon, probably won't cut it. It doesn't hurt to ask the principal or director where he or she taught before. The quality and philosophy of that school may be a guide to what the new school will be like.

When it comes to establishing a new school, the quality of teaching is probably more important than the level of achievement of the kids. A new school with good teachers will, as word gets out, attract bright kids. A school with bright kids and boring teachers will probably always remain a school with bright kids and boring teachers.

What Kids Should Be Studying

Middle schools are so different from the junior high schools that most of today's parents attended that it's hard for most of us to judge what's good and what's not. In some cases, teaching methods have changed dramatically. In others, the material that teachers believe should be mastered is different. How can parents determine—particularly on a brief tour—if a school is doing what it should be doing?

One of the biggest differences between today's middle schools and yesterday's junior high schools is the way in which different subjects are integrated. No longer are history and English discrete subjects, taught by teachers who never speak to each other. Rather, the history teacher and the English teacher (and possibly the math and science teacher as well) will meet frequently and plan lessons together. Children might read *To Kill a Mockingbird* in

Questions to Ask on a Tour

- How has the school changed since you've been here?
- What changes would you like to see in the future?
- I hear the transition to middle school can be difficult. Does the school do anything to help new students adjust?
- How much homework do you think is appropriate for children this age?
- Where do most of your graduates go to high school?
- How do you handle behavior problems?
- Are the bathrooms locked, or may children use them whenever they please?
- May children leave the building for lunch?
- Do you have any after-school activities?
- How often to children have physical education?
- Are there any sports teams?
- What music and arts programs do you offer?
- How do you recruit new teachers?
- Do you offer any Regents-level courses in math or science?

English class while they discuss the civil rights movement in history class. The science and English teachers might jointly assign a term paper that they both grade, with the science teacher judging its content and the English teacher judging its style, organization, and grammar.

In **English** classes (also called English Language Arts, or ELA classes), students are less likely to read the classics and more likely to read contemporary fiction than they were a generation ago. You may still see old favorites such as *The Diary of Anne Frank* and Shakespeare's *Julius Caesar* on today's reading lists. But you're increasingly likely to see books such as *Holes*, Louis Sachar's story of a boy sent to a detention camp after being wrongly accused of stealing a pair of sneakers, and *Monster*, Walter Dean Myers's novel (written in the style of a film script and diary) about a teenager who is accused of murder. You'll also see the influence of multiculturalism, with novels written by authors from Africa or Asia, or works such as *Shabanu: Daughter of the Wind*, Suzanne Fisher Staple's story of a Pakistani girl who rebels against an arranged marriage.

The method of teaching **writing** has also changed, influenced by the work of Lucy Calkins at Columbia University's Teachers College. In her method, known as the Writing Process, children are encouraged to write multiple drafts and to edit one another's work. At its best, the Writing Process teaches children to write the way professional authors do—constantly revising their work, always with a real audience in mind. A major benefit is the way in which the Writing Process allows children to work independently of their teacher. This gives the teacher time to help one child while the others in the class are working productively on their own. Most important, it gives teachers the courage to assign long papers. In schools that have incorporated the Writing Process well, children typically write longer and more complex papers than is common in junior high school—10 to 12 pages or more.

The subject matter in **history** (also called social studies) hasn't changed much. Kids mostly study ancient civilizations in 6th grade and American history in 7th and 8th grades. But the teaching methods have changed a lot. Textbooks are out. Primary source materials are in. Children are encouraged to read actual documents and contemporary accounts of events in the past: court records from colonial America, the diaries of Revolutionary War soldiers—now available as books published for young adults.

Kids may study the contents of an Egyptian tomb on a museum visit or perform a Greek play in translation. Many history teachers make good use of the excellent documentary films that have been produced in recent years, such as *Eyes on the Prize*, telling the history of the civil rights movement. Here, too, multiculturalism has made inroads. Children study ancient civilizations of India and China as well as Egypt, Greece, and Rome. Children study not only military and political history but the history of ordinary peoples as well, particularly the lives of women and children.

There is a great debate over how **math** should be taught in middle school, comparable in some ways to the phonics/whole-language debate over how reading should be taught in elementary school. Proponents of the "new math" say the methods by which most of today's parents studied mathematics were often dull, routine, and irrelevant. The old methods concentrated too much on basic arithmetic and memorizing formulas—pencil-and-paper work made obsolete by the introduction of the pocket calculator. A new math curriculum, proponents argue, would introduce elements of algebra, probability, statistics, and geometry to middle school children, engaging their curiosity and better preparing them for high school.

In schools that have adopted the new math, you'll see kids rolling dice to figure out problems in probability. You'll see kids constructing rectangles from small plastic tiles to find factors or to determine whether a number is prime. These methods are appealing. But teachers must also ensure that children have a good grasp of basic skills. Some parents have dubbed the new math "fuzzy math" and have complained that their children are unable to do long division if the batteries on their pocket calculator fail. If students don't master arithmetic, they won't do well in high school.

Some schools offer **Regents-level math,** or high school algebra, in the 8th grade. All students in New York State must take five Regents exams (one in math, one in English, one in science, and two in history) to graduate from high school. Students who take the Regents math exam in 8th grade are more likely to be prepared for Advanced Placement (college-level) Calculus in high school. Each district middle school directory lists which schools offer Regents-level math; I've listed them here as well.

The teaching of **science** is another area that has undergone tremendous change. In the past, critics say, many science classes concentrated on rote learning and memorization. Teachers focused on covering material in a textbook so kids could pass standardized tests intended to show their mastery of the facts. The teacher might do an experiment in front of the class, but the kids rarely got a chance to touch or feel any materials themselves.

Many schools still teach science this way. Schools that concentrate on learning from textbooks may prepare children fairly well for Regents exams—but some teachers complain that those exams rely excessively on children's mastery of facts.

Many passionate teachers of science say the old methods of instruction were boring and tedious—and missed the point of scientific inquiry. These teachers say textbooks shouldn't be the primary tools of instruction. Rather, they say, children should explore science with things they can see and touch. They should conduct experiments themselves—not just watch the teacher. They should take trips to the city's parks to learn how rocks are formed and how ecosystems work. They should learn to think the way scientists think—by posing questions, making their own observations and hypotheses, and predicting outcomes—rather than passively accepting information from the teacher.

Some middle schools offer **Regents-level science,** most commonly Earth science but sometimes Living Environment (biology). Like Regents-level algebra, these courses have the potential to give children a leg up on high school by getting basic requirements out of the way so they can take more advanced courses. However, many academically challenging schools, such as Salk School of Science, prefer a science curriculum that emphasizes exploration and discovery to one that concentrates on preparation for a Regents exam. The district middle school directories list the schools that offer Regents-level science; I've included them here as well.

Middle school is when instruction in **foreign languages** begins in earnest. Unfortunately, teaching was weak in almost every school I visited. Rarely did I hear the language the kids were supposed to be studying spoken when I entered a class. Rather, I heard the teacher—in English—rambling on about some arcane point of grammar as kids fidgeted. Obviously, kids learn languages best when they hear and speak them. English in the foreign-language classroom should be used sparingly.

How to Apply

Once you've visited the schools that interest you, you'll have to fill out applications for admissions—unless you decide on your zoned neighborhood school. Some of the schools have entrance exams. Some have auditions. Some accept children by lottery.

For the schools within your district, you'll fill out a one-page application ranking each program in order of preference. Be sure your child is eligible for a program before you list it: Some schools require certain test scores for admission, for example. In some cases, the school will contact you if an exam or interview is necessary; in other cases, it's your responsibility to schedule an exam. For programs outside your district (including charter schools), apply directly to the school. Parents are notified of admissions in May. Your child will be admitted to one school in your district. He or she may also be offered a spot at a boroughwide or citywide program, such as Philippa Schuyler in Brooklyn or New Explorations Into Science, Technology and Math (NEST+M). In that case, you may choose.

If your child is assigned to a school that is on a state list of "failing" schools, he or she may be eligible for a transfer to a better school under federal legislation called No Child Left Behind (NCLB). For further information, see Insideschools.org, or contact your regional office.

If you move to the city after the deadline for applications, in the middle of the school year, or after your child has already entered 6th grade, the office of student enrollment will help you find a place. Call 311, (212) NEW-YORK, or the Office of Student Enrollment, Planning and Operations (OSEPO) at (212) 374-2363 for the address of a placement office near you. (The offices are also listed in this book in the introduction to each borough.) Principals of individual schools no longer have the authority to enroll a particular child.

Making a Good Choice

So you've visited a bunch of schools, kibitzed with your friends, and agonized with your child, and you still don't know how to list the schools in order of preference? How do you decide? Take a deep breath and consider some basics.

Starting times. Is your child an early riser? Then a school that starts at 7:45 a.m. may be fine. If it's a struggle to drag your child out of bed in the morning, consider a school that starts later. Some begin as late as 9 a.m. Take note: As children enter adolescence, their biological clocks change. They need more sleep than younger children, but hormonal changes mean they have trouble falling asleep in the early evening. For many, early morning start times can be a killer.

Location. Close to home is nice. That leaves more time for work *and* play. Of course, if schools in your neighborhood aren't any good, you may have to travel. But make a trial run early in the morning to see if the commute is plausible.

School culture. If your child favors green hair, don't make him go to a school that has uniforms. If he relishes order, don't send him to a school where kids are sprawled on sofas.

Listen to your child. Remember, she's the one who has to attend—not you. Some parents pick a school that's perfect for them—but a disaster for their child. Take her concerns seriously.

Match the school and the child. Some children need structure. Others balk at too many rules. A shy child may hate working in groups. A sociable child might be miserable in a school where the teachers do most of the talking. An ambitious, competitive child may do well in a fast-paced school, but a more laid-back child may do better in a school where he can pause to smell the roses.

Think about what's fixable. Help your child weigh each school's strengths, and consider how you might mitigate a school's weaknesses. If a school has a poor sports department, you can sign her up for a private soccer clinic on weekends. But if she feels overwhelmed by the size of a huge school, or by a crushing home-work load, her concerns will be harder to address.

Beware of peer pressure. If your child wants to go to school with his friends from elementary school, that's understand-able. And it's certainly nice to start middle school with some old friends. But he shouldn't pick a school just because it's the trendi-est, or the most selective. Remind him that he can still see his old friends, even if they go to another school. And he will make new friends—wherever he goes.

Try to relax. There are more middle school options than you imagine. Large or small, traditional or experimental, well-established or brand new, the city has dozens of programs worth considering for your child.

The middle school years can be exciting and challenging, frightening and exhilarating, hopeful and frustrating—sometimes all on the same day! These years are the first, difficult steps on the bridge between childhood and adulthood. Help your child find a good middle school, and high school and college admissions may seem like a breeze.

District 1
1   NEST+M
2   Tompkins Square
3   East Side Community

District 2
4   Academy of Technology
5   IS 289
6   Greenwich Village
7   ICE
8   Salk School of Science
9   Simon Baruch
10 School of the Future
11 Lab Collaborative Studies
12 Clinton School
13 Professional Performing Arts
14 Robert F. Wagner
15 East Side M.S.
16 Hunter College

District 4
17 Manhattan East
18 Young Women's Leadership

District 3
19 Center
20 Computer
21 Anderson
22 Booker T. Washington
23 Mott Hall II

District 5
24 Columbia Secondary
25 Mott Hall
26 Frederick Douglass

Manhattan
Schools

MANHATTAN

When out-of-towners say New York City, they really mean Manhattan, that crowded, overpriced, exhilarating island of skyscrapers, tenements, and raw energy. Some aggressive Manhattanites are among the most competitive people on Earth. These are the folks who think nothing of sending their 4-year-old off for IQ tests to be placed in special kindergarten classes for the "gifted." So it should come as no surprise that some of Manhattan's middle schools are among the most selective and competitive anywhere. Manhattan is also a place where oddballs feel welcome, and, perhaps not surprisingly, there are some excellent schools for kids who don't fit the mold.

Manhattan middle schools vary tremendously in quality, and it's a rare situation when a parent can send a child to 6th grade without enduring an exhausting round of tours and applications. Application procedures vary from district to district and even from school to school. Luckily, there are some gems that make the agonizing search worthwhile.

The district in which you live must find a seat for your child. If your child attended elementary school outside your home district, he or she is entitled to attend middle school there as well. (You may also apply to citywide programs outside your district.) Middle school directories are available at the borough enrollment offices. These offices should also be able to answer any questions you might have. For the East Side south of 96th Street and the West Side south of 59th Street (Districts 1, 2, and 4), the borough enrollment office is at 333 Seventh Avenue, 10011, (917) 339-1755 or (212) 356-3788. The school choice coordinator, Jimmy Bueschen, jbuesch@schools.nyc.gov, is particularly helpful. For the West Side north of 59th Street, Harlem and upper Manhattan, the borough enrollment office is at 388 West 125th Street, 10027, (212) 342-8300. You may also try the central Office of Student Enrollment, Planning, and Operations (OSEPO) at 52 Chambers Street, Room 415, 10007, (212) 374-2363.

Each district has a middle school fair, usually in January. These fairs are jam-packed, but they are a good way to meet principals and students. Also check out tours at individual schools in the fall and winter.

Downtown and East Side

District 1 on the Lower East Side has long been home to an eclectic mix of poor and working-class Puerto Ricans, Orthodox Jews, Chinese immigrants, yuppies, squatters, and artists. The district has been in the forefront of school choice, and in recent years a multiracial group of parents has helped create new small schools that have attracted middle-class parents and begun to reverse a long exodus of neighborhood kids to other districts. The district is home to a gifted program that accepts children from across the city, New Explorations Into Science, Technology and Math (NEST+M). The district office is at 220 Henry Street, Room 134A, 10002, (212) 587-4046.

District 2 includes some of the most expensive real estate on the planet: the Upper East Side, Sutton Place, Gramercy Park, Greenwich Village, and Tribeca. Even the West Side south of 59th Street—once known as Hell's Kitchen—has been renamed Clinton or Midtown West by hopeful real estate agents who have been able in recent years to command astounding rents. The schools have a long history of excellence. Unfortunately, they rarely have room for children living outside the district. District 2 students may attend their zoned neighborhood school or choose another school in the district. The district office is at 333 7th Avenue, Room 713, 10001, (212) 356-3789.

District 4 in East Harlem includes public-housing blocks and run-down buildings, as well as some posh Fifth Avenue apartments near Mt. Sinai hospital. It also includes Spanish Harlem and a tiny Italian American enclave. An uncrowded district, it was one of the first in the country to allow parents to choose their child's public school, and there are some important and interesting middle schools here. Students who live in District 4 are also eligible for the new Columbia Secondary School for Math, Science and Engineering (p. 101). Unfortunately, District 4's 35-year history shows that "choice" is not a cure-all for failing public schools. Many schools in the district still have very low levels of achievement, and the system of "choice" may have exacerbated the gaps between the best and the worst. The district accepts applications from children who live outside its boundaries. The district office is at 319 East 117th Street, Room 402, 10035, (212) 828-3512.

West Side and Upper Manhattan

District 3 encompasses the West Side between 59th Street and 122nd Street. There are no zoned neighborhood schools and students are required to choose a school from the many options in the district. Most of the District 3 middle schools begin in the 6th grade. (The Center School starts in 5th grade.) The district office is at 154 West 93rd Street, Rooms 122 and 204, 10025, (212) 678-5857. Also, children who live north of 96th Street (in Districts 3, 4, 5, or 6) may consider Columbia Secondary School for Math, Science and Engineering.

District 5, in Central Harlem, has long had some of the lowest-performing and most poorly managed schools in the city. One notable exception: the Frederick Douglass Academy, a school for high-achievers that consistently ranks at the very top of middle schools citywide. The district office is at 425 West 123rd Street, Room 205, 10027, (212) 769-7500.

District 6, serving northern Harlem, Washington Heights, and Inwood, is one of the most crowded districts in the city. School construction didn't keep pace with the waves of immigrants who moved into the neighborhood in the 1980s and 1990s, and hundreds of pupils are bused to less crowded schools downtown and in the Bronx. Over the years, upper Manhattan has changed from being mostly Irish and Jewish to predominantly Dominican. Recently, Russian immigrants have moved to the area, along with artists and musicians escaping sky-high rents downtown. The most prosperous families live in large co-op apartments surrounded by formal gardens on Cabrini Boulevard and in Castle Hill Village overlooking the Hudson River. But most of the district consists of poor and working-class families living in rental apartments. The district office is at 4360 Broadway, 10033, (917) 521-3783.

New Explorations Into Science, Technology and Math (NEST+M)

111 Columbia Street
New York, NY 10002
(212) 677-5190
www.nestmk12.net

Admissions: citywide
High school choices: NA
Grade levels: K–12
Enrollment: 1,250 (projected)
Class size: 25

Test scores: R *****, M *****
Ethnicity: 54%W 9%B 18%H 19%A
Free lunch: 15%

New Explorations Into Science, Technology and Math (NEST+M) is one of a handful of "gifted" programs that accept children from all five boroughs. It serves children in grades K–12, and children may enter at kindergarten, 6th grade, or 9th grade. Housed in a sparkling, sunny building with up-to-date science labs, wide halls, and classrooms arranged around a central courtyard, NEST has smart kids, reasonable class sizes, and a challenging curriculum. NEST has an excellent elementary school, a good and growing middle school, and a high school that shows a lot of promise.

The elementary school classrooms have the feel of a progressive school: Each class in kindergarten through 2nd grade has a play area with lots of blocks. Parents are welcome; walk through the halls and you'll see parents reading aloud to small groups of children. Children call teachers by their first names, and lessons are woven around interdisciplinary themes such as bread (where it comes from, how to make it, how yeast makes it rise).

The middle school has a more traditional tone. Children mostly call teachers "Mr." and "Ms." and, while there are plenty of engaging projects, there is also an emphasis on accelerated academic achievement. Girls and boys are separated for math and science; Jared Rosoff, assistant principal for the middle school, said that, in particular, girls are more likely to speak in class if they are separated from boys. Children in grades 3–8 wear a dress code: khaki or navy blue trousers or skirts, and polo shirts of various colors emblazoned with a NEST+M logo.

Sixth- and 7th-graders follow the Singapore math curriculum, originally developed in the island nation from which it takes its name. Singapore Math emphasizes quick recall of arithmetic facts far more than the progressive TERC or Everyday Math programs used in most New York City schools, which emphasizes conceptual understanding.

Children take the high school algebra Regents exam in January of their 8th-grade year—6 months ahead of most other accelerated math programs. Students take the Earth science Regents exam in 7th grade and the Regents Living Environment exam in 8th grade. Science is further accelerated in the high school, with physics offered in 9th grade, chemistry in 10th grade, Advanced Placement (AP) biology in 11th grade, and AP physics and AP chemistry in 12th grade.

As in other New York City schools, in social studies, 6th-graders study ancient civilizations and 7th- and 8th-graders study American history. Children's writing projects are posted on bulletin boards: One student wrote a pamphlet on eating disorders; another wrote about how horses can be used in physical therapy for humans.

While the academics are challenging and the tone is formal, Rosoff wants to ensure that there is still plenty of nurturing in the middle school. Sixth-graders meet regularly with the school librarian and the guidance counselor to learn how to plan their time, to understand how to organize their work, or just to talk about how their week is going. Kids I spoke to said the homework load wasn't overwhelming, perhaps 2 hours a night. The middle school, which serves 125 children in each grade, offers music, studio art, and technology. Sixth-graders go on an overnight camping trip, 7th-graders visit Boston, and 8th-graders travel to Washington, DC. Rosoff has focused on creating an after-school program and introducing middle school sports. Class size in the middle school is 25.

Founded in 2001, the school underwent a period of turmoil in 2006, when the school's original principal, Celenia Chevere, left after a battle with Schools Chancellor Joel Klein over a plan, eventually dropped, to house a charter school in the NEST building. Dr. Olga Livanis, Klein's choice for new principal, clashed with parents over everything from class size to her decision to eliminate the college guidance counselor. Some parents withdrew their children. One-third of the teachers left, and those who remained filed dozens of union grievances against the principal.

By 2008, the school had stabilized. The teachers' union declared a truce with the principal, and, while there was lingering friction between the principal and some parents, the leadership of the Parents Association pledged to work with the administration rather than challenging it at every turn.

Formerly assistant principal for physics at Stuyvesant High School, Livanis had been accustomed to the parents-stay-out culture of that school and had trouble adjusting to NEST's hyper-involved parent body, who expected to be consulted about every decision. Public relations is not her strong suit, and she can be abrupt. For example, one mother complained that the principal refused to give parents details about a fight among children in the playground, saying only "Don't worry, we're taking care of it." At the same time, Livanis has won over some parents by hiring good teachers and strengthening the curriculum. "She's not an extrovert, and she can't communicate," said a mother who nonetheless was impressed with a program that allowed students to use a university research telescope by linking to the Internet. "You're not going to get a warm fuzzy feeling from her. But she's smart and she has good ideas," she added. Another mother said, "The kids are happy and the education is good."

Livanis hired three assistant principals (one each for the elementary school, the middle school, and the high school); bolstered the high school science program; and, at parents' urging, hired a part-time college counselor. The school was proud to have its first Intel science competition semifinalist—one of the top honors for high school science students. Increasingly, middle school students are deciding to stay at NEST for high school rather than transferring to specialized high schools like Stuyvesant.

Special education services are limited. One teacher offers Special Education Teacher Support Services (SETSS). Occupational therapy and speech therapy are also available.

For admission to the 6th grade, students must score in the 95th percentile on the Otis-Lennon School Abilities Test (OLSAT); the school also considers children's 4th-grade report cards, standardized test scores, and attendance records. The school website has information about testing, including an on-line sign-up form. The website also has details on open houses, generally offered in the late afternoon and on Saturday. Students come from every borough except Staten Island. A group of Brooklyn students (called Brooklyn NESTers) take the subway together, and their parents take turns accompanying them. Queens parents have hired a private bus.

Tompkins Square Middle School, IS 839

600 East 6th Street
New York, NY 10009
(212) 995-1430
www.tsmsonline.org

Admissions: District 1 priority
High school choices: Millennium, Beacon, Bard
Grade levels: 6–8   **Test scores:** R ****, M *****
Enrollment: 370   **Ethnicity:** 16%W 16%B 52%H 16%A
Class size: 30   **Free lunch:** 60%

A warm, intimate school with top-notch teachers, Tompkins Square Middle School builds on the progressive education offered at the alternative elementary schools in the neighborhood—including the Neighborhood School, the Earth School, and Children's Workshop School. Tompkins Square welcomes children of different races, family incomes, and skills levels and strives to challenge strong students while offering support to kids who are struggling.

"Kids learn a lot being in a real-world setting," says Principal Mark Pingitore, who previously taught at the Neighborhood School. "Our kids learn a lot from each other."

Located on the 3rd floor of a building that also houses the Earth School and PS 64, Tompkins Square Middle School has a new science lab, Smartboards (electronic whiteboards connected to the Internet), and a large new playground for basketball and handball. Each child is assigned an advisor, who does everything from answering a question about how to use a combination lock to giving advice about the high school applications process. Teachers are mostly young, and there is a strong emphasis on staff development. The whole staff meets every morning for 15 minutes. Everyone calls the principal by his first name.

Tompkins Square has been named a "mentor school" by Teachers College. That means teachers from other schools visit to learn about the school's writing program. Students may write a "persuasive essay" on a topic of immediate concern—such as the condition of their lockers—and then advance to a "lawyer's brief" based on their study of the U.S. Constitution. They may write a memoir based on their own experience, then write an imaginary immigrant journal based on their study of Ellis Island.

The school's curriculum is organized into 9-week blocks, or "modules," during which kids study a topic in depth, such as American Government and the Constitution or Westward Expansion. There is an emphasis on interdisciplinary work.

Administrators and teachers listen to the kids and take their concerns seriously. Seventh-graders mounted a petition to win the right to go out of the building for lunch. Their work paid off: Seventh-graders are now allowed out to lunch 1 day a week.

Another example: Kids took part in a grassroots campaign to expand their outdoor play space to encompass an area that had been reserved as a parking lot for the office of school safety, but was rarely used. They drafted letters to local officials and drew up a petition to ask for the playground to be given back to the school—and they were successful.

On one of our visits, a handful of students sat quietly in the hallway doing independent work while others peeked their heads into the principal's office to ask about organizing a meeting. "I think the kids are treated like adults more," answered a 7th-grader when asked how Tompkins Square compared with her former school. "The kids are given more respect."

Children with **special needs** may be assigned to a Collaborative Team Teaching (CTT) class with two teachers, one of whom is certified in special education. These classes, one in each grade, have a mix of general education and special education students.

Sports and arts are offered in a comprehensive after-school program every day until 6 p.m.

Millennium is the most popular choice for high school, but graduates also are admitted to Beacon, Bard, School of the Future, Manhattan/Hunter (in the Martin Luther King building), LaGuardia High School of Music and Art and Performing Arts, and the specialized science high schools.

Tours are offered from November through January. Prospective students submit a teacher recommendation and are interviewed in a group. "We're looking for kids who can work well with others," Principal Pingitore said.

Nearly all students come from District 1, but occasionally there is room for out-of-district students.

East Side Community High School

420 East 12th Street
New York, NY 10009
(212) 460-8467
www.eschs.org

Admissions: District 1 priority
High school choices: NA
Grade levels: 6–12
Enrollment: 570
Class size: 16–22

Test scores: R **, M ***
Ethnicity: 6%W 28%B 59%H 7%A
Free lunch: 70%

East Side Community High School has a good track-record taking in kids with low levels of achievement and preparing them to go on to college—even some prestigious colleges like Brown, the University of Pennsylvania, Wesleyan, and George Washington University. Small class size, talented teachers, and a focus on learning to read and write well have made this school a successful model for school reform.

Every day starts with 30 minutes of independent reading. Students may choose anything they like to read—graphic novels, fiction, nonfiction—the goal is to get them reading, and keep them reading. Principal Mark Federman has a book club for students who are interested, and teachers looking for a good book to read make their way to the school's well-stocked library—or to the principal's office, where one wall is lined with bins of books for students to borrow (categories include scary, real-life, social justice, sports fiction, and graphic novels) and another with books for teachers (categories include education policy and standards, literacy assessment, and social and emotional education).

East Side Community has such a successful writing program that it has been named a "mentor school" by Teachers College's Reading and Writing Project. That means teachers from around the country visit to observe classes in which children write multiple drafts of papers, revising them each time. Middle school students have monthly "publishing parties" to celebrate their final or "published" papers.

East Side Community is housed in a red brick building that spans nearly half a city block. Adjacent to the building is a new basketball court that leads into a community garden, which is used by science classes. On one of our visits, 7th-grade science students were studying the components of soil that had been gathered from the garden.

The day is organized so that teachers have only 40 students—two classes of 20 children. Teachers stay with the students for several hours a day and for 2 academic years.

The school is a member of the Coalition of Essential Schools, the national network of small progressive schools. Like its sister schools, East Side Community teaches that it's more important to study a few subjects in depth than to have a smattering of information about many topics. Teachers believe that kids need to learn to express themselves well and to defend their points of view competently—both orally and in print. Class discussions—rather than lectures—are the norm.

Children receiving **special education** services are completely integrated into regular classes. Most classes have two or three adults, including aides and student teachers, so the kids who need extra help get individual attention right in their classes.

The school has long admitted kids who other schools avoid—truants, low-performers, or difficult kids. The school helps kids stay in school, even when they have big personal problems, such as a 7th-grader who had a baby.

The school has a college counselor 5 days a week, paid for with a grant from Prudential Securities. Graduates have gone to private colleges such as Wesleyan, George Washington University, Alfred, Antioch, Hofstra, and St. John's.

Check the website for tour dates. There is no interview for admission, but interested students should send the principal an e-mail or letter saying why they want to attend the school.

Manhattan Academy of Technology, PS/IS 126

80 Catherine Street
New York, NY 10038
(212) 962-2188
www.ps126mat.com

Admissions: District 2
High school choices: Millennium, Baruch, School of the Future
Grade levels: 6–8   **Test scores:** R ****, M ****
Enrollment: 330   **Ethnicity:** 5%W 18%B 24%H 53%A
Class size: 25–30   **Free lunch:** 59%

A sweet, engaging school, the Manhattan Academy of Technology (MAT) is an increasingly popular choice for children who want to enjoy the intimacy of a small school and an impressive array of arts and sports. An art teacher who trained at the Rhode Island School of Design offers courses ranging from drawing to fashion design; an energetic athletic director manages 38 (yes, 38) sports teams and clubs, including table tennis and surfing (yes, surfing).

Manhattan Academy of Technology is the name given to the upper grades of PS/IS 126, a combined elementary and middle school. PS 126 is neighborhood school that serves mostly poor and working-class children from Chinatown and the Lower East Side. Most of the 5th-graders stay on for 6th grade, where they are joined by 50 or 60 children from other elementary schools in District 2. One striking feature of MAT is that it has managed to attract well-off children in 6th grade who willingly attend a school where most of the other children are poor enough to qualify for free lunch. The school serves a wide range of abilities, from high-achieving children bound for the specialized high schools to students needing remedial education.

The building, constructed in the 1970s, has wide, shiny corridors; clean white walls; and doors trimmed in yellow, red, blue, lavender, green, and purple. Large windows let in plenty of sunlight, and there are views of the Brooklyn Bridge just a few blocks away. The presence of the little kids gives the school a gentle tone. A climbing wall (with fake rocks) on the back of the stage in the auditorium gives kids a place to stretch their legs.

The middle school, with 330 students, offers honors classes for the strongest students, a small "self-contained" **special education** class for emotionally disturbed and other disabled students, and various options for everyone in between. Class size is 25 for regular classes, 30 for honors.

There are plenty of hands-on projects and class discussions. On one of my visits, children debated the pros and cons of child labor—and compared the global situation today to that of the Progressive Era in the United States, when laws limiting child labor were first passed. In a science class, kids learned about density by first filling a beaker with rocks, then adding pebbles, and then adding sand—increasing the weight of the beaker without increasing the volume. In a math class, children explored probability by flipping sets of coins and predicting how many would land one way or another.

The writing program seems to be particularly well developed. Children learn to write in a variety of genres, producing movie reviews, advice columns, letters to the editor, and poetry. In a social studies class, children made their own "advertisements" for a product from ancient China—silk or tea or gunpowder. In an English class, students wrote about their experiences in the style of Metropolitan Diary, *The New York Times* column about city life.

MAT is one of the only schools I have visited in which the writing of severely disabled children is posted, with pride, on bulletin boards in the corridor. Children from the self-contained special education class wrote their memories of a trip to Disneyland or of a fishing expedition. Like other children in the school, they were expected to write and revise multiple drafts. In addition to the self-contained class, special education services are offered in Collaborative Team Teaching (CTT) classes, which have two teachers and a mix of general education and special needs kids.

Each room has a rich classroom library, and children are given latitude in what they read. Children not only read in English and social studies classes, they also read silently for 15 minutes in science class, choosing books about, say, spiders, or rodents. In English class, the emphasis is on contemporary fiction, rather than the classics. "It's easier for them to relate to contemporary fiction," said Carlos Romero, assistant principal for the middle school.

Principal Kerry Decker says she is committed to educating the "whole child" by offering more than academics. "Middle school should be exploratory," she said. "The students should be able to try out everything." All students take music and technology electives, include painting, guitar, web design, and African drumming.

An extensive after-school program includes fashion design (taught by art teacher Nicole Schorr), Lego robotics, a science club, and a math club. In the "rock shop," kids write and perform their own songs. Athletic director John DeMatteo has assembled an amazing array of sports teams and clubs: usual ones like volleyball, track, and soccer, and unusual ones like swimming. He even has organized a surfing class at a Long Island beach.

A possible downside: Although classes were orderly the day I visited, parents say there is some roughhousing between classes and on the playground. One mother suggested that playground supervision could be improved.

A thoughtful guidance counselor, John Ngai, guides children through the high school admission process. Many children attend District 2 high schools, but increasing numbers are admitted to the specialized high schools. In 2008, 16 students were accepted into specialized high schools and 9 were accepted at LaGuardia High School of Music and Art and Performing Arts. The school offers regular tours. Admission is limited to students in District 2.

IS 289

201 Warren Street
New York, NY 10282
(212) 571-5659
www.is89.org

Admissions: District 2
High school choices: Beacon, Millennium, LaGuardia
Grade levels: 6–8   **Test scores:** R ****, M ****
Enrollment: 305   **Ethnicity:** 40%W 14%B 13%H 33%A
Class size: 32   **Free lunch:** 40%

IS 289 (sometimes called IS 89) is an unusually calm and gentle school, where children seem to be kind to one another and even the cafeteria is pleasant. "We try to keep it civilized," Principal Ellen Foote said with a smile, while she supervised lunch in the brightly lit space, with large windows and a soaring ceiling. Kids and adults actually carry on conversations in the cafeteria without shouting—a rarity in New York City public schools.

Parents choose IS 289 for its relaxed atmosphere and its attention to children's social and emotional development—as well as for its challenging academics. Parents appreciate the fact that the kids aren't overly competitive and don't have excessive amounts of homework (1½ to 2 hours a night is typical). Although classes are large, teachers are attentive and the principal knows every child.

"The kids treat each other with respect and are nice to each other," said one mother. "They bounce ideas off each other, and work together collaboratively. I like the fact that all the kids are expected to learn [together] and they are not segregated by ability."

PS 89/IS 289 is a combined elementary and middle school built by the Battery Park City Authority in 1998. The elementary school serves neighborhood children, but the middle school is open to students who come from across District 2. The building, adjacent to the site of the World Trade Center, has commanding views of New York Harbor, the Statue of Liberty, and Liberty Park.

One of the most attractive physical plants in the city, the building has nooks in the halls for kids to work individually or in groups; spaces for community meetings; and large, sunny, quiet classrooms designed so kids can move around. Gray Formica tables with red or gray plastic chairs, blue carpeted areas, and light gray tile give the building the downtown look of industrial chic. Each class has a rich classroom library with children's classics such as *A Secret Garden* and contemporary fiction such as the Harry Potter series and *Dave at Night*, set during the Harlem Renaissance. Copies of the science section of *The New York Times* and magazines with new research on the Civil War give students current materials with which to study.

The corridors are unusually wide for a middle school, and at various points there are carpeted steps where kids may sit and talk to one another, put on a small theatrical production, or meet with a teacher. Teachers are young and energetic and seem to have a good grasp of their subject matter and an affection and respect for the children in their care.

IS 89 emphasizes interdisciplinary projects. Sixth-graders create murals in the style of the ancient Egyptians, combining the knowledge they gain in social studies with the concepts they learn in math class to make scale drawings. Seventh-graders write and perform their own operas. They write the libretto, make the scenery (using scale drawings), and use their knowledge of science to make the light boards to illuminate the performance. The 8th-grade science expo combines science and literacy. Students pick a theme, such as the environment, and write pamphlets on related topics, such as an assessment of the likelihood of a natural disaster.

On one of my visits, 6th-graders studying ancient civilizations were preparing projects on topics such as the role of women in ancient Egypt and Greece. Two girls were sprawled on the floor of the corridor, with large sheets of paper spread around them with an outline of their project.

An 8th-grade science class was conducting an "energy audit" of the building, calculating, for example, how much heat was wasted when windows were open. (The kids told the principal that she would save energy if she climbed the stairs, rather than using the elevator.)

A class studying the Civil War worked on a project that involved making up an imaginary interview with a freed slave, a former master, or a politician, all based on material gathered from textbooks; biographies; and authentic documents of the period, such as slave narratives and actual letters from an ex-slave to his master.

IS 289 uses the Connected Math curriculum, an approach that encourages problem solving rather than memorizing formulas. Kids seemed happy and engaged in the math class I visited.

Instruction in instrumental music (woodwinds, brass, and strings) is offered twice a week.

There is a "self-contained" **special education** class for students. These students seem well integrated into the life of the school, and the classroom is as cheery and well equipped as others in the building.

Sixth-graders take an overnight camping trip; 7th- and 8th-graders go on overnight trips connected with their study of American history: to Boston and Salem or Philadelphia. Children have "advisory" periods once a week, in which they can talk with a teacher and a group of other students about social and emotional issues—and how to balance schoolwork with the rest of their life.

Graduates go to some 20 different high schools, including Beacon, Lab, School of the Future, Millennium, and Baruch. Although a few graduates attend the super-selective Stuyvesant High School nearby and LaGuardia High School of Music and Art and Performing Arts, most seem to prefer smaller, more intimate schools, Principal Foote said.

IS 289 has a free after-school program that offers an "open gym," track, soccer, and volleyball. It has an extensive drama program, arts and crafts, and robotics.

IS 289 is open to all children in District 2. Sign up for tours on the school's website. The administration is committed to having a range of academic abilities, a mix of children from different ethnic groups and income levels, and a geographic distribution of children within District 2. Students submit teacher recommendations and a writing sample. A tip for applicants: Don't say you want to attend the school because the building is pretty—try to find something else you admire.

Greenwich Village Middle School, MS 896

490 Hudson Street
New York, NY 10014
(212) 691-7384
www.gvms896.net

Admissions: District 2 priority
High school choices: Baruch, Lab, Beacon
Grade levels: 6–8   **Test scores:** R ****, M ****
Enrollment: 215   **Ethnicity:** 24%W 31%B 36%H 9%A
Class size: 26–28   **Free lunch:** 46%

The classrooms in this tiny school are clustered along one off-white corridor, lined with purple lockers, on the top floor of PS 3, a 100-year-old building. Hexagonal tables (rather than desks), high ceilings, large windows, and wood floors give the school a cozy feel. Well-stocked classroom libraries, offering such works as *The Pearl* by John Steinbeck and poetry by Robert Frost, have bins of novels and biographies and bins with labels like "fantasy" and "the Asian experience." Lots of children's work decorates the walls. The staff is young, enthusiastic, and idealistic. Posted prominently is the school's motto, attributed to Margaret Mead: "Never doubt that a small group of thoughtful, committed citizens can change the world; indeed, it's the only thing that ever has."

Greenwich Village Middle School prides itself on its diversity, and it attracts kids of different racial groups as well as children of different academic abilities. It's a school that emphasizes warmth and nurturing rather than an accelerated curriculum. It doesn't offer Regents-level math for 8th-graders, for example. At the same time, Principal Kelly McGuire closely monitors each student's progress and encourages teachers to keep careful track of whether each child has mastered each new concept before moving on to the next.

The school keeps parents involved. Parents must sign a log to ensure a child has read for 25 minutes each night. The school had a "family math night," when parents work on math games with their children, giving them a chance to meet teachers and better understand the math curriculum. The parents organize fundraisers, such as a Valentine's Day Comedy Night, and raise $15,000 to $20,000 a year for supplies.

McGuire has expanded the school's art offerings, and students have art, music, or dance two or three times a week. Sixth-graders take music, 7th-graders study dance, and 8th-graders learn digital photography. Examples of student artwork are posted on the school's website. The physical education program includes cooperative games using equipment such as hula hoops and ropes, as well as team sports.

Greenwich Village Middle encourages community service. Every year, students and teachers participate in the annual AIDS walk. Middle school children read with elementary school children in PS 3. The school's annual Thanksgiving dinner, prepared jointly by parents, teachers, and students, also serves as a fundraiser for not-for-profit organizations selected by the students.

Field trips are common: One year, the 6th-graders visited the Egyptian wing at the Brooklyn Museum as part of their study of ancient civilizations and the Brooklyn Botanic Garden for a science activity.

The school offers Collaborative Team Teaching (CTT) classes for students in **special education**, which have two teachers, one of whom is certified in special education. These classes have a mix of general education children and children with special needs.

An after-school program, from 3:30 p.m. to 4:15 p.m., includes homework help, a math club, robotics, guitar instruction, basketball, and (the most popular offering) cooking lessons. At the time of our visit, McGuire was seeking funding to introduce a YMCA-run tutoring program at the school.

Graduates tend to go to small high schools in District 2, including Baruch, Lab, Eleanor Roosevelt, and School of the Future. A few go on to the specialized science high schools or to LaGuardia High School of Music and Art and Performing Arts.

Priority in admission is given to District 2 residents. In recent years, there has sometimes been room for students from outside the zone. There is no test for admissions. Children are interviewed. They are asked to bring a sample of work of which they are proud, and a copy of their most recent report card. They work on a math problem in a group. A plus for late risers: The school's hours are 9 a.m. to 3:20 p.m.—a late start for a middle school.

Institute for Collaborative Education

345 East 15th Street
New York, NY 10003
(212) 475-7972

Admissions: citywide
High school choices: NA
Grade levels: 6–12   **Test scores:** R ****, M ***
Enrollment: 412   **Ethnicity:** 42%W 25%B 25%H 8%A
Class size: 18–22   **Free lunch:** 24%

The Institute for Collaborative Education (ICE) is a small school serving kids in grades 6–12 that focuses as much on children's emotional and social development as it does on their academic success. Small classes, dedicated and hardworking teachers, and classes that rely on projects rather than textbooks make this school an appealing place for kids who don't fit the mold.

ICE has an unusually good music program that includes an award-winning middle school jazz band. On one of my visits, music teacher Roy Nathanson, a professional jazz musician, worked with 6th-graders and their English teacher to put phrases from Lewis Carroll's *Alice in Wonderland* to music. A girl recited, "Speak roughly to your little boy and beat him when he sneezes!" accompanied by a boy playing a harp and a girl playing a clarinet. Nathanson, looking every bit the jazzman with his saxophone, a white goatee, nerdy black glasses, black jeans, and black sweater, said the school's jazz band was going to Paris to perform in the Banlieues Jazz Festival.

Down the hall, art teacher Jennifer Billow was working with middle school students on designs for stained glass windows that they would make using a real soldering iron. When Principal John Pettinato and I entered the classrooms, students presented him with a petition signed by several dozen kids who wanted to enroll in the class but couldn't because there wasn't enough space. "We teach them to stand up and fight for their rights and to tell us what they want to do," Pettinato told me as he took the petition and promised to figure something out for the kids.

A 6th-grade humanities class pondered philosophical questions such as "What is reality?" and "What would Socrates and Pythagoras think of each other?" The children constructed "proofs" of statements the kids made up such as "Homework causes mental breakdowns." An 8th-grade English class read *Fist, Stick, Knife, Gun,* Geoffrey Canada's memoir of growing up in the South Bronx, and discussed the statement "Violence is a learned behavior."

ICE is a member of the Coalition of Essential Schools, a national network of progressive schools organized by Brown University's Theodore R. Sizer, who believes that small schools that concentrate on teaching a few subjects well are more effective than large schools that attempt to teach a wide array of subjects.

It's an informal place. Students call teachers by their first names and sometimes use slang when speaking to adults. Blue jeans are the rule, on adults as well as on kids. Kids are boisterous and loud during class changes. Although some parents might find the atmosphere too relaxed, the kids seem happy. "If you are a quirky kid who is not going to fit in at a big school, this may be the place for you," one mother said. "The teachers' commitment to kids is extraordinary."

Teachers stay after school to help kids with their homework and often eat lunch with them. Even in the evening, teachers are willing to show their support for kids by attending their theatrical or musical performances outside school. The school has a nice mix of kids of different races and social classes.

Pettinato, who founded a school for kids released from juvenile detention and was assistant principal at City-as-School, an alternative high school, has an easy way with the students. "Kids love to hang out with him, especially kids who are having a hard time," said a teacher. Pettinato has master's degrees in both special education and social work. As he walked through the hall on one of my visits, he greeted students by name, stopping to drape an arm around a shoulder and to plant a kiss on a forehead.

The Institute for Collaborative Education occupies the 5th floor and part of the 4th floor of the former Stuyvesant High School, which it shares with the High School of Health Professions and a District 75 program serving 75 high school students with autism. A new paint job—yellow walls and blue lockers—has brightened the place up. Large papier-mâché sculptures, which the kids made and painted themselves, sit on top of lockers in the hall. Students' science projects are visible everywhere: towers made of straws; bridges made of Popsicle sticks to test loads; and posters about earthquakes, avalanches, and pollution in the city's Newtown Creek.

No textbooks are used in English or history, and the school has only recently introduced textbooks in math and science. In one English class, students read *Nickel and Dimed,* Barbara

Ehrenreich's best-selling memoir of life as a low-wage worker. They compared Truman Capote's *In Cold Blood* with the movie *Capote.* In a history class, they reenacted the Cold War–era trial of Julius and Ethel Rosenberg.

The school has a full-time **special education** teacher who offers individual help to children with special needs. One downside: The small size of the school means that course offerings are limited. For example, only 3 years of high school Spanish are offered. The only sports teams are girls' and boys' basketball.

Parents say that the college counselor, Jennifer Wells, is unusually helpful and accessible. Pettinato says that more than 90% of graduates go to 4-year colleges. College acceptances include Brown, Colby, Sarah Lawrence, Yale, the University of Chicago, Cornell, Penn State, Middlebury College, Hampshire College, Bard, Bucknell, and College of the Atlantic.

The school accepts children from all five boroughs, and kids travel from Brooklyn and even Staten Island to attend. The school offers monthly tours for prospective parents. Contact the admissions director, Meryl Meisler, at mmeisle@schools.nyc.gov. There are 60 seats in the 6th grade, and the number of applications is far greater than the number of seats. A student must submit an application and a two-page "personal statement" describing "the most important things for someone to know about him or her as a student and as a person outside of school." Applications are usually due in March.

Salk School of Science

320 East 20th Street
New York, NY 10003
(212) 614-8785
www.salkschool.org

Admissions: District 2
High school choices: Baruch, Stuyvesant, Lab
Grade levels: 6–8   **Test scores:** R *****, M *****
Enrollment: 385   **Ethnicity:** 42%W 15%B 14%H 29%A
Class size: 33   **Free lunch:** 25%

Walk into the office at Salk School of Science and you might think you're in someone's living room. There are comfy sofas, chairs, and potted plants, and, unlike in most schools, there's no counter to divide you from the people working there. Across the hall, Principal Rhonda Perry and Assistant Principal Julia Chun-Rhodes share an impossibly small office lined with bookshelves. The door is always open, and children feel free to drop by to say hello.

The school, on the top two floors of an elementary school, PS 40, has sky blue corridors lined with red lockers, recessed lights, yellow classrooms, and sparkling new science labs. The rooms are clean, airy, and newly renovated. There are piles of books everywhere. The rapport between students and staff is relaxed but respectful, and parents seem to be more welcome than in many middle schools. On one of my visits, a mother seated at a table in the corridor outside the main office sold tickets for a Halloween party. She seemed to know every teacher and every child. Nearby, the principal put her arm around a girl's shoulder, chatting with her about a book she'd just read.

Founded in 1995 with the help of New York University Medical Center, Salk School of Science was designed to encourage students who traditionally shy away from the sciences—particularly girls, poor and working-class children, and children of color—to consider careers in medicine. As the school has become ever more popular (and limited its enrollment to students living in District 2), its student body has become more prosperous (and Whiter). Still, Salk is a place where girls as well as boys learn to feel confident in science and where children, whatever their race, have role models in a multiracial faculty. Most schools that focus on science have an enrollment that's lopsided with boys; Salk has equal numbers of boys and girls.

True to its name, Salk has a rich science curriculum. Sixth-graders have two science classes each day, one that focuses on experiments, the other that teaches research and writing skills. Sixth-graders may, for example, research and write about how a particular animal, like Darwin's finches, adapt to their environment. They may go to the Bronx Zoo and observe how a gorilla eats and grooms itself, then write about their observations. Seventh-graders have a curriculum that includes an introduction to earth science, biology, and chemistry. Eighth-graders are required to give "minidissertations" to a panel of Medical Center professors, school staff, and parents at the end of the year. One child presented a plan for an invention that would trap and store electricity from lightning bolts. Another gave a plan for saving Chinese pandas from extinction by setting up wildlife corridors between their existing habitats.

Each class has a year-end "Exploratorium" similar to a science fair. The 8th-grade Exploratorium is held at the American Museum of Natural History. The Hall of Asian Mammals is closed to the public for the occasion, and working scientists and researchers come to ask children questions about their projects.

The humanities curriculum is equally rich, and parents need not fear their children are being shortchanged in English and social studies. History and English are integrated, so children studying the American Revolution may read historical novels about, say, a boy who fights in the Battle of Lexington along with real diaries of the teenage soldiers who witnessed the battles. Children are expected to do historical research from primary sources: soldiers' letters home, court records, and documents such as the Declaration of Independence that are available in their classrooms.

In English, kids keep regular journals and study creative writing from teachers who've had special training in the Writing Process at Teachers College. In one class, children wrote lyrical lines about the pain of war and the loss of childhood based on their readings on Revolutionary War battles: "It seemed my childhood had slipped away with the pull of a trigger," one poem began.

Salk has adopted the District 2 Connected Math curriculum, which attempts to give children real-world applications of problems in algebra and geometry. Eighth-graders may take the Regents (high school level) algebra exam.

Spanish is offered in 7th and 8th grade, but 6th-graders don't have time for a foreign language because they take two science courses. Art and drama are also offered. Drama students from

NYU's Tisch School of the Arts volunteer in the Salk drama program, teaching kids to act out scenes from *A Raisin in the Sun* or *A Midsummer Night's Dream*.

The school has one self-contained **special education** class, as well as Collaborative Team Teaching (CTT) classes. In the CTT classes, which have two teachers, children with special needs mix with children in general education.

The school makes a special effort to help new students acclimate. Seventh-graders are paired with 6th-graders and write their "buddies" letters of welcome over the summer. When the school year starts, the older children take care to invite the younger ones to lunch. The buddy system was developed at the suggestion of the student council—an example of how the administration listens to children and acts on their suggestions.

During the fall, the 6th-grade class goes on an overnight trip to an environmental camp in the Catskills, where they take walks and get to know one another. Back at school, children have advisors who help them with everything from opening their lockers to organizing their homework. The principal takes students for a walk around the neighborhood to introduce them to businesses nearby—preparing them for the middle school privilege of leaving the building for lunch. "We understand the transition from 5th grade to 6th grade is very difficult," said Perry.

Teachers don't pile on the homework here—a plus or a minus, depending on your point of view. One mother said that Salk didn't push her child hard enough and didn't focus on preparation for the specialized science exam. But another said that her son was happy at Salk because "not having burdensome homework after school allows him to be a kid." Perry says she values family time—particularly around the holidays.

She says that the school has been very successful at high school admissions. At the same time, the school wants to create an atmosphere in which children are happy and not too stressed. "We want them to love learning," she said. About 55% of 8th-graders are admitted to the specialized high schools, but LaGuardia High School of Music and Art and Performing Arts and District 2 high schools such as Baruch, Lab, and Eleanor Roosevelt are popular as well.

The school offers regular tours. Admission is limited to District 2 students. Applicants complete a writing sample, undergo a group interview, and take part in a science experiment. Successful applicants generally have scored a high Level 3 or Level 4 on 4th-grade standardized tests in math and English.

Simon Baruch Middle School, MS 104

330 East 21st Street
New York, NY 10010
(212) 674-4545
www.104m.org

Admissions: neighborhood school/District 2
High school choices: Stuyvesant, Eleanor Roosevelt, Baruch
Grade levels: 6–8   **Test scores:** R ****, M ****
Enrollment: 1,040   **Ethnicity:** 30%W 16%B 23%H 31%A
Class size: 25–33   **Free lunch:** 40%

A neighborhood school open to everyone who lives in the zone, MS 104 serves a wide range of students, from those in honors classes to those receiving special education services. It has a drama program that puts on ambitious productions such as *On the Town* and *Kiss Me Kate*, a ceramics room with a real kiln, and an orchestra and band that everyone can join.

The enrollment of the school has declined in recent years, as the city enrollment office has restricted out-of-district applicants to the school. Class size has been reduced to 25 in 6th grade and to about 30 in grades 7 and 8—a far cry from a few years ago, when classes often topped 38.

Still, it's a large school. There are 12 classes in each grade, about half of which are designated as honors or "special placement," for high-achieving students. The school is divided into "houses" of four classes and four teachers who work as a team. Each house has one or two honors classes, one or two regular "academic" classes, and a class for students receiving special education services. Children go from class to class within their house, so everyone gets the same teachers. Advanced students may take Regents-level math and Earth science courses, usually offered in high school. Children have lunch and recess with their whole grade. Teachers have a regularly scheduled 90-minute time period to plan together, when they may work together as a team or discuss individual students' issues.

"There's always help available and the teachers are so caring, it feels like a small school," said one mother. But unlike in some small schools, children are exposed to a range of experiences. "You can do sports. You can do art. You can do music. You don't have to choose," she said.

All 6th-graders take Latin and minicourses in ceramics, computer, art, and drama. Seventh- and 8th-graders take Spanish or French and may choose from the arts electives. No audition is required for the band or orchestra and children can choose whatever instrument they want. Similarly, anyone can join the track team or play basketball or tennis.

The style of teaching tends to be more traditional than in some other District 2 middle schools. There are plenty of textbooks and worksheets to supplement the novels and creative writing projects in each class, and you're just as likely to hear the teacher talking as the children. "You do have to have some direct instruction," said Principal Rosemarie Gaetani. "Kids only know so much. You need the teachers to expand and support what the kids do know."

At the same time, there is room for projects and group work. On one of my visits, an inspired math teacher helped students use small wooden blocks to derive the formula for the surface area of a rectangular solid. Children in an 8th-grade social studies class made their own scrapbooks of the civil rights movement and put together a pretend assembly line to learn about factory conditions in the early 20th century. The drama teacher led children in improvisation: One child read aloud from a fairy tale, such as *Goldilocks*, while the other children made up pantomime for the parts.

A number of seasoned teachers have retired in recent years. The new teachers have lots of energy and dedication, but some are still learning the ropes of classroom management. Still, the parents we spoke to were enthusiastic that the new teachers had invigorated the school and were willing to work far more than the hours required by their contract.

For example, one mother said that a 6th-grade science teacher runs an after-school science club, coaches the baseball team, and co-runs flag football intramurals. A guidance counselor coaches both the girls' and boys' basketball team and, during the holiday break, coached the boys' team in a tournament. A social studies teacher runs the yearbook and coaches the cheerleaders.

The school has self-contained **special education** classes, as well as two Collaborative Team Teaching (CTT) classes in each grade. CTT classes mix special needs and general education students and have two teachers, one of whom is certified in special education. About 60 students are classified as English Language Learners. A teacher of English as a Second Language works with them individually, in their regular classes, and offers strategies to classroom teachers.

MS 104 offers a free after-school program until 4:30 p.m. or 5 p.m. The theater program is particularly popular. There are many teams and clubs, including a chess club, a basketball team, a wrestling team, and cheerleading. One year, the science club spent the night at the American Museum of Natural History.

Many students are admitted to the specialized-exam high schools or to LaGuardia High School of Music and Art and Performing Arts. District 2 high schools, including Baruch and Eleanor Roosevelt, are popular as well.

MS 104 has regular tours. Any child who lives in the attendance zone (the East Side from 14th Street to 57th Street, as well as Tribeca and Battery Park City downtown) is entitled to attend. Students who live outside the zone but within District 2 may apply through the school choice process. A score of about 685 on both the 4th-grade ELA and the math exam is generally required for students applying for an SP (gifted) program, but the cutoff changes from year to year.

School of the Future

127 East 22nd Street
New York, NY 10010
(212) 475-8086
www.sof.edu

Admissions: District 2
High school choices: NA
Grade levels: 6–12   **Test scores:** R ****, M ****
Enrollment: 675   **Ethnicity:** 35%W 24%B 25%H 16%A
Class size: 25   **Free lunch:** 29%

The School of the Future makes an irresistible promise to prospective parents: Give us your child in 6th grade, and we'll return him or her to you in 7 years with a couple of college acceptances in hand. Indeed, the school makes good on its promise: Nearly everyone graduates on time and is admitted to a 4-year college—to schools like Cornell, Columbia, Hampshire, Colby, Middlebury, and Skidmore. The continuity—staying in one school for middle school and high school—is part of the school's charm; its welcoming attitude to kids who don't fit the mold is another plus.

Both teachers and students are encouraged to use their imaginations to design creative projects. In one class, students set off Alka-Seltzer rockets on the roof of the building to learn about velocity. In another, they made pinhole cameras out of cardboard and compared them with the human eye. A group of kids drafted a platform for an imaginary political party. Others reenacted the trial of a character accused of beating his wife in the classic African novel *Things Fall Apart.*

The School of the Future is a "mentor school" for the Coalition of Essential Schools, a national network of progressive schools organized by Brown University's Theodore R. Sizer and based on the principle that it's better to study a few topics in depth than a smattering of every imaginable subject. Teachers from School of the Future offer training to other coalition schools at workshops and seminars across the country.

Like those at other coalition schools, teachers at School of the Future says it's more important to learn "habits of mind"—various ways of approaching a new problem—than to learn a particular set of facts. Kids are encouraged to find their own solutions—not merely have the teacher pass information on to them. Students are expected to show their mastery of major subject areas through a "portfolio assessment" of written work and oral presentations.

In the past, the joyful, relaxed atmosphere of the school sometimes bordered on sloppy. Kids flopped and even slept on sofas in the classrooms. There were plenty of fun-to-read books, but hardly any textbooks. Now, a new administration is working to make academics more challenging for top students and to tighten discipline, while still keeping the inclusive, nurturing atmosphere for which the school is loved. Homework load is increasing, and there is more test prep than before. The staff has long visited other progressive schools to share ideas for teaching; now they also visit more traditional schools such as KIPP Academy Charter School in the Bronx.

"We're definitely pushing kids more, and pushing teachers more," said Stacy Goldstein, who became principal of the school and director of the middle school in September 2007. At the same time, she said, "We don't want to undermine the soul and the spirit of the place."

It's still a school with lots of room for class discussion, and, with classes of 23 to 26 students, kids get an unusual amount of attention from grown-ups. There are no bells, and kids don't have to ask permission to use the bathroom. At the same time, the classes are somewhat more focused on traditional skills than they were in the past.

The building is cramped, even claustrophobic. Housed in a former vocational high school for girls, the school is arrayed on ten floors of an aging building, and students and staff must negotiate crowded stairways (or a slowpoke elevator) to get to class. The kids' lockers are inconveniently located in the basement, but the building has a nice gym and an adequate cafeteria. The library is small, and students frequently use the public library nearby. The roof has been transformed into a garden, with a greenhouse and picnic tables—a nice place for science classes or lunch.

The classes are organized in ways that make it easier for teachers to give kids the attention they need. At most schools, teachers have five 43-minute classes of 34 students each day, or 170 students, and it's almost impossible to pay attention to each child's writing. At School of the Future, history and English are combined to form humanities. Humanities teachers have two 2-hour classes of 25 students each day—a much more manageable number that allows teachers to help kids from the early stages of forming a thesis through several drafts.

In grades 7–10, teachers stay with each group of students for 2 years. In 11th and 12th grades, students may choose a humanities elective such as The Civil War and Reconstruction, Writing for Radio, or a course examining the borderline between sanity and insanity that includes readings such as *Running with Scissors* and *One Flew over the Cuckoo's Nest*.

Future is known for giving particular attention to kids who don't fit the mold. About 25% of the students receive **special education** services. They are assigned to regular classes, and a special education teacher gives extra help both in and out of class. This teacher helps the regular classroom teacher modify lessons if, for example, the special needs students need help with organization.

Future has a parent body that seems to love the school. One mother said that the school devotes an unusual amount of time to teaching children to write well, and she described teachers as "tireless, energetic, and very creative." Another raved about the college office and said a counselor, who writes "extensive" letters of recommendation, takes kids personally to visit college campuses and persistently calls colleges on behalf of the students.

The downside of a small school is that it can't have a wide array of courses, although students may make special arrangements to take college courses at the City University of New York and New York University. The small library doubles as a "media room," with computer stations and a few shelves of books. Each classroom, however, has its own classroom library, which is the source of many of the books the students use.

A free after-school program offers some of the extras that are missing from the regular curriculum. Students participate in a rock-and-roll band, drumming, guitar, and hip-hop and step dancing, as well as sports such as volleyball, baseball, and softball.

The school prides itself on securing a college admission for every single graduate. About 92% of graduates go to 4-year colleges, while 8% go to 2-year colleges. Nine recent graduates won prestigious Posse Foundation scholarships. Recent graduates have been accepted to Columbia, Barnard, Skidmore, Hampshire, Middlebury, Cornell, New York University, Wesleyan, Amherst, Fordham, and Penn State.

Students from District 2 have priority. The school rarely has room for students from outside the district. Most students enter in 6th grade. About 25 to 30 students are admitted in high school. The school offers regular tours. E-mail the school at softours@yahoo. com to reserve a spot.

Lab School for Collaborative Studies

333 West 17th Street
New York, NY 10011
(212) 691-6119
www.nyclabschool.org

Admissions: District 2
High school choices: NA
Grade levels: 6–12   **Test scores:** R *****, M *****
Enrollment: 1,095   **Ethnicity:** 56%W 7%B 11%H 26%A
Class size: 33   **Free lunch:** 25%

New York City Lab School for Collaborative Studies is a selective middle and high school that consistently ranks in the very top in reading and math scores citywide. A demanding curriculum and creative instruction combine to attract some of the best students in District 2, including children from as far away as the Upper East Side. The school is a pioneer in special education inclusion and is particularly successful in ensuring that children with special needs get the same high-quality instruction and achieve at as high a level as everyone else.

The middle school has long been known as a place for driven, competitive kids, who are both academically talented and socially sophisticated. Brooke Jackson, who was named co-director in 2006, is working to change the culture of the school and to make it a less stressful place. The homework load has eased, and the administration is trying to pay as much attention to children's social development as it does to their intellectual work.

The school has an informal feel: Teachers don't make a fuss about kids wearing hats, for example, and students are permitted to leave the building for lunch. There is pleasant give-and-take between the teachers and students. Most classes are taught in a seminar style, with lots of class discussion. Class changes are pleasant, with kids talking quietly to one another and then settling down quickly to study. There are no bells, no PA announcements to interrupt the day, no passes required to go to the bathroom.

Two of the six middle school classes in each grade are designated as Collaborative Team Teaching (CTT) classes. These have two teachers, one of whom is certified in special education. About one-third of the students in these classes have special needs, such as dyslexia, dysgraphia (difficulty writing), Attention Deficit

Disorder, or Asperger's syndrome. Parents say the CTT classes work well for all kids: Kids who need the extra attention get it and everyone benefits from having a low ratio of grown-ups to kids. Special education students have their own "skills classes" in which they review classwork they may have not understood or preview work to come.

The surroundings aren't beautiful. Teachers and kids call Lab "the concrete donut," because it's housed in a square, fortress-like gray concrete building with a central courtyard. Classrooms feel cramped, with 33 in a typical class. But the rooms are cheerful and well equipped, with colorful bulletin boards, hanging mobiles, fish tanks, and plants. New science labs have perked up the place. A refurbished gym, where the middle school students have physical education, makes the school's facilities seem almost adequate. The Parent Association takes advantage of the courtyard for events like the annual auction.

Lab encourages students to delve deeply into a subject, "cultivating intellectual curiosity [rather than] accumulating more and more advanced credits," said Jackson, a long-time teacher at Lab who was named co-director in 2006 along with Gary Eisinger, former assistant principal of the High School for Environmental Studies in Manhattan. "If you are looking to move ahead faster and faster, this is not the place for you," she said. However, the school offers a number of Advanced Placement classes, and able students may take college courses at New York University, Baruch College, and the Borough of Manhattan Community College.

Imaginative projects keep the kids engaged. In a 6th-grade math-science class, students worked in groups of four to draw "flow charts" of where New York City tap water comes from. Some gathered at tables while others worked on the floor. In a 6th-grade humanities class, kids demonstrated their knowledge of Hammurabi's code, the ancient law of Babylon, with a mock game show called Wheel of Torture: Live from Mesopotamia.

Seventh-graders breed trout in tanks in their classroom, learning firsthand about natural selection when, for example, deformed fish die quickly. When the trout get big, the students release them into a river. Eighth-graders work on interdisciplinary projects in groups: One group studied the local food supply, interviewed local farmers at the Union Square Market, and presented a report on organic farming.

The math program follows the progressive Connected Math curriculum commonly used in District 2 schools; Lab also offers Regents-level math to 8th-graders.

A popular music director leads a rock band for middle school students. Sixth- and 7th-graders study instrumental music for half the year and art for half the year. The Spanish program is better than most I've seen: Students converse almost entirely in Spanish and gain a fair degree of proficiency.

A free after-school program offers homework help, chess, and arts and crafts until 6 p.m. Sports include basketball, soccer, and track.

The homework load, once oppressive, appears to have eased in recent years. Students I interviewed on one recent visit said that the workload was manageable, perhaps an hour or two a night in the middle school and 2 to 3 hours a night in the high school. (Although I did speak to one father who said his 7th-grader was swamped with more than 4 hours of homework a night.)

Some middle school parents have complained that the social scene can be cliquey. For years, even 6th-graders have been permitted to leave the building for lunch, and divisions have been created between the children who can afford to spend $15 a day at nearby Chelsea Market and those who stay inside to eat free lunch in the cafeteria. Jackson said she planned to keep all 6th-graders inside for lunch, giving them a better chance to make friends across class lines and eliminating one source of division. Older children will still be permitted out for lunch. Moreover, parents say Jackson and Einsinger are much stricter than the previous administration about cracking down on disciplinary infractions ranging from the minor (tardiness) to the serious (drug use).

Between half and three-quarters of the middle school students stay for high school; those who leave tend to go to the specialized high schools. In 2008, 45 students—nearly one-quarter of the 8th-grade class—were admitted to Stuyvesant High School; a total of 131 students, nearly two-thirds of the class, were offered seats at one of the specialized schools. But many of those offered seats at the specialized schools elect to stay at Lab. One 11th-grade girl we met turned down a seat at Bronx Science because she preferred the chance to take part in student government, the school newspaper, and model U.N. without competing against huge numbers of other students.

Lab has an attentive college counselor who encourages students to apply widely to colleges—not just to "the same 20 schools that everyone applies to." About 95% of Lab graduates attend 4-year colleges. About half go to CUNY or SUNY schools and half to private or nationally known state schools, such as New York University, Michigan, Georgetown, Wesleyan, and Penn State. The school has an excellent record, ensuring that special education students graduate with a regular diploma (rather than the less rigorous special education diploma) and go on to 4-year colleges.

Lab's enrollment has increased in recent years, and there are now 580 students in the middle school and 515 in the high school. A downside to the size: Communication between the administration and parents is uneven, and parents sometimes complain that their e-mails go unanswered. Parent-teacher conferences are a mob scene.

Admission is limited to children living in District 2. Most successful candidates score at Level 4 on both English and math 4th-grade standardized tests. Lab gives its own entrance exam to incoming 6th-graders, which consists of a writing sample and some math problems. Children are also interviewed. About 1,000 children apply for 200 seats.

Special education students have a separate but parallel application process and are tested apart from the general education students. There are 24 seats for special needs children in the 6th grade. Lab has a full-time teacher for speech and occupational therapy.

Check the website carefully for details about tours. It's devilishly difficult to make an appointment for a tour by telephone, but keep trying. Be sure to bring your child: Parents without children are not admitted.

The Clinton School for Writers and Artists

320 West 21st Street
New York, NY 10011
(212) 255-8860
www.theclintonschool.net

Admissions: District 2
High school choices: LaGuardia, Baruch, Eleanor Roosevelt
Grade levels: 6–8   **Test scores:** R *****, M *****
Enrollment: 250   **Ethnicity:** 40%W 16%B 34%H 10%A
Class size: 32–33   **Free lunch:** 33%

The Clinton School for Writers and Artists is a tiny middle school where children may put on their own musical theater production, study ballroom dancing, or create art projects with students from the School of Visual Arts. One year, some kids even traveled to Sardinia on a 10-day exchange program to study art and Italian—and Italian students visited Clinton. Many Clinton graduates—perhaps 20% to 25%—are admitted to the highly selective LaGuardia High School of Music and Art and Performing Arts.

Clinton has a strong academic program and students are well prepared for high school. But what really distinguishes Clinton is the attention the staff pays to students' social and emotional development. The staff works hard to make sure that children get along with one another and that no one is bullied. The kids seem to be happy and engaged—and nice to one another. "The social scene for kids at the school seems very healthy," one mother said. Another mother marveled at how much time teachers are willing to spend with students. She recalled a potluck supper for parents and staff at which teachers chatted informally with kids—even though they had just spent the whole day in the classroom.

The school is known for its arts curriculum. In addition to their regular coursework, children study visual arts, creative writing, and performing arts. Each of these classes meets three times a week: Children rotate among them, sampling each in 6th and 7th grade and concentrating on one in 8th grade. The visual arts curriculum combines art history with studio classes in drawing, collage, watercolor, and wire sculpture. Creative writing includes playwriting, poetry, and fiction. Performing arts include drama and ballroom dancing.

Children say they love the way the arts are integrated into the curriculum. Students illustrate almost every project: In one social studies class they made travel brochures with facts about African countries. In another they made "neighborhood guides" with street maps that labeled schools, houses of worship, and other points of interest. In science they made posters illustrating global warming, recycling, and the water cycle. Even math projects include drawings.

The academic teaching staff is young and energetic, and many have experience in the arts. Principal Jeanne-Marie Fraino directs a church choir on weekends and used to coach ballroom dancing, The 7th-grade English instructor, Jerry Maraia, teaches theater at New York University in the summer; at Clinton, he directs ambitious after-school musical productions such as *Into the Woods* and *Once on This Island*. Even the Spanish teacher plays the piano.

The English and social studies programs are particularly strong. "The writing program is better than strong. I think it's fabulous," said a mother who is a professional writer. "The language arts teachers are so encouraging and excited about good writing."

The school has long served kids with a wide range of academic ability: Some kids read sophisticated books like *The Catcher in the Rye* or *The Call of the Wild*, while others read books typically read by younger children such as *Charlotte's Web* or *A Year Down Yonder*. In a history class on the Civil War, some students read very challenging historical fiction, while others read easier books on the same topics. The teacher managed to include everyone in the discussion, drawing expertly on what each child had read.

The math curriculum combines the progressive Connected Math program used by most District 2 schools with Impact Math, which offers more practice drills. The kids seemed focused as they multiplied fractions on one of my visits. In science class, kids examined a metamorphic rock and filled out a worksheet. A new science lab is planned, and that promises to add some excitement to the science curriculum.

Located on the 5th floor (with a few classrooms on the 4th floor) of an elementary school, PS 11 in Chelsea, Clinton has basic but pleasant facilities. Tall windows let in lots of light and wooden cupboards give a homey feel. Children's artwork and projects are posted on the walls, and there are rich classroom libraries. There's no elevator in the building and the gym is tiny, but kids may play basketball on a rooftop playground.

Clinton has just two or three classes in each grade. It is one of the few middle schools in which no racial group predominates, and its diversity is a source of pride. Every teacher knows every child, and every child knows every teacher. Sixth-graders have "advisories," small classes in which they may talk about anything that's on their mind. Parents can get advice during regularly scheduled "Friday morning chats" with the guidance counselor and parent coordinator. Recent topics included Internet safety and adjusting to middle school.

The school shuns oppressive amounts of homework. One parent said her son averages 1 to 1½ hours of homework a night—and that the homework is interesting and challenging but not time-consuming.

One of Fraino's goals is to improve the after-school program. She hired a Latin dance instructor to teach salsa and meringue, for example, and expanded an after-school music instrumental program. In addition to the Latin dance and music classes, the program includes basketball teams, a spirit squad, a newspaper club, and an art club. Audition and portfolio prep sessions are offered to assist students applying to specialized art schools. "We really wanted a soccer team, and when I suggested it to the principal she followed up immediately, called a coach, and hopes to have a team in place by the fall," a mother said.

The school has one self-contained **special education** class. The room is nicely equipped, with plants and plenty of books. The children receiving special education services mix with the other children for art, drama, and physical education. One child who was particularly strong in math joined the general education class for math. A Collaborative Team Teaching (CTT) class was added in 2008.

A large number of graduates go on to LaGuardia High School of Music and Art and Performing Arts. One recent year, one child was admitted to Bronx Science, one to Brooklyn Tech. Baruch, School of the Future, and Eleanor Roosevelt are also popular choices, and a few children go on to small schools, such as Lower Manhattan Arts Academy and Essex Street Academy.

Clinton conducts regular tours for prospective parents. See the school's website for dates. District 2 students are given priority. The school looks for children with an interest in writing and the arts. Incidentally, one mother said that the school tours don't do justice to the school, because it's hard to see how extensive the art programs are. "On the school tours, you don't get a sense of what makes the place tick," she said.

Professional Performing Arts School

328 West 48th Street
New York, NY 10036
(212) 247-8652
www.ppasnyc.org

Admissions: citywide
High school choices: NA
Grade levels: 6–12   **Test scores:** R *****, M *****
Enrollment: 428   **Ethnicity:** 53%W 25%B 18%H 4%A
Class size: 25   **Free lunch:** 18%

The Professional Performing Arts School (PPAS) provides excellent professional training in acting, vocal music, ballet, and musical theater, along with a solid academic program. The school's partnerships with the Actors Institute, the Alvin Ailey School, the School of American Ballet, and the Songs of Solomon Academy of the Arts offer unusually strong opportunities for students who are passionate about performing. Graduates may go on to professional careers, to conservatories, or to liberal arts colleges.

Serving children in grades 6–12, PPAS has a tiny middle school, with just 75 children (25 each in grades 6, 7, and 8). All middle school students take drama, singing, and dancing in addition to a full academic load. They take academic classes in the morning, and in the midafternoon, after an early lunch, they study performing arts during a 90-minute block, from 11:45 a.m. to 1:15 p.m. In 9th grade, the school grows to serve about 80 students in each grade.

High school students have academic classes from 8:30 a.m. to 1:15 p.m., followed by 2 hours of instruction in their major: drama, vocal, dance, or musical theater (which combines acting, dancing, and singing). Acting, musical theater, and the vocalist program are offered in the building; dancers travel to the Alvin Ailey School on West 55th Street.

Students are admitted by audition, rather than by their academic record. That means there is a wide range of academic abilities in each class—from high-achieving students who are bound for Ivy League colleges, to those who are just scraping by. Luckily, teachers are unusually imaginative in finding ways to address the wide range of skills in their classes and, because class size is small, all students seem to get the attention they need.

PPAS, just off Broadway in the Theater District, shares a building with a popular and successful elementary school, Midtown West. The 100-year-old building is clean and the rooms are airy, with a new library, a newly renovated auditorium, and a black box theater. The science labs are new and brightly lit. Some of the classrooms are equipped with a Smartboard, an electronic device that combines the functions of a chalkboard with webpages from the Internet. There are no bells, and bathrooms are open. Students in grades 8–12 may leave the building for lunch. Teachers are available to give individual help to students during lunch.

The academic classes are solid, particularly in the humanities. Math and science instruction has improved substantially in recent years, and parents need not fear that their children will be short-changed academically if they choose PPAS. The teachers prepare students for the realities of show business, said Charles M. Vassallo, the school's artistic director. Yet, at any given time, only 5% of union card–holding actors are working. So the school wants to ensure that the kids can write well and master algebra so they can go into other lines of work if their performing careers fizzle.

Some of the students—about 5%—are already working in film, television, or theater productions, both on and off Broadway. The school makes accommodations for them with a flexible schedule to ensure that they keep up with their schoolwork.

The school has a few students receiving **special education** services who are integrated into regular classes. The performing arts traditionally attract more girls than boys and the school is more than 70% female. The ratio is even more lopsided in the middle school.

About 90% of graduates go on to 4-year colleges and 2% go on to 2-year colleges. Some, particularly the dancers, go directly to professional work, for example at the School of American Ballet. Many of the graduates pursue performing arts at conservatory programs such as at Julliard, Berklee College of Music, SUNY–Purchase, the University of Michigan, and North Carolina School of the Arts. Others attend liberal arts programs. Top students are admitted to colleges such as Columbia, NYU, Oberlin, Carnegie-Mellon, Cornell, and Northwestern.

Some recent graduates include singer Alicia Keys; Lee Thompson Young (The Famous Jett Jackson); Jesse Eisenberg (The Emperor's Club); Sean Nelson, who starred in HBO's *The Corner* and was admitted to Temple University; and Sara Zelle, who played Liesl in *The Sound of Music* on Broadway and was admitted to

Harvard. Two alumni, Jessica Lee Goldyn and Paul McGill, were cast in the Broadway revival of *A Chorus Line*.

About 100 students have auditioned for 25 seats in the middle school in recent years. Middle school students must audition again to be considered for admission to the high school. More than half stay; some leave for specialized high schools such as Stuyvesant and LaGuardia High School of Music and Art and the Performing Arts.

Auditions are scheduled in November and December for the high school and in January for the middle school. Successful applicants are asked for a call-back, followed by an interview. There are regular tours during the day for prospective parents and an evening "showcase" and information session in October. Call the parent coordinator for details.

Robert F. Wagner Middle School, MS 167

220 East 76th Street
New York, NY 10021
(212) 535-8610
www.wagner167.org

Admissions: neighborhood school/District 2
High school choices: Eleanor Roosevelt, Stuyvesant, LaGuardia
Grade levels: 6–8   **Test scores:** R ****, M ****
Enrollment: 1,256   **Ethnicity:** 31%W 15%B 24%H 30%A
Class size: 28–33   **Free lunch:** 38%

The largest school in District 2, Wagner has one of the biggest instrumental music programs in the city; an extensive physical education department with instruction in gymnastics and tennis; and a free after-school program that offers courses such as dance, improvisational theater, and yoga.

A neighborhood school that is open to everyone who lives in the zone—the East Side from 59th Street to 96th Street—Wagner has a range of academic courses to serve everyone, from high-achievers to those with special education needs. Wagner attracts children from all over District 2; some parents from Chinatown see Wagner as their children's best chance of gaining admission to the city's specialized high schools.

As a neighborhood school serving a large swath of Manhattan, Wagner serves kids whose parents can afford to take vacations to Europe as well as kids who can't afford a new winter coat. One mother said she was pleased that her son had a "nice eclectic group of friends" that included a child from Martinique, a child from Colombia, and a child who had one Jewish parent and one African American parent.

The well-kept building, constructed in the 1950s, has a large gymnasium and an auditorium, tennis courts, and several music rooms. About three-quarters of the students enrolled at Wagner are in "special progress," classes for children who score at Level 3 or 4 on standardized tests. Of these, some are assigned to honors classes and take high school or Regents-level math and Earth science. Students in the "academic" track, as the general education classes are known, benefit from a smaller class size, with 28 students. (The SP classes have as many as 33 students.)

An able and competent administration, led by Principal Jennifer Rehn, strives to make the most of the school's many resources while minimizing the chance that students will get lost in the crowd. While the school is large, the administration has taken steps to make it feel smaller. In 6th grade, students have "humanities," combining English and social studies, for 90 minutes a day. Each teacher has only two humanities classes, so teachers get a chance to know students better. Students are organized into "houses," with all their classes near one another, so when children move from class to class they move a few doors down rather than halfway across the building.

There are four assistant principals, three assigned to a particular grade, who follow students from 6th grade through graduation, plus one who oversees special education and other special programs. These assistant principals seem to connect well with kids and seem to know the names of all students in their care. The assistant principals have their offices on the floor with the classrooms of the grade they serve, and each year they move offices to be with their students as they move to another grade. In addition, the school's guidance counselors follow the children from 6th grade through 8th grade, when they help them apply to high school.

The school has a reputation as being somewhat more traditional than other District 2 schools, but under Rehn's leadership it has moved firmly into the progressive camp. Teachers encourage group work, class discussions, and projects to supplement work from textbooks. One girl was thrilled with a science project in which she made an "edible cell," making her own model of a cell with different-shaped candy—which she then ate. Another girl enjoyed a debate in which students researched the political positions of various presidential candidates, then pretended they were the candidates answering questions from classmates. "The teachers are so caring," said an 8th-grade girl. "If you need help after school or in the morning they are always there."

Rehn, principal since 2004, is both a strong administrator and a good educational leader. She has worked hard to improve communication between parents and the administration in a school where both parents and students have sometimes felt disconnected in the past. Rehn attends PTA meetings and invites parents to monthly "coffee hours" in the morning. More than 700 parents are signed up for an e-mail Listserv, and the school has a potluck dinner and a "curriculum night" for parents to meet teachers. Teachers are encouraged to give students their e-mail addresses.

The Parents Association is unusually active and raises money for projects such as renovating the library. Parents say the school has evolved from a place where parents are expected to stay away into one in which parents are welcome. "I think the school is a warmer place to be," said one mother who is active in the PA. "I think the teachers are more open to having parents in the classroom." One downside: Parent-teacher conferences can feel like a mob scene, with hundreds of parents struggling to get a few minutes with their children's teachers. Still, the administration has extended the hours of parent–teacher conferences to make them a little more manageable.

The school has extensive **special education** services, including services for the hearing impaired, self-contained classes only for children with special needs, and Collaborative Team Teaching (CTT) classes. The CTT classes have two teachers, one of whom is certified in special education, and a mix of children in general education and those with special needs. The special education classrooms I visited seemed to be as cheerful and well equipped as the regular classrooms.

About 40% of the students take part in the school's extensive instrumental music program, with classes five times a week. The school plays host to the boroughwide band, which has played at Carnegie Hall. On one of my visits, kids were playing "Seventy-six Trombones" from *The Music Man* in a band that included trombones, tubas, and kettle drums. Unfortunately there isn't room for every student who wants to be in music. The students are screened for musical aptitude and sense of rhythm. No prior music experience is needed.

Seventh- and 8th-grade children with their parents' permission may leave the school grounds for lunch. There is a free after-school program, paid for by the PTA. Teams include volleyball, wrestling, flag football, tennis, track, and basketball. "There is always some team for everyone," said an 8th-grade girl. "For the track team, you don't have to try out, you just show up for practice. Same for the wrestling team."

Wagner prides itself on the number of graduates who are admitted to the specialized high schools, such as Stuyvesant and Bronx Science, and on the number of music students who are admitted to LaGuardia High School of Music and Art and Performing Arts. A large number of graduates also attend Eleanor Roosevelt High School, just two blocks away.

The school offers regular tours. Children applying for the "special progress" program must have reading and math scores of Level 3 or 4 on the 4th-grade standardized tests for math and English.

East Side Middle School

1458 York Avenue
New York, NY 10021

331 E. 91st Street
New York, NY 10128
(212) 439-6278
http://114m.r9tech.org

Admissions: District 2
High school choices: LaGuardia, Bronx Science, Eleanor Roosevelt
Grade levels: 6–8 | **Test scores:** R *****, M *****
Enrollment: 540 (projected) | **Ethnicity:** 59%W 13%B 13%H 15%A
Class size: 28 | **Free lunch:** 15%

Principal David Getz likes to tell prospective parents and students that the Good Humor man selling ice cream in the neighborhood insists that East Side Middle School kids are the nicest middle school kids around. It's a claim that's impossible to prove, of course, but the fact that Getz tells the story suggests that he thinks niceness counts—and that niceness is a value he wants to foster at the school.

Academics count a lot, too, and the classes at East Side Middle are as challenging as those you'll find anywhere. But a sweet tone permeates the school, from the parent coordinator who calls kids "honey" to the stress-busting catered breakfast for 8th-graders who are anxious about the specialized high school entrance exam.

Long housed in cramped quarters on the 4th and 5th floors of PS 158, a 100-year-old elementary school at 1458 York Avenue (at 77th Street), East Side Middle School is scheduled to move to a 5-story, $45 million building at 331 East 91st Street in the fall of 2009. The new building, with a gym, library, science labs, and art and music rooms, is adjacent to a 32-story apartment complex called the Azure. The new building accommodates 200 more students than the old, so the enrollment will grow to 540 students.

Whatever the benefits of the new building, East Side Middle has long been known for the high quality of teaching and the high level of discussion among the kids—not for its physical plant. When you visit, look at the samples of their writing, the artwork on the bulletin boards in the halls, and the mountains of books in each classroom—books that are both serious and fun to read.

Listen to the class discussions. Talk to teachers about the passion they have for their students and their work. Look at the kids—serious, articulate, engaged in their work.

East Side Middle was founded in 1991 as an antidote to what one teacher called "the Henry Ford model of education." Parents who feel that traditional middle schools are too big, too anonymous, and too much like factories are attracted to the idea of an intimate, cohesive alternative. The principal plays baseball with the children on the playground during lunch and seems to know every child by name. The parent coordinator is like a school den mother, attentive and alert to any problems a child might have. (On one of my visits, she told Getz her concerns about a child's father who was very ill.) Teachers meet regularly to plan lessons—as a whole staff, as a team teaching one grade, and as a team teaching one subject. "There's a real *esprit de corps* because everyone knows everyone," said one mother. At some middle schools, you get the feeling that the teachers are frustrated high school teachers. At East Side Middle, you get the sense that the teachers really like early adolescents—and really like one another.

Children ease into middle school routines with a homeroom teacher who also teaches 90-minute classes in humanities (combining English and social studies) and with specialists for 47-minute classes in math, science, art, and foreign languages. This arrangement gives students an anchor in a teacher who knows them well (as they had in elementary school), while offering the benefits of specialization they need as subject matter becomes more complex.

Getz, principal since 2003, has the rare ability to connect with both students and parents, never patronizing them, and using his understated humor to cope with the inevitable vicissitudes of running a public school in New York City. An accomplished author, he has written seven books of interest to middle school students—two novels and five science discovery books. *Frozen Man*, for example, is the true story of a 1991 discovery in the Italian Alps of a mummified 5,000-year-old body. Getz describes how archaeologists determined the age of a body and how they used the man's tools and clothing to learn about how humans may have lived at the time.

East Side Middle encourages an interdisciplinary approach to learning, with an emphasis on primary source materials and current scholarly debates. On one of my visits, humanities students were reading a clipping from that day's science section of *The New York Times*, outlining an archaeological discovery of prehistoric tools. Students debated whether the invention of tools may have allowed humans to get a better diet and ultimately a bigger brain, or whether the bigger brain came first and allowed humans to invent better tools. The discussion was part of a class on the history of ancient civilizations, but the emphasis was on how historians or scientists gather the information they need, rather than on facts or dates. "I want students to see history as an active pursuit," said Getz. "I want them to ask, 'How do we know about the past?'"

East Side Middle uses the Connected Math program (a continuation of the TERC math used in most District 2 elementary schools), supplemented with more traditional textbooks. The school has recently introduced Regents (high school–level) algebra in 8th grade. A teacher said that the math curriculum "combines theoretical study with real-world applications." In a 7th-grade math class, for example, students were calculating the potential profits of an imaginary tour company, depending on the number of visitors and various costs. The students seemed to be engaged and the material seemed to be challenging.

Students are expected to write papers in all subject areas—not just humanities. In science, for example, students may write a research paper on hurricanes. In addition, students are encouraged to submit their book reviews, short stories, and poems for publication in children's literary magazines such as *Stone Soup* and *Potluck*. History and literature are integrated, and children studying the Civil War might write a piece of historical fiction based on their research.

Getz hopes to make the middle school years memorable for children and has put in place engaging projects and assignments to that end. One 6th-grader did a math project based on the board game Monopoly; he developed winning strategies by determining the return on investment of various properties—and the most opportune time to buy and sell them. Students choose "electives," special classes that meet once a week, that include math club, soccer, magic tricks, and a history of comedy in cinema. The school has a particularly good drama program, and an art department that inspires kids to paint and draw, even those who have never shown an interest in art before. The art teachers help students prepare portfolios for LaGuardia High School of Music and Art and Performing Arts.

The school offers Collaborative Team Teaching (CTT) classes. These classes, with two teachers, one of whom is certified in **special education**, integrate children with special needs and those in general education.

About 40% of the school's graduates are admitted to specialized high schools, including Stuyvesant, Bronx Science, Brooklyn Tech, and LaGuardia. Many others go to District 2 high schools such as Eleanor Roosevelt.

Children who have their parents' permission may go out for lunch or to John Jay Park next to the school. (Although Getz, by playing baseball with kids at lunch, makes it seem just as cool to stay in.)

Tours are offered in the fall and winter. Admission is limited to children living in District 2. Although there is no cutoff to be considered for admission, most successful candidates score 660 or above on the 4th-grade reading and math test. Children who pick East Side Middle School as their first choice are asked to visit the school, where they write a brief essay, solve a math problem, and take part in a small-group interview.

Hunter College High School

71 East 94th Street
New York, NY 10128
(212) 860-1400
www.hchs.hunter.cuny.edu

Admissions: citywide
High school choices: NA
Grade levels: 7–12   **Test scores:** R *****, M *****
Enrollment: 1,212   **Ethnicity:** 40%W 6%B 4%H 50%A
Class size: 25   **Free lunch:** 15%

Hunter College High School is a highly successful, very selective, and competitive school that prepares its students for the country's most elite colleges. It's known particularly for its strength in the humanities, but it also offers high-level math courses and sometimes fields semifinalists for the Intel Science Talent Search (a high honor known as the baby-Nobel), like student David Bauer, who won first prize in 2005. Students may conduct research in genetics or biotechnology as interns at Mt. Sinai Hospital, Sloan-Kettering Memorial Hospital, or Rockefeller University. Hunter consistently sends one-quarter to one-third of its graduating class to Ivy League schools. *The Wall Street Journal* recently named it as one of the top schools in the country—public or private—for admission to selective colleges.

Teachers encourage discussion and debate, and there is an emphasis on learning to write well and to think critically, not only in English classes but in science as well. Students learn to edit as well as to write, and they typically edit one another's papers through several drafts.

Hunter has an unusually strong program in music and art. The drama department offers students the chance to write and perform their own plays and musicals. Student musicians have performed from France to Senegal. Art history classes take trips to Florence and Siena. Students may sing medieval and Renaissance music *a cappella*; play American jazz in an orchestra; or take a college-level studio art course in nude figure drawing.

Unlike schools where students are required to specialize in science or math, dance or singing, Hunter requires students to have a balanced course of English, social studies, math, science, foreign language, and the arts. A wide variety of sports are offered. Students may choose as many extra projects as they feel they can handle. At Hunter, you can both be in the class play and conduct an independent research project in science.

Classes are smaller than the public high school norm. Most classes have fewer than 25 kids, and many upper-level courses have only 15 to 20. "Hunter is great because it combines the class size and academic quality of a private school with the diversity of a public school," said a student.

It's a high-pressure place, where lots of kids are chronically sleep-deprived by mountains of homework and commutes as long as 2 hours each way. However, a new administration—led by Randall Collins, who is acting director of both the elementary and the high school, and Sonya Mosco, acting principal of the high school—has taken steps to make the place a bit more forgiving. There is a new position of "learning specialist," to give extra help to kids who might otherwise founder. Psychological counseling is available to children suffering from stress or emotional problems. Teachers give letter grades rather than number grades to ease the competition.

The guidance department offers an unusual level of attention to juniors and seniors as they navigate college admissions. There is one college advisor for every 36 students—a ratio that's much smaller than at other public schools, where one advisor may serve hundreds of students. Kids get into top colleges, not only the Ivy League, but also highly selective schools such as MIT and Rhode Island School of Design.

The school is predominantly White and Asian, with smaller numbers of Blacks and Hispanics. About half of the students' parents were born outside the United States; about 30% of the students are the first in their families to go to college. While some families are rich enough to pay for private school, others are poor enough to qualify for free lunch. Students may be academically competitive and even intellectually "arrogant," but there's no competition over clothes or fancy vacations, and "no one talks about which Prada bag is the best," one girl said.

Like Hunter College Elementary School, Hunter College High School is touted as a "laboratory" school for the study of "gifted" education. It is tuition-free and supported by tax levies, but it's not part of the Department of Education. Instead, Hunter College, part of CUNY, administers it.

The school hires its own teachers, sets its own admissions criteria, and writes its own curriculum. Students may take college courses at Hunter while still in high school.

The surroundings are austere, and the kids affectionately call the school "the Brick Prison." The building, a former armory, is an ugly brick high-rise with tiny slits for windows. Classrooms have no windows at all. But the alumni association and the PTA have done a lot to improve the physical plant: The stairwells have been painted, the library has been renovated, new carpets have been installed, and new books have been purchased—finally replacing reading materials that were photocopied 25 years ago and books that were held together with tape. Classrooms now have Smartboards—electronic chalkboards connected to the Internet. The cafeteria has been renovated and a more appealing menu has been added.

Still, kids go to Hunter for the life of the mind, not for the physical stuff. And most kids are grateful to be there. What the school offers very bright kids is one another's company, some very good teachers, and a consistently high level of intellectual excitement. Several parents said that they were envious of their children's experiences—like the passion one girl developed for biology, or the thrill of studying Asian art at the Metropolitan Museum of Art.

The school offers students an unusual degree of independence and freedom. Students may spend their free periods in the library, hanging out in the halls, or at a coffee shop down the street. The corridors serve as the student lounge, as kids chat seated cross-legged in front of their lockers. For 7th-graders, the responsibility can make for a difficult transition as they struggle to organize their time, but most of the high school students I interviewed cherished being treated like adults.

For many years, 7th- and 8th-graders were treated like miniature high school students, and the transition to middle school was tough. Now, the administration has launched an initiative to ease the transition. There is an orientation for new students. Younger students have a "skills class" twice a week, in which they learn how to organize their time, develop good work habits, and get homework done without distraction. A new position of assistant principal for the middle school has been created; one guidance counselor follows kids through 7th and 8th grade. There is a push to encourage kids to join middle school sports teams, as well as a chorus, orchestra, jazz ensemble, and drama program designed for the younger students.

Tony Fisher, assistant principal for the 7th and 8th grades, said he is encouraging the teachers to do "less lecturing, more group work and more hands-on activities" for the younger students. Teachers meet to plan lessons for 7th- and 8th-graders and discuss individual students' progress. While homework still follows a "boom and bust" cycle (because teachers may all assign big projects due on the same day), Fisher said he is working for better coordination among the staff.

Still, 7th- and 8th-graders are given far more responsibility than is typical for children of this age. It's an "open campus," which means children are allowed to leave campus anytime they don't have a class. (Part of the middle school initiative includes scheduling younger students so they don't have too many free periods.)

The 7th- and 8th-grade classrooms look like high school or even college lecture rooms—simply furnished with desks and chairs, but with no student work posted. Because teachers aren't assigned to their own rooms, they cannot decorate them or stock them with classroom libraries.

The teaching style is traditional for the most part. On one of my visits, students worked on math problems on floor-to-ceiling blackboards that covered the walls. Students read aloud from *Julius Caesar* in one English class. In another, students learned to write their own mystery stories and discussed techniques of how to build suspense in a narrative. In 7th-grade science, students dissected a squid. In a theater class, students worked in groups to write their own skits; some sprawled on the black floor (painted to resemble a black box theater), while others sat in the corridors.There are no electives in 7th and 8th grades. All 7th- and 8th-graders take algebra, science, social studies, English, music, and art.

Children may study Latin, French, or Spanish. (Italian is offered to juniors and seniors. Mandarin is offered as an after-school elective.) Readings in 7th grade include *The House on Mango Street*, *Of Mice and Men*, *Lord of the Flies*, and *A Midsummer Night's Dream*. Eighth-graders read *The Joy Luck Club*, *Black Boy*, and *The Chosen*. Children are expected to have at least a nodding acquaintance with icons of Western civilization, such as Plato and Aristotle. One year, children read not only the Bible but also early Irish myths and sagas, the Arabian nights, stories of Islam, and tales of dragon gods and spirits from Chinese mythology.

"It's a perfect balance between a classical curriculum and innovative teaching methods," said one mother.

Because it's administered by CUNY—not the Department of Education—Hunter isn't bound by the Department of Education's requirement to teach American history in the 7th and 8th grades. This means that teachers can use these years to introduce children to topics that form the foundation of social studies—such as political philosophy, cultural anthropology, and a smattering of economics—and can give them tools to use for research—such as how to study documents and primary sources. Children investigate these "global studies" for 3 years before they look at American history in the 10th and 11th grades.

Kids study 2 years of algebra in 7th and 8th grades, as well as elementary probability and geometry. The most advanced 8th-graders also study less traditional topics, such as logic, groups, and fields.

Kids study life science in 7th grade and physical science in 8th grade. On one of my visits, kids were working in groups, chatting happily and animatedly with one another. One girl in blue jeans was digging for earthworms in a pile of dirt on the lab table as her group investigated ways to estimate the number of earthworms without counting every one. (They divided the dirt into quadrants, counted the worms in one quadrant, then multiplied it by the number of quadrants.)

Hunter has some brilliant teachers—as well as a few who are a bit dull. One mother said that her daughter got "one dud teacher every year." But she added that the good teachers were extraordinary, and even the classes with dud teachers were salvaged because the kids were so smart that they were able to learn from one another.

The workload is heavy. "I think [my daughter] is working harder at middle school than I did at college," one mother said. "Unless you're incredibly motivated and organized, it could be a horror." Another mother said that her 7th-grader's homework load ranged from 1 to 5 hours a night.

The school can be a stressful, intense place. One teacher described an "insane careerism" about where kids go to college and a "hysteria about having a 1350 SAT score"—a score that would be considered very good indeed almost anywhere but Hunter. I met a child who was visibly disappointed that he would be going to Swarthmore (he'd been hoping for Yale). One teacher said that the "parents are just nutso" about their kids' college admissions. The college office has made a concerted effort to keep the hysteria under control by encouraging students to apply widely. One counselor visited 50 colleges—just so she could give firsthand reports about places students might not have considered.

"College advising was very good and highly personalized," said the mother of a senior who was admitted to Yale. "The counselor rejected [my son's] initial college list of all elite or nearly elite schools, and forced him to add more safety schools to the list. As it happened, we didn't need those, but it was a wise move."

Still, everyone agrees, it can be tough to be a kid in a school filled with overachievers. "You have to be self-sufficient and a little thick-skinned to survive," another mother said.

Children in the elementary school are generally admitted to the high school, although, going forward, admission may no longer be automatic. Others are admitted in 7th grade based on the results of a test administered to children in January of their 6th-grade year.

Only Manhattan residents may apply to the elementary school; children living anywhere in the five boroughs who meet the eligibility requirements may apply to the high school. About 45 children enter Hunter College High School from the elementary school, while about 180 are chosen from other schools.

Children who score in the 90th percentile or above on the standardized reading and math tests given in 5th grade are eligible to take the entrance exam in January of their 6th-grade year. Students applying from private schools must score in the 90th percentile on the ERBs or a similar standardized test. (The cutoff scores vary from year to year.) Your child's 6th-grade teachers should notify you if your child qualifies. There is a fee to take the exam.

With the new administration, there is a heightened awareness that very bright kids are still, after all, kids, with the same range of social and emotional problems that any other kids might have. Increasingly, Hunter is making accommodations for students who are "twice exceptional," that is, intellectually gifted but challenged in other ways. For example, a very bright boy with behavior problems was assigned an aide to help him control his outbursts. A handful of children are formally classified as needing **special education** services; others receive extra help informally. A learning specialist is available 3 days a week for children with learning difficulties

The school makes accommodations for children in special education whose reading and math scores meet the cutoff. If, for example, a child is blind or hearing impaired, an appropriate aide may assist during the exam. The school is wheelchair accessible.

Each year 2,000 kids take the exam, which consists of multiple-choice questions and an essay. The 150 children who score the highest on the multiple-choice portion of the test and who write acceptable essays are offered admission. In addition, about 30 seats are set aside for children who are "economically disadvantaged"—children from low-income families. Those children must have standardized test scores high enough to be eligible for the exam and must pass the essay part of the test, but may have slightly lower scores on the multiple-choice section. Students must apply for economically disadvantaged status before taking the multiple-choice exam. Seventh grade is the only year for which children are admitted. Students hear whether they are admitted in mid-February. Increasingly, students who are successful have taken private prep classes.

Manhattan East School for Arts and Academics, MS 224

410 East 100th Street
New York, NY 10029
(212) 860-6047
www.manhattaneastschool.org

Admissions: citywide
High school choices: LaGuardia, Eleanor Roosevelt, Frederick Douglass
Grade levels: 6–8   **Test scores:** R *****, M *****
Enrollment: 266   **Ethnicity:** 23%W 34%B 37%H 6%A
Class size: 28   **Free lunch:** 41%

You climb five flights of stairs. Your heart still pounding, you're greeted by a sign that says: "Congratulations! You've made it to the top!" Everyone at Manhattan East, a small school on the top floor of a junior high school built in 1923, is proud of the place—and it shows. There's a joyful spirit that's shared by parents, teachers, and students. The building is immaculate, classrooms—all lined up along one corridor—are large and cheery, and children's work is displayed throughout.

There's an intimacy among students and staff that's unusual even among small schools. Students and teachers even eat lunch together. The staff of 18 teachers is small enough that they can fit around one table for their regular staff meetings.

Consistently one of the top-ranked middle schools in the city, Manhattan East attracts students from all five boroughs to its creative art, drama, dance, and music programs and its accelerated academic classes. Rare for a city school, the student body is roughly one-third White, one-third Black, and one-third Latino.

In English, children read a mix of classics and contemporary fiction: 6th-graders read *The Odyssey*, *The Giver*, *Animal Farm*, and *To Kill a Mockingbird*; 7th-graders read *Romeo and Juliet*, *The House on Mango Street*, *Freak the Mighty*, and *Twelve Angry Men*; 8th-graders read *Hamlet*, *Of Mice and Men*, *The Catcher in the Rye*, and *Bless Me Ultima* (the story of a Mexican *curandera*, or herbal healer).

Although the school has long been known for the arts, one mother called the science teachers "inspiring." Each grade participates in an impressive end-of-the-year science fair. There is a new, well-equipped science lab. Eighth-graders take the Earth science Regents exam.

The math program is accelerated, and 8th-graders take the Regents exam in algebra usually given in high school. In 2006, the school began asking 8th-graders to take the U.S. history and government Regents exam, usually given in 11th grade. "Needless to say, the 8th grade is quite challenging," said a mother who is active in the PTA. "While it may seem like a lot of pressure, it does prepare them well for high school."

The art, music, and drama classes are favorites, and many of the school's graduates go on to performing arts schools such as LaGuardia. All 6th- and 7th-graders study instrumental music and may choose woodwind, brass, or percussion. Electives include studio art, band, jazz ensemble, ceramics, sports conditioning, dance (including ballet and jazz, but not hip-hop), environmental action (which fosters recycling in the school), yearbook, and sewing. The jazz ensemble has traveled to Florida and Massachusetts to take part in national competitions. The school has a kiln and pottery wheels.

Every year, the school puts on a dance production, an art show, and a musical (featuring the jazz band, the orchestra, and the chorus). One year the students put on a production of *Annie*.

The kids I spoke to were happy and enthusiastic about the school. "I never want to graduate, it's so warm and cozy," one girl said. "It's like a family and you can trust everyone," said another girl. "It's a community and we all work together."

The school has an unusual level of parent involvement. The principal has an open-door policy for parents—indeed, with no secretary to intercept visitors, anyone can walk into her office. Parents even have a say in how the budget is spent and what needs to be emphasized in the curriculum. If, for example, parents want more concentration on writing, the staff tries to oblige.

Parents had a part in designing a new playground built by the Trust for Public Land that features a basketball court, artificial turf field, running track, fitness and play equipment, trees, benches, and a stage. They also found funding to renovate the building's auditorium and to build the new science lab.

Manhattan East shares the JHS 99 building with the Academy for Environmental Science Secondary High School. While the building is well kept, there has been some tension in the past between the administrations at both schools regarding the maintenance of shared facilities. Manhattan East students do not interact much with the high school students, one parent told us.

Students go to a variety of high schools, including LaGuardia High School of Music and Art and Performing Arts; Beacon;

Bronx Science; the High School of Math, Science and Engineering at City College; the High School of American Studies; and Frederick Douglass Academy.

About 400 students apply for 90 spots in the entering 6th-grade class. Prospective parents tour the school, then children sit in on classes for a whole day to see if the program is appropriate for them. Children are interviewed and must take a math and writing test to be admitted. The school attempts to keep a good racial balance and in recent years has maintained a population that's roughly a third white, a third African American, and a third Hispanic. Applications are accepted citywide.

Young Women's Leadership School
105 East 106th Street
New York, NY 10029
(212) 289-7593
www.tywls.org

Admissions: citywide, District 4 priority
High school choices: NA
Grade levels: 7–12   **Test scores:** R ****, M ****
Enrollment: 407   **Ethnicity:** 2%W 35%B 61%H 2%A
Class size: 15–20   **Free lunch:** 63%

Founded in 1996 as one of the few all-girls public schools in the nation, Young Women's Leadership School has quickly gained a reputation as a serious, academically challenging college-preparatory school for girls who believe they can achieve more without the distraction and competition posed by having boys in their classes. Cheerful and well-equipped rooms, small classes, attentive teachers, and a no-nonsense atmosphere combine to make this school an attractive choice for girls.

The school has received a number of honors: It was ranked number 1 in the city in a report by Insideschools.org entitled *Against the Odds*. That report recognizes the achievements of schools that admit average or struggling students and graduate them on time. In 2005, Young Women's Leadership was named a Breakthrough High School by the National Association of Secondary School Principals (NASSP), as one of 10 nationally recognized schools that serve mostly poor students of color and send most of them to college. The New York State Education Department named it a High Performing/Gap Closing School in 2006 for its success in closing the racial gap in student performance. Also in 2006, *Newsweek* called it "one of the best public schools in the city."

Occupying five floors in an office building on 106th Street between Lexington and Park Avenues, the school has pleasant quarters with commanding views of Central Park. Girls wear uniforms—plaid skirts or navy blue trousers with blue blazers or blue sweatshirts, emblazoned with a crest on the breast pocket. Good manners are emphasized and I heard lots of "Excuse me's" as girls passed one another in the halls.

But there's a relaxed feel to the school, as well. The walls are painted in soothing pastels of light pink and mauve, with navy blue trim. Classrooms have framed art prints on the walls, cozy sofas, and tables instead of desks. Girls call their teachers by their first names and think nothing of plunking themselves in a favorite teacher's office without an appointment to ask advice.

Instead of eating in a noisy cafeteria, girls have lunch in a place they call their "dining room"—with round tables suited for conversation rather than the long, institutional tables typical of public schools. Large windows let in the sun.

Classes offer an unusual degree of discussion and debate, and students feel free to interrupt a teacher if they don't understand. There is a strong emphasis on learning to write well, and the class size of 20 to 25 in the high school means teachers can edit student papers without becoming overwhelmed. In the 7th and 8th grades, classes are split in half for English, math, and science. With no more than 15 students in each of these classes, girls can get the attention they need.

In an 8th-grade humanities class, girls worked on research projects on the history of slavery and the Middle Passage, between Africa and America. The girls worked in groups, and the atmosphere wasn't competitive. In a class on Earth and marine science, each student was assigned to study a creature in an aquarium in the back of the room, including turtles, clown fish, dragon fish, and frogs. The school has fully equipped science labs and a growing science research program.

Some classes have a feminist twist. In an 11th-grade humanities class, girls studying 18th-century philosophers of the Enlightenment read an excerpt from Mary Wollstonecraft's *Vindication of the Rights of Woman*. For homework, they had to create an imaginary dialogue between Jean-Jacques Rousseau and Wollstonecraft on the role of women in society.

Girls sometimes discuss topics that might be embarrassing in a co-ed class. In a biology class on the digestive system, for example, a teacher spoke candidly about the pain of hemorrhoids during pregnancy.

"They are taught to be young ladies," said a grandmother who is active in the PTA. "They are treated with respect, and they are respectful in return." Standards are high. In one 11th-grade class in which girls studied the use of character development in essays, the teacher told students that she was available to help them—but that anyone who didn't turn work in on time would receive an F.

While there aren't a lot of electives, girls may study string instruments in the school's music program or videography with

Metropolis Studios, housed in the building. Advanced Placement offerings include Spanish language, Spanish literature, English literature, U.S. history, calculus, and environmental science—a large number, considering how tiny the school is, with just 60 students in each grade. Students receiving **special education** services are integrated into regular classes. Sports include basketball and soccer.

The school is the brainchild of Ann Rubenstein Tisch, a philanthropist who believes that single-sex education is an important way to counter what researchers see as a crisis of confidence that strikes young adolescent girls. "It seems to be where the unraveling begins, right out of elementary school," Tisch said. "Kids can go from being fairly stable, to getting into trouble—socially and academically."

Carol Gilligan at Harvard University's School of Education, among others, has said that girls who are self-assured as preteens begin to change as they reach adolescence. Once fearless about raising their hands in class, some girls become shy and withdrawn. They begin to worry more about their looks and pleasing boys than about academic achievement. Girls who are high-achievers in elementary school often begin to stumble in middle school, overtaken by boys whose confidence is increasing, researchers say.

Tisch believes that single-sex education can overcome some of these problems. With the cooperation of what was then called the Board of Education, she helped found the Young Women's Leadership School.

A foundation she heads, the Young Women's Leadership Foundation (www.ywlfoundation.org), pays for the college advisor and some of the after-school programs. With funding from the Bill and Melinda Gates Foundation, Young Women's Leadership has replicated its success with new schools of the same name in the Bronx; in southeast Queens; and in Astoria, Queens.

The school has the luxury of a full-time college counselor, Chris Farmer, who meets regularly with each girl in her junior and senior years. His office, with a comfy couch and shaggy throw pillows, contains a mailbox for each senior for college applications and information. The foundation also supports student trips to tour colleges and universities, including Yale University, Smith College, and Connecticut College. Smith College offers students summer school classes on its campus in Southampton, Massachusetts. Skidmore College and NYU offer summer classes as well.

Nearly every graduate attends college, and more than 90% attend 4-year schools. Students have been accepted to such schools as Fordham, Mount Holyoke, Howard, Columbia, Williams, Amherst, and Haverford. YWLS graduates have a good record staying in college and graduating on time, said Farmer.

All prospective students must attend a tour with their families. Most students enter in 7th grade, but there are a few openings for 9th-graders. Priority is given to students in District 4. Parents as well as students are screened: The administration wants to ensure that parents support the school and that their daughters will conform to the dress code and are committed to the idea of single-sex education. Students are interviewed. Most successful candidates score at least at Level 2 for reading and math on standardized tests. "Our typical student is an average student who really wants to be here," Farmer said. "We have hardworking, nice kids. They may not be gifted academically, but their work ethic is strong."

Center School, MS 243

270 West 70th Street
New York, NY 10023
(212) 799-1477
www.thecenterschool.org/

Admissions: District 3
High school choices: LaGuardia, Beacon, Bard
Grade levels: 5–8   **Test scores:** R ****, M ****
Enrollment: 200   **Ethnicity:** 50%W 22%B 19%H 9%A
Class size: 10–27   **Free lunch:** NA

A tiny gem of a place, the Center School is worth a visit just to see how beautifully teachers work to combine challenging academics with a warm and nurturing atmosphere. With very small classes and lots of attention for each child, the school has a progressive attitude toward *how* children learn and a classical view of *what* they should learn.

This means that teachers expect the kids to move around the classrooms and to chat with one another as they work, rather than sit silently in rows and absorb knowledge. Teachers and kids alike wear blue jeans. At the same time, the subject matter is traditional: Latin is mandatory. Everyone is expected to spell properly and to learn conventional geography and algebra.

Founded in 1982, the school has changed little over the years. The founding principal, Elaine Schwartz, is still there—and vows never to retire. Many talented, passionate teachers have been there for years, joined by younger equally talented staffers. Perhaps the only thing that has changed is the rest of the world, which has finally come to understand what Schwartz has long known, that the traditional junior high school—with more than 1,000 kids, 40-minute classes, and lectures from textbooks—is simply the wrong model for teaching young adolescents.

Children this age, Schwartz says, can't sit still and need to talk to their friends. They are beginning to move from concrete to abstract thinking, but they can't absorb material solely from textbooks. They need materials they can see and touch. Schools that fail to recognize the realities of young adolescent development, she says, won't be able to teach them.

"If you accept the fact that they must socialize and they must make noise, you've won half the battle," says Schwartz. "Sitting still for hours and being quiet is not the way adults work, so why should children do it?"

The school allows 6 minutes for class changes—not the 3 minutes allocated at most schools. That gives children a chance to stretch their legs and chat a bit, so when their next class starts they're more ready to concentrate. Classes vary in length from 45 minutes to 2 hours.

The school goes from 5th to 8th grade, and children of different ages are assigned to classes together for most subjects. The administration believes there is an advantage to keeping children in a middle school for 4 years rather than the more typical 3. There's more continuity, and it's easier to build a sense of community if children stay for 4 years.

The mixing of ages in classes gives children a sense of family and belonging. Classes that are clearly sequential—math and Latin—are separated by age, but others, including English and social studies, have children of different ages.

"Children this age are a mess of anxiety about everything," said teacher Judith Hartmann. "They are insecure emotionally, physically, every which way they can be. Most schools tend to make that even worse, exacerbating their insecurities."

Having classes with children of different ages, she said, eases competition and allows children to relax about who they are. "What it teaches them is that not everyone is at the same place. They see 5th-graders who know the answers and 8th-graders who don't," Hartmann said. "I don't hold everyone to the same standard."

Teachers pride themselves on their ability to teach different subjects. One year, Gabrielle Castelnau, an English and social studies teacher, gave a science unit on coral reefs, boning up on the subject herself over the summer.

"We're expected to be flexible and to have enough intellectual curiosity to delve into new subjects," said Castelnau. "We're not tied to one subject here." Interdisciplinary work comes naturally in a setting such as this. The unit on coral reefs, for example, included a lot of geography as well as science.

The teachers seem particularly well attuned to the quirks of young adolescents—and adapt their lessons to appeal to them. "They are really captivated by mayhem and disasters, so I did a science curriculum based on earthquakes, volcanoes, and tidal waves," said Hartmann.

The school has no science labs, but the science curriculum is rich nonetheless. Posters, researched and illustrated by the children, display the history of rockets—from the ancient Greeks until modern times. In one class, children learned about jet propulsion by filling soda cans with water, suspending them by strings, then poking holes in them with nails. They measured the speed at which the water poured out and the cans spun, depending on the size and placement of the holes. Another class went on a "video Safari," studying the habitat of crocodiles by observing them—on tape—in the wild. Children built bridges from folded paper, then tested their strength by piling them high with wooden blocks. They studied the form and function of birds' wings and sketched parts of a feather they observed under a microscope.

Each teacher serves as an advisor to 10 to 12 children and meets with them as a group regularly. The advisor acts as an advocate for the child, helping resolve any difficulties with other children or other teachers. The advisors help develop study skills, particularly planning how to organize long assignments.

Instead of receiving conventional report cards, children write their own evaluations in November. At the end of each trimester, teachers write long comments, and children add their own notes.

There are very few textbooks, except for math and Latin. Instead, teachers rely on works of literature and primary source materials, such as diaries and historical documents. The whole school takes an annual overnight trip, to Boston; Washington, DC; or an environmental camp.

The school has one teacher certified in **special education**, and about two dozen children receive services, integrated into regular classes.

The Center School is on the top floor of a well-regarded and well-kept elementary school, PS 199. White tiles, white floor, and good lighting make the classrooms bright and appealing. Children's work covers the wall.

High school choices include Beacon, Bard, LaGuardia High School of Music and Art and Performing Arts, and Eleanor Roosevelt. One year, six students were admitted to Stuyvesant, but none decided to go, preferring small schools, Schwartz said.

Prospective students are asked to sit in on classes for the morning (prospective parents, meanwhile, look in on other classes). Prospective students are asked to write the answer to a question such as "How did you feel when you came to the Center School?" The teachers interview applicants, asking them questions such as why they wanted to come to the Center School and what kind of books they like to read. Call the school to arrange a tour and interview in the fall of your child's 4th-grade year. The school has about 200 applicants for 45 spots in the 5th grade. One downside: Children are admitted only in the 5th grade.

Computer School
100 West 77th Street
New York, NY 10024
(917) 441-0873
www.thecomputerschool.org

Admissions: District 3
High school choices: Beacon, LaGuardia, Bronx Science
Grade levels: 6–8   **Test scores:** R ****, M ****
Enrollment: 332   **Ethnicity:** 32%W 24%B 35%H 9%A
Class size: 24–30   **Free lunch:** 39%

When the Computer School was founded in 1982, the idea of using computers in every classroom was considered offbeat, even weird. Now, of course, everyone recognizes the importance of computers—and it's hard to remember how radical the idea was when the school opened. The Computer School is still a leader in the use of technology. Students have computer classes twice a week in which they learn programming and web design and create their own blogs and "wikis," or collaborative websites.

They may study the history of animation (including 19th-century zoetropes—spinning cylinders with drawings on the interior), create sound effects and moving images, and even make simple animated cartoons. They use computers to make bar graphs and pie charts from Excel spreadsheets showing, for example, the percentage of different races in different New York City neighborhoods. In one class, they used Photoshop to place photos of themselves into historic scenes. One girl put a photo of herself sitting on the famous bus next to civil rights leader Rosa Parks. Another stood with Washington crossing the Delaware.

The Computer School has become one of the most popular and successful schools in the city, with far more applicants than seats available. It has an energetic and talented principal, a cohesive staff, and a varied and imaginative student body. There are no bells.

For many years the school was awkwardly housed in two sites, sharing space with PS 9 on 84th Street and MS 44 on 77th Street. Now the school is united on one cheery floor of MS 44. Sixth- and 7th-grade classes are mixed—half 6th-graders, half 7th—for English and social studies, as a way to integrate the youngest students into the life of the school. "We don't want them to feel like low man on the totem pole," said Principal Henry Zymeck, a former science teacher at the school. They follow a 2-year curriculum, studying colonial history one year, immigration the next. While humanities and science classes mix children of different abilities, children are grouped according to their level of skill in math. Struggling students get the attention they need in classes as small as ten students, while advanced students may master high school algebra in a Regents-prep class. All students take Regents (high school–level) Earth science and advanced students take Regents Spanish.

The school collaborates with the Lincoln Center Institute to integrate the study of visual and performing arts into the academic curriculum. In a math class, a group of students used their bodies to illustrate math concepts such as parabolas—combining dance and math. Trips are a big part of the curriculum: Kids visit the American Museum of Natural History and the New York Historical Society (both a short walk from the school), Ellis Island, the Guggenheim, and the Metropolitan Museum of Art. One 8th-grade class took an overnight camping trip to Montauk and enjoyed watching the stars—visible on the beach but invisible to kids in Manhattan.

One year, on a day trip to Central Park, students observed the effects of erosion and glaciers on different rock formations—part of the Earth science curriculum. At the Metropolitan Museum of Art, they looked at different kinds of rocks and minerals in the Egyptian wing—granite sarcophagi and clay pottery and beads made of various minerals. "Rather than passing around a little piece [of a rock] in class, they can see what it's used for," said Zymeck. "We ask, 'Where did these rocks come from? Where does clay come from?'"

Teachers say they appreciate the flexibility to create their own lessons. "I feel like I have the freedom to teach in a deep, thoughtful way without having someone over me saying, 'What about the test? What about the test?'" said social studies teacher Jessica Shalom. The teachers are knowledgeable and concerned, constantly reevaluating and adjusting their teaching techniques to accommodate different kinds of students. The staff seems to care as much about the low-achievers as about the high-achievers, and teachers manage to make lessons interesting and exciting for all.

A member of the Coalition of Essential Schools, the Computer School adheres to the principles of Brown University's Theodore R. Sizer, who believes schools should be small, democratic communities where decisions are made collectively by the staff. "The teachers genuinely like each other and communicate with each other," one mother said.

The relationship between the Computer School and MS 44, with which it shares a building, has improved in recent years. For several years, MS 44 had a revolving door of principals, a demoralized staff, and students who took out their resentments on Computer School kids after school. Now, MS 44 has a much smaller enrollment with fewer troubled kids and a principal who gives her students the same perks, such as class trips, that Computer School kids have. "The kids downstairs are happier" and friction has eased, said a Computer School parent. Arrival and dismissal times for the two schools are staggered: Computer kids arrive at 8 a.m. and leave at 2:20 p.m. MS 44 kids arrive at 8:30 a.m. and leave at 3:10 p.m.

The Computer School has no lockers or science lab. The cafeteria is tiny and noisy, but children are allowed to leave the building several times a week for lunch.

There is one self-contained **special education** class for 12 special needs students. About 30 students receive Special Education Teacher Support Services (SETSS). Students in the self-contained class have advisory periods and electives and go on class trips with other students, and they may be mainstreamed in academic classes when appropriate.

After-school classes in drama, art, dance, and sports are offered Monday through Thursday until 5 p.m.

About one-quarter of the graduates go to Beacon, a highly regarded progressive school founded by a former Computer School teachers. Others choose LaGuardia High School of Music and Art and Performing Arts, Facing History, Environmental Studies, and Millennium. One recent year, 25 graduates were admitted to the specialized schools.

Tours are offered in the fall and winter. Teachers interview children in groups of eight to ten. "They don't have to be high-achieving, but we like inquisitive kids," said an administrator. "A kid who needs a lot of constant, direct supervision is not likely to do well here." There are typically 300 applicants for 120 seats.

Anderson School

100 West 84th Street
New York, NY 10024
(212) 595-7193
http://www.ps334anderson.org/

Admissions: citywide
High school choices: Stuyvesant, Bronx Science, LaGuardia
Grade levels: K–8   **Test scores:** R *****, M *****
Enrollment: 517   **Ethnicity:** 62%W 8%B 11%H 19%A
Class size: 32   **Free lunch:** 15%

A school for "gifted" children that accepts applicants from all five boroughs, the Anderson School is one of the most sought after in the city. Housed in a neighborhood elementary school, PS 9, the Anderson School has creative teachers; a hyper-involved parent body; smart kids; and cheery, well-equipped classrooms. It's an intense place: The academic program is accelerated by at least a year. An enormous proportion of graduates are admitted to Stuyvesant High School or Bronx Science. At the same time, with just two classes in each grade in kindergarten through 8th grade, the school has a cozy, intimate feel, and teachers get to know the students well. The administration has taken steps to limit homework, and parents say it's not a pressure cooker. The middle school dean (who functions as an assistant principal), Aimee Terosky, gets high marks from parents; one mother said that she "manages to be there for every child."

The middle school, serving just 180 children in grades 6–8, has its own entrance, its own staff, and its own lunchtime (an impossibly early 10:30 a.m.) Most of the children in Anderson's 5th grade continue on to middle school, so there isn't a lot of room for new students. Don't get your heart set on the place: With 400 applicants for about a dozen seats in 6th grade and another dozen in 7th grade (the precise number varies from year to year), it's a long shot even if your child is very, very bright. Still, it doesn't cost anything (except your time and effort) to apply.

The curriculum is imaginative. In one social studies class, children mummified a chicken as part of their study of ancient Egypt. In another, children wrote their own family's history, interviewing elderly relatives about, for example, their experiences in World War II. An 8th-grade English class focused on "banned books"—with children choosing to read books that had once been banned, including *Huckleberry Finn*, *The Catcher in the Rye*, and Stephen King's *Carrie*. Sixth-graders interviewed meteorologists as part of a study of the weather. Seventh-graders study philosophy once a week for 12 weeks. The school also offers weekly electives, such as documentary filmmaking, drama, cooking, crime scene investigation, and debate club. All 6th-graders learn to play the piano in the "keyboard lab." Students may also take semi-private music lessons in flute, clarinet, saxophone, trombone, trumpet, cello, and violin.

The math curriculum is particularly fast paced. Seventh-graders may take the algebra Regents exams, commonly taken in 9th grade, while 8th-graders may take the geometry Regents exams, commonly taken in 10th grade. Eighth-graders take the Living Environment (biology) Regents, usually taken in 9th grade.

Still, the tone of the school combines playfulness with serious study, and the kids seem to be relaxed and happy. The school once had a reputation as a place with mountains of homework. Terosky said that the school responded to concerns that homework was excessive by drawing up a policy that limits homework to about an hour a night. Parents I spoke to said homework might creep up to 2 hours a night, but it's not the nightmarish quantity of work that they had feared.

Sports include tennis, volleyball, soccer, baseball, basketball, and track. Children may have lunch outside the school building, with certain restrictions.

Parents are actively involved in the school and were, in fact, the catalyst for the opening of the middle school program in 2003. Parents volunteer in the classroom and cafeteria as "learning leaders," raise money for the school, and serve on a committee that hires the staff.

The school has an excellent record of sending graduates to the specialized high schools. "Almost everyone gets their first choice," Terosky said. One year, out of 60 graduates, 20 were admitted to Stuyvesant, 16 to Bronx Science, and 14 to LaGuardia High School of Music and Art and Performing Arts. Others were admitted to Beacon; Bard; the High School of American Studies at Lehman College; Townsend Harris; Brooklyn Tech; and the High School of Math, Science and Engineering at City College.

An open house is held in January. Students applying for admission must score at Level 4 on both reading and math on 4th-grade standardized tests (or a combined score that in previous years was set at 1385), and must also take an exam administered by the school. Students from anywhere in the city may apply. Check the school's website for tour information and an application. Admissions procedures change from year to year. Students may apply to 6th or 7th grade. Some students leave for Hunter College High School or private schools in the 7th grade, leaving a few spots open.

Booker T. Washington School, MS 54
103 West 107th Street
New York, NY 10025
(212) 678-2861
www.ms54.org

Admission: District 3
High school choices: Bronx Science, Stuyvesant, LaGuardia
Grade levels: 6–8   **Test scores:** R ****, M ****
Enrollment: 900   **Ethnicity:** 39%W 24%B 31%H 6%A
Class size: 28–30   **Free lunch:** 64%

MS 54 houses one of the most challenging middle school programs in the city: Delta Honors, a traditional, structured place where kids study Latin, take high school–level courses in math and science, and learn to write 5-paragraph essays before launching into 10- or 15-page term papers. Reading lists include Shakespeare's *Hamlet, Richard II, Othello, Macbeth,* and *Romeo and Juliet,* as well as *Antigone* and modern classics like *Tom Sawyer, The Great Gatsby, The Catcher in the Rye,* and *Lord of the Flies.* The workload is heavy, but the payoff is great: Nearly three-quarters of graduates go on Stuyvesant, Bronx Science, or other specialized high schools.

For years, MS 54 was a school of haves and have-nots: The kids in Delta Honors got the best teachers and the best books and supplies, while kids in the rest of the building seemed to get whatever was left over. Resentments sometimes spilled over into fights outside the building. Dr. Elana Elster, who became principal in 2005, has worked hard to build a sense of community in the building and to create more equity between Delta and the rest of the school, and, while the results aren't perfect, she's been pretty successful. Parents say the school is much safer, particularly since children must now have lunch in the cafeteria and recess in the playground. (They are no longer permitted outside in the neighborhood.) The total enrollment in the building has been reduced, and with the easing of overcrowding, tensions have eased as well.

There is one PTA for the building; all students—not just those in the Delta program—have a chance to go on class trips, and all classrooms are well stocked with books and supplies. All students have access to music and art. All 6th-graders sample chorus, percussion, strings, and band.

Elster consolidated three small programs into one, called CORE (which stands for Creating Opportunities for Rigorous Education). CORE serves students with a range of abilities, including new immigrants who are just learning English and some students with severe disabilities. Delta and CORE teachers plan their lessons together. Delta is no longer housed on its own floor; each floor has both Delta and CORE classes.

The building, constructed in the 1950s, is rather drab, with gray walls and flickering florescent lights. Class changes are orderly but noisy, and the tiny cafeteria is really too small for all the students it must serve.

Delta, with 550 students, is one of the most selective middle school programs in the city, and, while it faces competition for students from the Anderson Middle School and the new Columbia Secondary School, it continues to attract some of the best students in the district. Delta has long had a reputation of being a pressure cooker, but the administration has made efforts to ease the homework load on students, and parents I spoke to said their children averaged 1½ to 2 hours of homework a night. Teachers are asked not to assign any homework over the weekend or on school vacations.

"We heard all the nightmare stories about kids getting lost in the 6th grade and mountains of homework, but it hasn't been the case," said a mother. Teachers help ease 6th-graders into middle school routines with tips on how to plan their time, how to study for tests, and how to organize their homework. Every Monday, teachers are available for half an hour before the regular school day begins, to help students individually in what is called an "open house."

"It's not a sink-or-swim kind of place," said a father. "The level of compassion among the 6th-grade faculty is amazing."

Long-term projects have been restructured in a way that allows children to do some of the work in school, rather than at home. Research papers emphasize "quality, not quantity," one teacher said. Children are given step-by-step instructions on how to organize note cards and write a bibliography.

All Delta 8th-graders take the Earth science and math Regents, and many take the Spanish Regents as well. (French and Latin are also offered.) On one of my visits, 8th-grade Delta students analyzed the cultural and historical context of Willa Cather's *My Ántonia*. In a social studies class, students tested their knowledge of the Civil War by filling out a worksheet on the Battle of Gettysburg. In a science class, kids made graphs on their laptops showing the phases of water from ice to vapor over time.

Delta has an excellent record of high school admissions: One recent year, out of 190 graduating 8th-graders, 52 were admitted to Bronx Science and 40 to Stuyvesant. More than a dozen were admitted to LaGuardia High School of Music and Art and Performing Arts, and the rest went to sought-after schools like Bard, Eleanor Roosevelt, Townsend Harris, and Beacon.

The CORE program has 350 students. In nearly all the classes we visited, the kids seemed happy and engaged, and the quality of teaching was good. Imaginative teachers brought lessons to life using hands-on activities in the math classes we visited.

The school has six self-contained **special education** classes for children with special needs, and two Collaborative Team Teaching (CTT) classes that mix special needs and general education pupils. About 120 students receive services, including Special Education Teachers Support Services (SETSS), occupational therapy, and speech. Some students are hearing impaired, some have learning disabilities, and some have emotional problems. The building is not wheelchair accessible. There is a bilingual special education class, as well as two classes for students in English as a Second Language.

After-school activities include sports such as soccer, track, and basketball; a math team; a creative writing club; and a visual arts club.

Tours are offered in the fall and winter. Applicants to Delta Honors must have a teacher recommendation, must score at Level 4 on the 4th-grade standardized writing and math tests (or have a combined score of 1385), and must also pass a writing and math exam administered by the school. About 250 students apply for 180 seats in the Delta program. Priority in admission goes to District 3 students, but there are occasionally spots for out-of-district students.

Mott Hall II, MS 862

234 West 109th Street
New York, NY 10025
(212) 678-2960
http://mott.echalk.com

Admissions: District 3
High school choices: Beacon, Mott Hall High School, Urban Assembly
Grade levels: 6–8   **Test scores:** R *****, M ****
Enrollment: 296   **Ethnicity:** 21%W 27%B 45%H 7%A
Class size: 25   **Free lunch:** 42%

Created as a clone of Mott Hall, a selective middle school that has long prepared kids from upper Manhattan for the city's best high schools, Mott Hall II combines the order and decorum for which traditional schools are known with the warmth and creative teaching that makes progressive schools attractive. Opened in September 2001, Mott Hall II has quickly become one of the most popular middle schools in District 3. It has a solid, enthusiastic group of teachers who have a nice rapport with the kids, and an eager, curious student body.

Mott Hall II has a nice mix of different ethnic groups and family incomes, and kids say that's part of the school's appeal. In an essay posted on the wall, one student wrote, "I feel like Martin Luther King's dream has been achieved. . . . I have friends that come from many different races and ethnicities."

While expectations are high and class work is demanding, parents say Mott Hall II is somewhat less pressured than schools like Delta Honors and Anderson. Teachers place an emphasis on skills and quick recall of facts: There are spelling quizzes and old-fashioned geography lessons, in which kids are expected to memorize the 50 states and their capitals.

At the same time, class work is engaging. One year, 8th-graders read *Fast Food Nation*, an exposé of the fast food business, then tried the industry in a mock court. On one of our visits, 7th-graders dissected owl pellets and played math games, and 8th-graders worked together in small groups to create book discussion guides. Seventh-graders reading the novel *The Catcher in the Rye*, for example, had written essays from the point of view of protagonist Holden Caulfield's school headmaster, created playlists for Holden's imaginary iPod, and were beginning to write ballads in the style of one mentioned in the book. "In every class we visited, students we talked to understood the reasons behind what they were doing and could explain those reasons articulately," Philissa Cramer reported on the Insideschools.org website.

Mott Hall II occupies the 4th floor of PS 165, a 100-year-old Gothic-revival building. (Crossroads, another middle school, is on the 5th floor.) The rooms are large and pleasant, and a new paint job has spruced the place up. Students follow a dress code that forbids jeans, baggy pants, or gear emblazoned with sports logos. Rules of behavior are posted prominently, and children are given detention if they break the rules, such as chewing gum in class. It's a strict school. "They give detention very freely," one mother said. To prevent children from spending an inordinate time in the bathroom—as middle school students sometimes do—children receive ten "bathroom bucks" each quarter. They may use the bathroom whenever they like during lunch, but if they want to go during class time they must use one of the "bathroom bucks."

Teachers are accessible. "If you need help with anything, the teachers are always there," one student said. "The kids feel the teachers really like them," a mother said, adding that the principal, Ana De Los Santos, "is young and peppy and the kids adore her." Parents appreciate that teachers respond promptly to e-mails, and the school's website keeps them informed about homework assignments. Students are assigned to an "advisory" group of 12 students and one teacher, who meet regularly to discuss academic as well as social and emotional issues. Students are present at parent-teacher conferences; in fact, the students start the meetings by describing what they see as their accomplishments.

Students take the math and Earth science Regents exams in 8th grade, and they can get Spanish proficiency certification that prepares them for advanced Spanish courses in high school. Students are expected to complete 2 to 3 hours of homework a night.

Because increasing numbers of middle-class families have enrolled their children, the school no longer qualifies for federal antipoverty funds known as Title I. Parents have made up some of that difference. The PTA raises money for equipment and supplies, teacher training, and field trips to Philadelphia and Washington, DC. Parents are also involved in putting on the school's annual musical.

The school offers a self-contained **special education** class for students with special needs, as well as Collaborative Team Teaching (CTT) program. CTT classes have two teachers, one of whom is certified in special education, and a mix of students with special needs and general education students. Special Education Teacher Support Services (SETSS, formerly called resource room) are also available.

The school has an extensive enrichment program, both during and after school. Courses include digital photography, cinematography, trivia, chess, community service, and dance. The Manhattan School of Music offers low-cost music lessons after school in drums, guitar, and violin.

Early on, the school encourages students to aim high for college: 6th-graders tour Columbia University, 7th-graders tour Princeton, and 8th-graders tour Yale. "They say, 'This is what you need to get in and you can do it,'" one mother said.

High school preparation begins with an orientation in 7th grade, and guidance counselors meet with students individually. The school offers test prep throughout the year and a portfolio preparation program for students interested in the arts high schools. (One parent told us that many kids take private test prep for the high school admission exams.)

About one-quarter of students are admitted to the specialized high schools, and about another quarter go to Beacon. An increasing number are opting for private and boarding schools. Open houses are held for prospective students. Call the school for more information. Admission is limited to children living in District 3. Children must score at least at Level 3 on 4th-grade standardized tests for both English and math. They must submit teacher recommendations and be interviewed.

Columbia Secondary School for Math, Science and Engineering

425 West 123th Street
New York, NY 10027
(212) 666-1278
www.columbiasecondary.org

Admissions: Manhattan north of 96th Street
High school choices: NA
Grade levels: 6–12   **Test scores:** new school
Enrollment: 650 (projected)   **Ethnicity:** 20%W 18%B 55%H 7%A
Class size: 30   **Free lunch:** NA

Columbia Secondary School for Math, Science and Engineering (not to be confused with a public high school of almost the same name at City College, or with the private K–8 school at Columbia University) is a partnership between the New York City Department of Education and Columbia University. Opened in 2007 on the fifth floor of an elementary school, PS 125, with a 6th-grade class, the new school will add a grade each year, eventually serving 650 students in grades 6–12 in a new building to be constructed on Columbia's Manhattanville campus.

A strong teaching staff, talented students, and lots of fun trips and projects combine to make this one of the most promising new schools to open in recent years. Sixth-graders designed and constructed cardboard chairs (without glue or fasteners) strong enough for a grown-up to sit on (they auctioned off the chairs and gave the proceeds to charities like UNICEF). They collected edible plants on one trip to Central Park, and on another they studied geology while climbing on rocks. They even planned camping trip to Puerto Rico, where they would hike in the rain forest and study marine biology by snorkeling around a coral reef.

Temporarily housed in a drab but well-kept elementary school building just north of Columbia University's Teachers College, the new school's facilities are basic. Some classrooms have shiny hardwood floors, others have institutional-looking green linoleum. There are wooden cubbies instead of lockers, and some classrooms have battered wooden desks and chairs (painted in bright colors by students and parents.)

The curriculum blends traditional and progressive teaching methods. In a 6th-grade engineering class, students built catapults with plastic spoons, rubber bands, and bits of wood and had a competition to see whose machine could launch a marshmallow the farthest. The students devised cardboard packages to drop eggs from a window to the sidewalk without their breaking. A social studies teacher raised provocative questions for class discussions, such as "Does gentrification promote diversity?" At the same time, teachers offer plenty of emphasis on basic skills, with arithmetic drills in math and spelling and grammar lessons in English. An imaginative Spanish teacher who came to the United States from Spain as a Fulbright scholar managed to challenge both native speakers of Spanish and those who are learning the language for the first time. In a philosophy class, children pondered questions such as "Does the universe have a beginning?" and "Is the universe finite or infinite?" Most classes have two adults, a certified teacher and a student from Teachers College.

In its first year, the majority of Columbia Secondary School students were Latino—attracted in part by the principal, Jose Maldonado-Rivera, a Puerto Rican who spoke Spanish at recruitment fairs for prospective parents. Maldonado-Rivera, who has a Ph.D. in science education from Teachers College, says the school is committed to attracting a mix of different ethnicities and is particularly trying to recruit more African American students.

Students are expected to wear uniforms of blue trousers or jeans and a long-sleeved dress shirt. (The principal wears his version of the uniform: blue jeans with an Oxford cloth shirt and a necktie.) Teachers are called "professor" and several are Ph.D. candidates at Teachers College. Children are divided into "houses" named after famous scientists: Newton, Darwin, and Leonardo da Vinci.

Columbia University, which plans to make some of its science and technology resources, as well its fitness facilities, available to the school, is helping the school develop courses. High school juniors and seniors who qualify will be able to take credits at the university free of charge—quite an opportunity considering the cost of an Ivy League education. A perk for the teachers: They may take graduate courses at Teachers College and Columbia for free. They may also use Columbia's gym and library.

Kids attend a summer "bridge program" one week before school opens, a program intended to ease their transition.

"Our proximity to Morningside Park provides us with tennis courts, basketball, racquetball, baseball, and soccer fields," as well as jogging trails, Maldonado-Rivera said. Electives include science fiction, multimedia design, film, photography, theater, orienteering, Spanish cuisine and culture, and mural painting, as well as a fitness program that includes jogging, Pilates, yoga, dance, swimming, and ultimate Frisbee.

Maldonado-Rivera said there is a high level of parent involvement at the school; out of a student body of 94, 82 parents showed up for curriculum night and a potluck supper.

The principal acknowledged that there has been some friction between Columbia Secondary School and PS 125. Kids at PS 125, possibly envious of the opportunities offered to kids at Columbia Secondary School, occasionally call them names. Administrators of the two schools sometimes squabble over the use of shared space, such as the auditorium. But Maldonado-Rivera said these incidents are rare. On the positive side: PS 125 has a swimming pool that Columbia Secondary students may use twice a week, and there are two gyms in the building, one used exclusively by CSS. (The building also houses a charter school, KIPP S.T.A.R., which has its own entrance.)

Tutoring and homework help is offered after school on Tuesday, Wednesday, and Thursday. There are also after-school electives, such as architecture, math team, Lego robotics, and journalism. No **special education** services are offered.

Priority in admissions is given to students who live or attend school north of 96th Street. Applications are available on the school's website. Students must take a writing exam in March. Most successful candidates score at Level 4 or a high Level 3 on 4th-grade standardized tests. In the first year, about 700 students applied for 100 seats.

Mott Hall School, IS 223

71 Convent Avenue
New York, NY 10027
(212) 281-5028
www.motthall.org

Admissions: District 6
High school choices: HSMSE, Bronx Science, Mott Hall High School
Grade levels: 6–8   **Test scores:** R *****, M *****
Enrollment: 429   **Ethnicity:** 5%W 5%B 85%H 5%A
Class size: 27   **Free lunch:** 81%

Consistently one of the top-ranked middle schools in the city, Mott Hall is a source of pride in the Dominican communities of Washington Heights and Inwood, where most of its students live. Most of the students and many of the teachers are of Dominican heritage.

Founded in 1985 as a small, specialized program for gifted children, Mott Hall is housed in a graceful brick building at 131st Street on the edge of the campus of the City College of New York. Mott Hall has placed many of its graduates in specialized public high schools and in selective private schools, often on full scholarships.

The school is traditional in tone, but many of the teachers use progressive methods in their courses. Teachers work in teams to offer children projects that cut across the disciplines of art, math, science, and literature.

One year, children studied Islamic art as a way of understanding geometry. They designed, built, and launched their own model rockets as an introduction to Newton's three laws of motion and the basics of trigonometry. They researched the history of their school building, which was once a convent, and wrote and performed a cantata based on what they found.

Expectations are high. By 8th grade, kids are reading such complex literature as Shakespeare's *Titus Andronicus*. They discuss the works, write about the characters, and confer with each other or the teacher if something is not understood.

Math, science, and technology are the major focus. In a 6th-grade math class, children used a series of numbers called Fibonacci numbers to predict patterns found in nature. They first examined pinecones, then, using their laptops, researched other places in nature where the patterns might be found. Pineapples were on hand for the next exploration.

In the Stars program, 8th-graders work on projects with mentors in City College science labs. Each week, the junior scientists meet with their Mott Hall advisor to discuss the projects. One team—a student, mentor, and Mott Hall advisor—planned to visit the Dominican Republic during the summer to pursue their research further.

The school uses technology in imaginative ways. Children have access to their own laptop computers, which they may take home. Video equipment is available for students to produce tapes of their projects. Students took part in the First Lego League city-wide robotics competition, and chatted online with an expedition to Mt. Everest. One year, students won the "eCybermission" competition sponsored by the U.S. Army. In this project, students used data they collected from surveys of other students to create a map to help law enforcement and community groups pinpoint blocks in upper Manhattan with gang activity.

Chess is big at Mott Hall. Students have won the national championship several times, and they are coached by a poet who brings literary allusions to his lessons. A small orchestra is taking shape, there is an outdoor garden-like area for science and recreation, and Mott Hall students share an ongoing relationship via Internet and teleconference with students in Japan.

After-school programs include dance classes sponsored by the National Dance Institute, acting classes sponsored by the Tisch School of the Arts at New York University, and chess.

The school has a mentoring program. One year, volunteers from Morgan Stanley & Co. visited the school on a weekly basis to teach basic concepts of business, finance, and economics. The volunteers helped children open their own small businesses, including a keychain company and a T-shirt business.

The school understands that young adolescents need to connect classroom learning to experiences outside school—and that one way to encourage children to act grown up is to give them grown-up responsibilities. Eighth-graders perform community service in places such as day care centers, elementary schools, and nursing homes.

One possible downside: The school seems to keep parents at arm's length. "Teachers don't make time for parents," a former teacher said.

The school once served children in grades 4 to 8. The 4th and 5th grades have been eliminated, saddening some teachers who believed that the school's success was based on having students for 5 years.

In recent years, about 35% of graduates have been admitted to specialized high schools, including Brooklyn Tech; Stuyvesant; the High School for Math, Science and Engineering (HSMSE) at City College; and Bronx Science. Some go to Mott Hall High School, the new school designed as a continuation of the middle school. Others go to private and boarding schools on scholarships.

Only District 6 residents may apply. (The district boundaries are from West 136th Street to West 212th Street, and from Tenth Avenue to Riverside Drive.) Students are admitted on the basis of their test scores, teacher recommendations, a written exam, and an interview. The school accepts about 100 pupils from 500 applicants each year. Applications, due in February, are available from elementary school guidance counselors or at the school. They may be downloaded from the school's website, www.motthall. org. Parents should call in early fall to reserve a spot on one of the school's scheduled tours, which generally take place in November and December.

Frederick Douglass Academy

2581 Adam Clayton Powell Jr. Boulevard
New York, NY 10039
(212) 491-4107
www.fda1.org

Admissions: District 5 priority
High school choices: NA
Grade levels: 6–12 **Test scores:** R ****, M *****
Enrollment: 1,434 **Ethnicity:** 2%W 72%B 25%H 1%A
Class size: 20–34 **Free lunch:** 38%

Frederick Douglass Academy gives the children of central Harlem the kind of rigorous preparation for college that's all too rare in low-income urban neighborhoods. FDA regularly sends more than 90% of its graduating class to college, many on scholarships, some even to the Ivy League. The school has been so popular that school reformers have cloned it, setting up a series of FDA spinoffs throughout the city.

Frederick Douglass Academy is a serious, traditional, and highly structured place, where rules of behavior are carefully spelled out and infractions are swiftly punished. Children are expected to complete 2 hours of homework a night—and they are sent to detention if they don't. A child arriving at school wearing boots rather than the regulation black shoes (no sneakers allowed!) is sent home to change.

Before enrolling a child, parents must sign a form agreeing to show up for parent-teacher conferences and to make sure that homework gets done. The child must agree to abide by the written rules, called the "12 non-negotiables." Children who can't keep up with the heavy workload are asked to leave.

Crisp blue-and-white uniforms, with mandatory neckties for boys and skirts for girls (except in the winter months, when trousers are permitted), are a hallmark of Frederick Douglass. An administrator explained that uniforms eliminate competition over clothes and therefore act as a great equalizer between poor and middle-class children. Having children wear uniforms also allows the grown-ups to spot at a glance anybody who doesn't belong at the school—an important way to ensure safety. (Provisions are made for those students who cannot afford to buy uniforms.)

Hardworking students, dedicated teachers, and a wide array of courses account for FDA's success. The building is open until 7 p.m. and on Saturdays. Students often stay for homework help and to use the facilities. Coursework is demanding. In a social studies class you may hear students respond to such sophisticated questions as, "How did feudalism shape medieval society?" or "How was the Mali Empire formed and why did it collapse?" Kids are required to take 4 years of math, science, and a foreign language, double the state requirement. Advanced Placement classes are offered in a number of subjects, including biology, chemistry, and physics, and the school has a separate lab for each of these sciences.

It is not uncommon to find teachers working in the building as late as 10 p.m. One history teacher, unhappy with textbooks that gave insufficient recognition to the contributions of African Americans, made it his business to seek out donations for textbooks focused on the Black experience in America. A devoted literacy teacher challenged her students with readings from writers ranging from George Orwell to Toni Morrison and crafted a project around the lyrics from "Strange Fruit," the haunting song about lynchings in the South that is perhaps best known through a rendition by Billie Holiday. Extracurricular activities include fencing and top-notch boys' and girls' basketball teams.

After-school activities range from gardening in the greenhouse and rapping in the recording studio to working out in the weight room. Music, art, and dance are mandatory subjects in the middle school for boys and girls. (One co-ed dance class had a particularly creative piece of choreography.) Trips include excursions to Paris, San Francisco, Israel, and South America. A trip to Japan was sponsored by a Japanese airline that was impressed that 400 African American students were learning Japanese.

Students run the school store in collaboration with the Gap, which supplies the school uniforms. Students learn business techniques by running the store, and one was flown to San Francisco to meet with Gap executives. Profits help pay fees for college applications.

There are four **special education** classes for children with learning disabilities. Every year a handful of special education students receive regular diplomas and college acceptances.

The school is housed in the former IS/HS 10, where poet Langston Hughes once taught and where writer James Baldwin and New York State Supreme Court Justice Bruce Wright attended as children.

Today, the school's motto is "Without Struggle There Is No Progress." Principal Gregory Hodge, who was raised in poverty and lost both his parents before he finished high school, is very familiar with the difficulties facing many of his students. Images of Frederick Douglass, painted by students, are posted throughout the building, along with other Black heroes and "sheroes." Students are constantly reminded that the opportunities they have today stem from the accomplishments of those who have gone before them.

Hodge knows better than most just how important a school can be in transforming a life. When Hodge was young and practically homeless, a high school counselor, the first person to tell him he was smart, pushed him to go to college, and Hodge went on to receive a series of master's degrees and a Ph.D. Particularly sensitive to the problems confronting African American boys, Hodge has worked to boost the percentage of male students at FDA. When the school was first founded, it had a disproportionately large number of girls. Thanks in part to a project he launched to recruit District 5 boys into a special summer preparatory program, FDA now has almost as many boys as girls.

Hodge's manner can be gruff: One student we talked to recalled how intimidated she felt when she first met him. Over time, however, she learned that he feels great compassion for his students; a staffer affectionately called Grandma says, "Hodge is always working for the kids. He's the one to push for them. If there is a kid with a need, Mr. Hodge will find a way to help." He knows his students well enough to be able to recount the details of their lives and the personal and academic challenges they have overcome.

FDA offers solid college counseling, and its graduates regularly win scholarships from the Posse Foundation, which sends young people to top universities. Students start taking the PSAT in middle school and the SAT and ACT college entrance exams every year in high school. The school was honored (in a report called *Against the Odds* by the website Insideschools.org) as one that does a particularly good job graduating students on time, considering the skill level of the entering class.

The school has open houses from October to March, usually on Friday evenings and Saturday afternoons. Most FDA middle school students come from District 5. There is some room for out-of-district students in 9th grade, and preference is given to the 8th-grade students from the FDA replication schools who want to attend. There are mandatory summer school sessions for both middle and high school students.

SCHOOLS WORTH WATCHING

Here are some additional Manhattan middle schools that are new or noteworthy. Some serve grades K–8 and have only a handful of seats open for new students in the 6th grade. Others were going through a period of transition—a new building or a new principal—when we visited.

The Thurgood Marshall Academy for Learning and Social Change, 200-214 135th Street, 10030, (212) 283-8055, was founded in 1993 with the support of the Abyssinian Baptist Church. The church, a Harlem institution led by the Reverend Calvin Butts, managed the construction of the school and still helps the staff with details, such as repairing the school's photocopy machine. The school, serving 590 students in grades 7–12, is housed in a beautifully renovated building with state-of-the-art technology on every floor, from Smartboards to fully stocked science labs. Each floor is painted in a different pastel color, with comfortable furnishings to match. Large artworks depicting African American heroes hang prominently. Principal Sandye Johnson empathizes with struggling students and believes firmly in the power of a second chance. The school has a good record with kids who are struggling: Only about one-quarter of the students begin 9th grade reading on grade level, but 84% graduate on time. Parents are welcome in the building. Graduates have been admitted to Monroe, Adelphi, and Franklin Pierce.

The Special Music School of America, 129 West 67th Street, 10023, (212) 501-3318, www.kaufman-center.org/sms.htm, a partnership between the Department of Education and the Kaufman Center, combines regular academic classes with unusually rigorous classical music training, including individual lessons from conservatory-trained musicians. The school serves 135 children from all five boroughs in grades K–8 and usually has a handful of seats open for new 6th- and 7th-graders. Originally modeled on the "spetsshkola," or special schools, of the former Soviet Union, the Special Music School has evolved under the leadership of Jenny Undercofler, the school's first American-born music director. Without abandoning a commitment to classical musical training, Undercofler has added more contemporary music, music theory, and music history to the curriculum. Once all the musicians were Russian-born; now about half are. Because of the school's tiny size, course offerings are limited. There is no science lab, and Italian is the only foreign language offered. Still, with only 15 children in each class, students get lots of attention. Eighth-graders take the math Regents exam generally offered in 9th grade. There is a student chorus, and one year children performed in an operetta by Gilbert and Sullivan. Graduates typically go on to LaGuardia High School of Music and Art and Performing Arts, Bard, Beacon, and Stuyvesant. Some leave after 6th grade for Hunter College High School.

Open houses are offered from October to March, and applications are due in March. Students applying for middle school must audition on a musical instrument; successful candidates generally have at least 3 or 4 years' experience on piano or violin or at least 1 or 2 years on wind or brass instruments.

The Future Leaders Institute Charter School, 134 West 122nd Street, 10026, (212) 678-2798, is a small, ambitious school in a community that is home to many schools with very low achievement levels. It was founded in 1999 by a husband-and-wife team: Marc Waxman, who had taught at the respected KIPP Academy in the Bronx, and Gianna Cassetta, a former teacher at PS 198 in Manhattan's successful District 2. They wanted to combine the progressive academics that are a hallmark of District 2 with features that made KIPP successful—an extended day and extra financial support from a non-profit organization. The result is a pleasant, well-financed school where students attend classes from 8:15 a.m. to 5 p.m. and participate in a summer session as well. It has 298 students in grades K–8. Founded as an alternative public school, Future Leaders converted to charter status in 2005 after quarrels with the Department of Education over, among other things, class size. As a charter school, Future Leaders has been able to keep elementary school classes at 20 and middle school classes at 25. With its strong leadership and dedicated staff, Future Leaders Institute is working hard to give all children the tools they need to succeed. Students are admitted by lottery in April. See the school's website, www.futureleadersinstitute.org, or call.

Two good Harlem choices are **KIPP S.T.A.R. College Prep Charter School**, 433 West 123rd Street, 10027, (212) 991-2650 and **KIPP Infinity Charter School**, 625 West 133rd Street, 10027, (212) 991-2600. Both are modeled on the original KIPP Academy in the Bronx; both serve children in grades 5 to 8 in an orderly, disciplined environment. Both have long days, starting at 7:30 a.m. and lasting until 5 p.m., with Saturday and summer classes. Expectations are high and good behavior is rewarded. Children in the upper grades visit Utah and California, but unruly students are not allowed to go.

KIPP S.T.A.R., opened in 2003, shares a building with PS 125 and the new Columbia Secondary School. With blue floors and freshly painted lavender and yellow walls, KIPP S.T.A.R. (which has its own entrance) is a cheerful place where children wearing khaki pants and black sweatshirts follow a traditional curriculum with plenty of emphasis on grammar and spelling. Even though most students enter 5th grade reading well below grade level, graduates go on to challenging high schools and some are offered scholarships at private boarding schools.

KIPP Infinity, opened in 2005, shares space with IS 193. Teachers snap their fingers to get children to sit up straight; when teachers clap their hands for attention, students respond by clapping their own hands. "Classrooms are whimsically decorated; the math teacher displays his extensive action figure collection in his classroom, and another classroom featured a softly gurgling fish-tank and soft cloth curtains over a closet," Insideschools.org reporter Philissa Cramer wrote. "In the nonfiction studies classroom, the teacher played classical music while students read quietly and answered questions in a workbook about Washington, DC, the destination of the annual 5th-grade trip."

Admission to both KIPP schools is by lottery, with preference given to children living in District 5.

PS/IS 187, Hudson Cliffs School, 349 Cabrini Boulevard, 10040, (212) 927-8218, is a zoned school that's worth considering if you live in the neighborhood. "The school manages to hit a lot of high notes—good academics, strong parent involvement, and a cheery, calm environment—the likely reasons that most students stay put through the 8th grade," wrote Laura Zingmond on the Insideschools.org website. "The tone throughout the old, well-maintained building is sweet and calm; everywhere we visited students seemed engaged and well-behaved." A former teacher and assistant principal at the school, Principal Cynthia Chory grew up in the neighborhood and attended PS 187 through the 8th grade. Even though the school serves children as young as 4, it manages to give older students a traditional middle school experience. Starting in 5th grade, children change classes for some subjects, and students in grades 5 through 8 are assigned lockers and get to leave school for lunch. Teachers volunteer to patrol the streets during the middle school lunch period.

Harbor Science and Arts Charter School, 1 East 104th Street, Suite 603, 10029, (212) 427-2244, is a welcoming school where adults greet one another with pecks on the cheek and teachers know every child by name. A charter school serving K–8 children,

Harbor has managed to establish a comfortable balance between pushing kids to perform academically and allowing them to cultivate strengths in the arts. Through collaboration with the Harbor Conservatory, a privately run theater and arts program located in the same building, students are exposed to drama, art, dance, and percussive music twice a week. During our visit, we saw students play conga drums and dance to African music. In the theater class, students read aloud their ideas for scenes in a play. Eventually they would write a script that would include staging. Student art is displayed throughout the building. A major perk to sharing space with Boys and Girls Harbor is that the charter school kids get to participate in the building's after-school and summer school programs, as well as take part in 6-week cycles of swimming lessons in the indoor pool. Anyone in the city may apply. Admission is by lottery. Call the school for details.

The **Talented and Gifted School**, also known as TAG, 240 East 109th Street, 10029, (212) 860-6003, www.teacherweb.com/ny/tagyoungscholars/tag, has long been one of the most sought-after elementary schools in the city, serving mostly African American and Latino students. One of three citywide programs for gifted children, TAG attracts children from as far away as the Bronx, Brooklyn, and Queens. Principal Janette Cesar knows every child by name, and the school is both warm and orderly. TAG elementary school combined with a Talented and Gifted middle school in the building in 2004 to form a K–8 school; now, after a few years of growing pains, the 6th, 7th, and 8th grades are as strong as the early grades. The day of my visit, some 8th-graders were reading *A Raisin in the Sun* and discussing the civil rights movement. In a spirited social studies class, 7th-graders discussed the way in which the Constitution balances states' rights against the power of the federal government—using Massachusetts's experience with same-sex marriage as an example. Children worked on science projects on topics such as "How allergies affect the skin" and "How drugs and alcohol affect the teen brain." There are a handful of seats open to students entering in 6th grade. Middle school admission is based on grades, standardized-test scores, and a teacher recommendation.

Bronx
Schools

District 10
1   David A. Stein
2   TAPCO
3   William Niles

District 9
4   Urban Assembly
5   Bronx Prep. Charter
6   Mott Hall III

District 7
7   KIPP Academy

District 8
8   MS 101

THE BRONX

From the mansions of Riverdale to the tenements of the South Bronx and the seaside bungalows of City Island, the Bronx encompasses rich and poor, urban and suburban, new immigrants and long-time New Yorkers. Many of the schools, particularly the middle schools, have suffered from poor leadership and very low levels of student achievement. Good teachers and principals often learn their craft in the Bronx, then leave after a few years for schools in Westchester, just a few miles to the north, where class size is smaller, working conditions are easier, and salaries are higher. A few excellent private schools in Riverdale are a magnet for good teachers and students as well, and they drain the public schools of talent.

Still, some Bronx public schools manage to buck the trend. A number of first-rate middle schools have opened in the past few years. Several of these are open to students in the entire borough, whereas others are open to students from an entire district. So, if your neighborhood school is a disappointment, shop around. You don't have to move to the suburbs or pay private school tuition to get a good education for your child—even if you live in the Bronx.

Each district in the Bronx offers middle school choice. Directories for each district are available from the borough enrollment offices at 1 Fordham Plaza, (718) 741-8496 (for Districts 7, 8, and 10); 1230 Zerega Avenue, (718) 828-2975 (for Districts 8, 11, and 12); or 3450 East Tremont Avenue, (718) 794-7420 (also for Districts 8, 11, and 12). The directories can also be downloaded from the Department of Education website: http://schools.nyc.gov/enrollment. (Check back frequently. The Department of Education doesn't leave them up all year.) These directories don't include charter schools, so contact charter schools directly for admissions information.

David A. Stein Riverdale/
Kingsbridge Academy, MS/HS 141
660 West 237th Street
Bronx, NY 10463
(718) 796-8516

Admission: neighborhood school/some by lottery
High school choices: NA
Grade levels: 6–12   **Test scores:** R ****, M ***
Enrollment: 1,238   **Ethnicity:** 27%W 14%B 47%H 12%A
Class size: 30   **Free lunch:** 64%

The Riverdale/Kingsbridge Academy serves children in grades 6–12 who are zoned for MS 141, as well as several dozen out-of-zone children who are admitted by lottery. Perched on a hill, the school has gorgeous views of the Hudson River. A new addition provides a cafeteria, a library, two high school science laboratories, and additional classroom space. The area has an almost suburban feel, with a small field and public parks adjacent to the building.

The school has close ties to the community: Students volunteer in the neighborhood's senior centers and tutor at local elementary schools. A local newspaper, *The Riverdale Press*, prints the student paper for free. The Riverdale Community Center offers an after-school program for middle school students, a teen center on weekend evenings, and a family literacy program for English Language Learners on Saturday mornings.

"The middle school is bright, cheery, and racially diverse," Philissa Cramer wrote on the Insideschools.org website. "Writing is emphasized in every subject, and we saw interesting writing projects, such as creative book reports and brochures advertising the functions of cells." Test scores are high, attendance is solid, and the middle school has a good record of getting students into specialized high schools. Administrators call that "a mixed blessing": It shows that the school is successful, but also deprives the high school of some of RKA's best middle school students.

The sunny library is open to students during lunch and after school until 5:30 p.m. The librarian runs several popular book groups, including one in which students and parents read together and another where high school students determine whether new books are suitable for middle school readers. The videoconferencing capability of the library also allows students to communicate with children in other schools—for instance, in a regional poetry slam.

The arts are strong. The school has spring and winter arts festivals. Sixth-graders may sample two of the arts offerings—including music, dance, drama, and visual arts. The school recently received $50,000 to turn one classroom into a fully equipped dance studio. Children get instruments for free—they don't have to rent them. One mother said that her saxophone-playing son—who wasn't an early riser—leapt out of bed eagerly to go to band practice 2 mornings a week before school. The Riverdale Community Center sponsors the drama club, which puts on performances like *Oklahoma!* and *The Wizard of Oz*. The cafeteria has round tables—rather than the long tables typical at public schools—to encourage quiet conversation.

One mother praised the "terrific" parent coordinator, Julie Prince, who "sends out constant e-mails," keeping parents informed about events and the school, and who organizes monthly workshops on topics such as Internet safety and bullying.

MS 141 was rezoned in 1999, excluding children from poorer neighborhoods such as Marble Hill, in order to make room in the building for a neighborhood high school that would serve Riverdale and Kingsbridge students. Neighborhood parents say that the school is smaller and more cohesive, and that discipline has improved. "It's really nice to have a community school," said one mother, Rita Pochter Lowe. "Kids think, 'I can't do something bad because my aunt Molly might be walking by.'" One administrator said, "There is more continuity now because children stay for 7 years instead of 3, and administrators get to know them better."

The school offers a range of **special education** services, including self-contained classes for children with special needs.

In the middle school, three out of seven classes in each grade are honors level. About 40% of the students in the honors program are admitted to specialized high schools.

Students zoned for the school are automatically admitted; 25 seats for students zoned for IS 368 are available through a lottery. There are weekly tours in October and November.

Theatre Arts Production Company (TAPCO)
2225 Webster Avenue
Bronx, NY 10457
(718) 584-0832
www.tapconyc.org

Admission: Bronx priority
High school choices: NA
Grade levels: 6–12   **Test scores:** R ****, M ***
Enrollment: 485 (projected)   **Ethnicity:** 5%W 25%B 68%H 2%A
Class size: 22   **Free lunch:** 55%

The Theatre Arts Production Company (TAPCO) has a creative staff, an engaged student body, and a wide range of courses in music, drama, dance, and art. Founded as a middle school in 1997, it has since become the top school for the performing arts in the Bronx, serving children in grades 6–12.

Each semester, middle school students choose from ten areas of specialty, which they study for a double period, 3 times a week. The specialties include playwriting, acting, filmmaking, technical theater, chorus, dance, painting, sculpture, photography, and set design.

Academics are integrated with the arts, and the staff works together to an unusual degree. When students put on a production of *The King and I,* they also studied Thailand. When they performed *Helen of Troy,* English and social studies teachers helped students write the script, a math teacher helped students to construct a huge Trojan horse, and a science teacher taught students the difference between the bone and muscle structures of humans and horses.

In an impressive class in set design, students prepared for a production of *Beauty and the Beast* that incorporated scenes from *Macbeth.* The teacher, Bud Thorpe, a set designer who said he has worked with Samuel Beckett and David Mamet, was patient with students as they decided how to mingle the Shakespeare soliloquies with the *Beauty* set.

Most teachers have both a background in arts and a certification in their subject area, and they seem to take an interest in students both inside and outside the classroom. One teacher lets kids visit the film company he owns, and the chorus teacher takes kids to watch recording sessions. The students go to the

New Victory Theater in Manhattan and write essays about the plays they see.

Housed in the same building as MS 391, TAPCO has its own entrance, as well as its own starting and dismissal times. TAPCO has large windows and high ceilings. Couches, tables, and bookshelves are placed along curved corridors. The cafeteria, which doubles as a performance space, has round tables and a spiral staircase leading up to classrooms. Stage sets from past productions add color to the cafeteria. Teachers eat with the students, adding to the homey feel. The school has a lounge area, three theaters (including a black box stage fully equipped with portable sound and lights), a dance studio, and many art studios. One drawback: Not all of the walls go up to the ceiling, so noise travels easily.

Principal Lynn Passarella is committed to providing small classes and lots of individual attention. Academic classes generally have fewer than 22 students, and art classes generally have 15. Twice a week, students are grouped by ability in classes of 8–15 for extra attention in their academic subjects. "We really put a premium on social and emotional development," Passarella said. "Students are known incredibly well" by their teachers.

The staff is a mix of seasoned teachers and those from Teach for America, the non-profit organization that recruits recent graduates from selective liberal arts colleges to work for at least 2 years in the public schools.

Students with **special needs** may be place in a regular class with extra support or in a Collaborative Team Teaching (CTT) class. CTT classes have two teachers, one of whom is certified in special education. Teachers try to accommodate children with special needs. For example, a 6th-grader who was diagnosed with Attention-Deficit/Hyperactivity Disorder was allowed to participate in a 7th-grade class because he was particularly attached to the 7th-grade teacher.

Teachers give ideas for projects, and then stand back a little to allow students to make what they call "safe mistakes." For example, a group of students tried to make a large teepee with lightweight paper. When it started to rip, they switched to a heavier material and built wood braces inside.

Students even help plan the curriculum. They meet with their teachers after school to discuss, for example, how they will study ancient civilization. "Kids here get to be judged by what kind of worker they are," said assistant principal Monika Fisher. "If a kid is doing their personal best, that is what is recognized."

The academic classes we saw seemed solid. In math class, students were focused and articulate, and the teacher clearly enjoyed his subject and the kids. Some of the children come in with low levels of skills, but make good gains by 8th grade.

Sixth-graders are bused to the school. The school has an extensive after-school and Saturday program, sponsored by the Children's Aid Society and Boys and Girls Clubs. After-school programs include dance, set design, yoga, boys' and girls' basketball, and academic support. The after-school program also offers students help in preparing an art portfolio, should they wish to apply to colleges such as the Rhode Island School of Design. The Children's Aid Society offers a medical and mental health clinic and a summer program at the Wagon Road Camp in Chappaqua, NY.

About 85% of TAPCO's middle school students stay for high school; a few leave for LaGuardia High School of Music and Art and Performing Arts or other specialized schools. TAPCO graduates its first high school class in 2009.

Applications are available in October and are due in February. The school offers regular tours. Students have a combined audition and interview. They need not have prior experience, but they must be committed to the performing arts. Priority is given to students living in the Bronx.

William W. Niles School, MS 118

577 East 179th Street
Bronx, NY 10457
(718) 584-2330

Admissions: District 10
High school choices: DeWitt Clinton, Bronx Center, Bronx Science
Grade levels: 6–8   **Test scores:** R ***, M ***
Enrollment: 1,170   **Ethnicity:** 3%W 27%B 63%H 7%A
Class size: 28   **Free lunch:** 89%

MS 118 is best known for its two gifted programs, the Pace Academy and Spectrum, both of which attract bright kids from across District 10 and prepare them for demanding high schools. About half the graduates of these two programs go on to private schools, often on full scholarship; many of the rest go on to the specialized public high schools. An unusual program within Spectrum offers honors-level classes to new immigrants who are learning English as a Second Language.

MS 118 also serves as a neighborhood school for children who live in the zone. Every semester, students choose an elective such as sewing, digital filmmaking, costume design, theater, chorus, Spanish, dance, or ceramics. The elective classes mix students from all the programs. The first floor of the building, constructed in 1938, is dedicated to art rooms where the electives are taught. The building is a bit worn: Some desks are scarred with graffiti and the playground is closed because of huge potholes.

In the **Pace Academy**, on the 3rd floor, the corridors have black linoleum floors and buff-colored wall tiles. Classrooms, painted a cheery yellow with blue trim, have old wooden coat closets and large casement windows that let in lots of light. There's a nice library and an adequate gym, and kids' work is displayed on bulletin boards in the halls. Pace serves 360 students.

The Pace students are eager and unusually mature. Teachers guide lively discussions and instruction is fast paced. Eighth-graders take Regents-level (9th-grade) algebra and Earth science. The program's teachers are organized in teams for the 6th, 7th, and 8th grades. Each team meets formally each week, and informally each day, to plan lessons and discuss each kid's progress.

There is a sense of camaraderie among the staff: Old teachers help young teachers with tips like how to build students' vocabulary or teach grammar, while young teachers help older teachers use new technology to create student blogs or put the student newspaper online.

Pace has prizewinning robotics and math teams; both have an unusual number of girls. "We have really good teachers, and girls aren't afraid of math and science here," said Pace program director and assistant principal Erin Balet, a former management consultant who has a bachelor's degree in history from Yale and an MBA from Cornell.

Parents praise the staff's tireless efforts at getting kids into good high schools: About 20% of the Pace graduates go on to specialized high schools, and another 50% go on to Catholic schools or other private schools. Other popular high school choices are the Macy's honors program at DeWitt Clinton and Bronx Center for Science and Mathematics. The Pace Academy's promotional leaflet boasts that Pace graduates have gone on to universities such as Colgate, Cornell, Fordham—and even Harvard and Yale.

On the 4th floor, the **Spectrum Academy** has lively teaching and imaginative class projects. In an 8th-grade math class, students competed in a game of "Deal or No Deal," trying to decide whether it was better to buy 12 AA batteries for $8 or 20 for $15. Spectrum students may take the algebra and Earth science Regents exams. Spectrum serves 310 students, but the administration plans to increase enrollment to 500.

Part of the Spectrum program is dedicated to about 50 students who are learning English as a Second Language. Insideschools.org reporter Vanessa Witenko said, "Top-notch classes are taught by dedicated, organized, and experienced teachers who excite their students with challenging lessons." Students complete multiple drafts of their essays—up to seven, in one case—and the final versions were "extremely polished, with good detail, proper grammar, and creativity," she wrote.

Anne Piotrowski, assistant principal and director of Spectrum, said her academy attracts outgoing, well-rounded students who are interested in extracurricular activities such as sports, music, and student council, as well as academics. The Spectrum students may not have test scores as high as the Pace students when they begin middle school, but their "strong work ethic" means that they make great strides and are sought after by private high school admissions departments, Piotrowski said.

The classes for neighborhood students zoned for the school were being reorganized at the time of our visit, and the administration acknowledges it is still trying to find a way to reach all the kids. In some classes we visited, bored students stared at the ceiling or drew on their desks, adding to the graffiti that was already there. However, there were some lively classes as well: In one science class, students raised tilapia fish and used the nitrates from fish waste to fertilize cucumber and basil plants.

An impressive program called the Unity Center offers help to children facing serious social problems. A team consisting of a social worker, a psychologist, a guidance counselor, and five to eight student interns from Columbia University School of Social Work meets regularly to draw up a plan for each troubled child. The school also works to help needy children get housing and medical services.

Tucked in the southernmost corner of the district in East Tremont, MS 118 is in a neighborhood that's undergone devastation and renewal, hallmarks of the Bronx in the past 30 years. The blocks around the school burned during the 1970s—a time of arson and waves of abandonment by landlords.

More recently, new immigrants have moved to the neighborhood from the Dominican Republic, West Africa, Bangladesh, Southeast Asia, the Caribbean, India, and Latin America. Vacant, garbage-strewn lots and boarded-up buildings are being replaced with trim brick townhouses and new apartment buildings. Greengrocers and clothing stores along the main commercial streets are bustling.

Children living in the zone for MS 118 are automatically accepted to the school. Children from across District 10 who score at Level 3 or 4 on standardized tests and who have good attendance may apply to Pace. Children are interviewed, take an entrance exam, and must submit a teacher recommendation. Most students admitted to Spectrum score at Level 3 or 4, but some scoring at high Level 2 are admitted. ESL students may be tested in their native language. The school offers regular tours. Call (718) 584-2568 for more information.

Urban Assembly School for Applied Math and Science

1595 Bathgate Avenue
Bronx, NY 10457
(718) 466-7800
www.urbanassemblymath.org

Admissions: Districts 9 and 10
High school choices: NA
Grade levels: 6–12   **Test scores:** R ***, M ****
Enrollment: 570 (projected)   **Ethnicity:** 5%W 36%B 52%H 7%A
Class size: 20   **Free lunch:** 91%

The Urban Assembly School for Applied Math and Science (AMS) has a stunning new building, a dynamic principal, and teachers who spark kids' interest with plenty of projects and trips. Opened in 2004 with just one 6th-grade class, the school is quickly building a reputation for its high academic standards, stellar attendance rates, and noteworthy student achievement in math and science. Students wear uniforms of gray, white, and burgundy, with black shoes.

Located near Crotona Park, AMS shares the Bathgate Education Campus with two other schools, Validus Prepatory School and Bronx Mott Hall. The striking canary yellow and lime green building has new labs, spacious classrooms and giant skylights. The three schools all use the building's library, cafeteria, and multipurpose room. Each school has its own entrance.

Math and science concepts are woven into various subject areas, such as the study of Greek and Egyptian civilizations. Students learned about angles at an exhibit at the New York Hall of Science, in which lasers were bounced off mirrors. They learned about aerodynamics by launching rockets on another trip to the New York Hall of Science; they used homemade sextants (protractors with a straw attached, or "height-o-meters," as the students call them) to measure how high the rockets are propelled and to calculate their results using the trigonometric function of tangents.

"It's really amazing to hear students yell, 'teach me the tangent function!'" Principal Ken Baum said. Baum, a graduate of Bronx High School of Science, taught college math and worked as a mountain guide in the Adirondacks before attending the

Department of Education's Leadership Academy, the training program for new principals.

Baum has worked to keep staff morale high by keeping class size small, creating a collegial atmosphere, and offering time for staff development and shared lesson planning during the school day. Instead of hiring new teachers in the fall, he hires them in the spring so they can work alongside a more senior teacher before being assigned their own classroom. New teachers have both formal and informal chances to share their struggles with more senior staff members; senior teachers are encouraged to deepen their skills by, for example, taking graduate courses in how to teach English as a Second Language—paid for by the school.

Although a large percentage of students enter 6th grade reading below grade level, by 8th grade most have caught up. This means that 9th grade begins with real high school work—not with the remedial work that is typical in new small schools.

Chrystodara, an environmental education foundation, sends several 7th- and 8th-graders on a 2-week summer camp and about 80 kids to a weekend camp, all free of cost.

Among the new school's accomplishments: A team of 7th-graders earned first place at the 2007 IBM EWeek Design Challenge, where they competed against middle school students from across the tristate area. AMS was recognized by the New York State Education Department as being a "High Performing/Gap Closing school" for the 2005–06 school year. "We get good test scores with an incredibly low amount of test prep," Baum said.

The school offers Collaborative Team Teaching (CTT) for children with **special needs**. In these classes, two teachers, one of whom is certified in special education, work together with a mix of general education and special needs youngsters.

The school was founded with the help of the Urban Assembly, a not-for-profit group that supports the creation of small, public, college-prep high schools. The Bathgate Education Complex is located between Claremont Parkway and East 172nd Street, far from the nearest subway stop. Despite the remote location, kids make every effort to get to school every day: The 96% attendance rate is a testament to how much the kids love being there.

Students living in Districts 9 and 10 may apply. Call the school for tour dates. Children who express an interest by attending a tour, an open house, or a middle school fair have preference.

Bronx Preparatory Charter School

3872 3rd Avenue
Bronx, NY 10457
(718) 294-0841
www.bronxprep.org

Admissions: citywide, District 9 priority
High school choices: NA
Grade levels: 5–12   **Test scores:** R ***, M ***
Enrollment: 587   **Ethnicity:** 0%W 52%B 48%H 0%A
Class size: 25   **Free lunch:** 82%

Bronx Preparatory Charter School offers children in grades 5–12 a structured, formal education and the opportunity to go to top colleges. Opened in 2000 in one of the poorest neighborhoods in the city, Bronx Prep graduated its first high school class in 2007. One 2008 graduate was accepted to the Massachusetts Institute of Technology. Others have been accepted at Georgetown, Holy Cross, Howard, Syracuse, and Hobart.

The school day is long: Fifth- and 6th-graders have classes from 7:55 a.m. to 4:55 p.m., while 7th- and 8th-graders have classes from 8:15 a.m. to 4:05 p.m. The school year begins in mid-August, and children who have three or more absences in the summer school session forfeit their seat, according to the school's website. Children wear uniforms of blue or white polo shirts and black or khaki pants. Classes are held in a sparkling new $19 million building. Parents are welcome at the school and must sign an agreement when a child enrolls promising to help enforce consistent student behavior and support the child's academic achievement. The school begins in 5th grade because administrators believe children need to start early to be fully prepared for college.

In its first years, the school suffered from attrition: Of the first entering class of 50 students, only 20 graduated in 2007. Others were held back or transferred to less demanding schools. But administrators are taking steps, including implementing "individual improvement plans" to help kids who are struggling, and more children are staying and being promoted, said Dr. Samona Tait Johnson, who became head of the school in 2007. "There's less focus on slogans and more on instruction," she said. "There's more [emphasis on] critical thinking and less memorization." Tait Johnson attended nearby PS 49 as a child, then won a scholarship to attend the private Riverdale school Horace Mann and the University of Pennsylvania. She received her doctorate from the Harvard School of Education.

Each grade has five classes of 25 students. Many children enter 5th grade with weak skills, and teachers work hard to make sure the students master phonics and the multiplication tables before they move on to more difficult material. But most catch up, and by 8th grade many are taking Regents-level (high school) algebra and even chemistry. Children read both classics, among them Eleanor Estes's *The Hundred Dresses*, the story of prejudice faced by a poor Polish girl who has only one shabby dress to wear, and contemporary fiction, such as Gary Paulsen's *Nightjohn*, the haunting story of a 12-year-old American slave girl.

The school has a rich program in the arts. Students study piano on the 35 keyboards the school has available. Instruction in instrumental music is also offered in violin, wind instruments, and percussion. The school has choir, art, step teams, and a drama program.

The school employs two counselors to help students navigate the college application process—an unusually large number for such a small school. It also provides support to students once they are attending college. Most students visit at least 15 colleges before they graduate.

One parent complained that the school day is too long and that children simply cannot concentrate for so many hours a day. A teacher said classroom management is a challenge, particularly late in the afternoon. But other parents are grateful for the education their children are receiving.

Students from anywhere in New York City may apply, but siblings of current students and children living in District 9 have priority. Applications are available in January. Open houses are held in January and March. The deadline for submitting applications is April 1. Students are selected by lottery. Check the school's website for dates. Children must apply for 5th grade; the school also has a waiting list. In recent years, 300 children have applied for 125 seats.

Mott Hall III

450 St. Paul's Place
Bronx, NY 10456
(718) 992-9506
http://mh3.echalk.com

Admissions: District 9
High school choices: Bronx Center, Beacon, Mott Hall High School
Grade levels: 6–8 **Test scores:** R ****, M *****
Enrollment: 280 **Ethnicity:** 0%W 38%B 62%H 0%A
Class size: 25 **Free lunch:** 81%

Launched in September 2002 with just 60 students, Mott Hall III is a clone of other successful Mott Hall programs in Manhattan (see www.motthall.org). Like them, Mott III aims to combine a traditional tone with progressive teaching methods. Instruction is more than teacher lectures; students work in teams for many projects.

Housed on the top floor of an elementary school, PS 55, Mott Hall III focuses on mathematics, technology, and science. Each classroom is named for a college, such as Stanford or Howard. The day we visited, the classrooms, filled with students working diligently, were so quiet that we felt almost like intruders. In a literacy class, groups of kids were writing reviews of the movie *Holes*, based on a well-regarded young people's book that they had also read. The classroom library held a healthy supply of books.

Elsewhere, students were preparing projects for a science fair. The science classroom contained an ant farm, as well as newly sprouting potatoes and legumes—an experiment on radiation's effect on plant growth. "Since we are very project based, there is room for a child to just meet the basics or go much deeper into it," a teacher said. Science reports containing bibliographies of web resources covered such topics as black holes. "I like it here," one girl said. "There are more hands-on experiments. My other school was more from the textbooks."

In a social studies class, the teacher told students to take out their passports to "visit" France, the last destination of a unit in which they had become familiar with countries ranging from Peru to Australia. Kids had traveled the world virtually, thanks to a website featuring a young girl who, with her family, had toured the globe by sailboat.

In math, teachers drew on issues of the day—how many people approve, disapprove, or are undecided about city budget cuts—to teach such skills as charting graphs or calculating percentages. The school community enjoys celebrations and throws costume and holiday parties. Significant classroom events might be celebrated with pizza or an entertaining gingerbread house–building activity.

Many graduates go to Bronx Center, Beacon, and Mott Hall High School. Students have also been admitted to specialized high schools.

Mott Hall III is open to District 9 students who are hardworking and whose families are committed to helping them succeed. Students must submit two teacher recommendations and be interviewed. Tours are available by appointment.

KIPP Academy Charter School
250 East 156th Street
Bronx, NY 10451
(718) 665-3555
www.kippnyc.org

Admissions: citywide, District 7 priority
High school choices: most attend private schools
Grade levels: 5–8 **Test scores:** R *****, M *****
Enrollment: 250 **Ethnicity:** 1%W 53%B 45%H 1%A
Class size: 32–38 **Free lunch:** 92%

KIPP Academy is for children who are willing to get up early, work late every day, come in for 4 hours on Saturdays, and attend summer school in July. Classes start at 7:25 a.m. and last until at least 5 p.m. on Mondays through Thursdays (dismissal is at 3:30 p.m. on Fridays). Homework is assigned even during school vacations: One class was asked to read 100 pages and fill in a 12-page workbook over the February break.

The hard work pays off. The school has been very effective in taking kids who are reading below grade level and boosting their skills enough to prepare them for demanding high schools, including private boarding schools and selective Catholic schools.

KIPP was founded by David Levin, a Yale graduate who believes the average child is often neglected by an educational system that offers special classes for the gifted and for children with learning disabilities. KIPP is out to prove that children in the middle 80% can outperform the so-called gifted-and-talented kids. A charter school, it operates independently of the Department of Education and accepts students by lottery. Blanca Ruiz, who was a teacher and dean at KIPP, was named principal in 2007, succeeding Quinton Vance, who left to become Executive Director of KIPP NYC elementary schools, overseeing all KIPP elementary schools in the city.

The school music conductor, McClenty Hunter, is a jazz drummer who has performed at Lincoln Center. "The kids are very disciplined," Hunter said. "I want to expose them to as much as possible, from classical to contemporary jazz."

All students learn to play an instrument: violin, viola, cello, bass guitar, piano, xylophone, or drums. Students have performed at Lincoln Center and Carnegie Hall. The school has attracted considerable support from corporations and foundations to pay for its extended-day and summer school programs, as well as special activities, such as a hiking and camping trip to Zion National Park in Utah, or class trips to Washington, DC, and Boston.

Located on the 4th floor of IS 151, KIPP is an orderly school where rules of conduct are strictly enforced. Students receive weekly progress reports called "paychecks"; if their attendance, homework, and classwork are good, they receive tickets that can be used to purchase snacks.

Children walk silently through the halls in single file and are reprimanded if they talk out of turn in class. On a recent visit, Vanessa Witenko of Insideschools.org said that she saw a group of children forced to stand single file in the corridor for an entire period because they had talked inappropriately in class. A husky male teacher scolded them, shouting: "I've had enough! Do you hear me?"

At the same time, students have the chance to forge close relationships with teachers. Teachers give students their telephone numbers so they can call them after school hours. There is a pleasant give-and-take between teachers and students in many of the classes, and lots of one-on-one tutoring during the day.

Not everyone can keep up the pace, and a handful of students in each grade leave each year. (Class size gets smaller, too: Fifth-grade classes have as many as 38 children, while 8th-grade classes have about 32.) But for those who stay, the rewards are great. A large number of students go on to private boarding schools on scholarship, including Choate-Rosemary Hall, Phillips Academy, and the Ethel Walker School, or to Catholic day schools like Cardinal Spellman and Fordham Prep.

The academy has a strong alumni group that encourages former students to mentor current students. KIPP to College is a program that helps students to apply to high school and KIPP alumni to apply to college. KIPPsters currently attend schools like Barnard, Brown, Cornell, NYU, and Temple.

Applications are available in January. Students are accepted by a lottery, held in April. Siblings and students living in District 7 have preference in admissions. There are typically 250 applicants for 75 seats in 5th grade.

MS 101

2750 Lafayette Avenue
Bronx, NY 10465
(718) 829-6372

Admissions: District 8
High school choices: Lehman, Pelham Prep, Bronx Science
Grade levels: 6–8   **Test scores:** R *****, M *****
Enrollment: 445   **Ethnicity:** 17%W 22%B 54%H 7%A
Class size: 25–29   **Free lunch:** 65%

MS 101 attracts the top students from across District 8, which includes both poor neighborhoods like Hunts Point and more suburban neighborhoods like Throgs Neck. Half the students are admitted to the school's gifted and talented program because they have high test scores. The school strictly enforces a uniform policy of white tops and navy pants or skirts. A magnet for science and technology, the school requires students to take seven to nine periods of science and math instruction a week. Students use computer technology as much as possible, from decorating the hallways with digital pictures to producing the student newspaper.

There is an emphasis on group work. Textbooks are used sparingly and children learn to use both primary and secondary sources. Teachers of different subjects and age groups meet frequently to coordinate and integrate their lessons. For instance, social studies, math, and English were combined for a study of colonial times. In the social studies class students read diaries and historical accounts of the era, in the math class they learned how to use grids to make a map of a colonial city, and in the English class they read the work of writers of the period.

Children have about 1 hour of homework a night, and some have trouble adapting when they first enter the school. "There was a tremendous adjustment period. It's not just cut and paste and throw something on a board. You really have to think," one mother said. Nonetheless, parents are enthusiastic.

Students in District 8 who have a combined score of 1408 on standardized tests may apply to the gifted and talented program. Children applying to the general academic program are selected from throughout District 8, but children attending PS 14, PS 71, PS 72, and PS 304 have priority.

SCHOOLS WORTH WATCHING

City Island School, PS/IS 175, 200 City Island Avenue, 10464, (718) 885-1093, is a zoned neighborhood school serving 400 children in grades K–8. It's one of the few zoned schools for middle school children in the Bronx to which parents feel confident sending their children. City Island, connected to the mainland by a bridge, looks like a New England fishing village, and the school reflects the small-town feel of the community. It's the kind of place where lots of mothers stay at home with their kids, where parents keep an eye on one another's children, and where kids can walk or ride their bikes to school. The school has a long-standing tradition of welcoming parents into the building every morning to recite the Pledge of Allegiance with their children. Admission is limited to children living on City Island. No application is required.

The Hostos-Lincoln Academy of Science, 475 Grand Concourse, 10451, (718) 518-4333, housed on the campus of Hostos Community College in the South Bronx, offers 500 students in grades 6–12 talented teachers and the chance to participate in college life. Older students may take college courses for free and some graduate with both a Regents diploma and an associate (2-year) college degree. Although most students come from poor families and speak Spanish rather than English at home, about 84% graduate from high school on time and 85% of graduates go on to 4-year colleges—including Columbia, Fordham, NYU, Harvard, and Brown. Founded as a high school in 1985, Hostos-Lincoln Academy of Science recently added 6th, 7th, and 8th grades. After-school activities include dance, yearbook, student government, basketball, chorus, and photography. Students may use the college swimming pool, cafeteria, and library. Admission is limited to students living in District 7. Preference is given to students who attend an open house and behave well, according to the principal. There are typically 400 applicants for 50 seats in 6th grade.

Young Women's Leadership School, Bronx Campus, TCU Campus, 2060 Lafayette Avenue, 10473 (718) 239-8101, www.ywlfoundation.org, is the second in a network of schools founded on the model of the successful all-girls school of the same name in East Harlem. Opened with 75 students in 7th grade in 2004, the Bronx school is expanding to serve 450 girls in grades 7–12. The school emphasizes math, science, and technology—fields traditionally dominated by men. Principal Arnette Crocker was a member of the first graduating class of New York City's Aspiring

135

Principals Leadership Program and spent a year shadowing Kathleen Ponze, the former principal of Young Women's Leadership in East Harlem. The girls take physical education through a program called Energy Up, which combines instruction in aerobics, nutrition, and health. Girls wear uniforms of navy blue sweaters, white blouses, plaid skirts, and crested blazers. Attendance is high at 94%. The school is located in District 8, but girls living anywhere in the city may apply. Students are admitted in 7th grade and must attend an open house. Open houses are held in January and February,

Bronx School for Law, Government and Justice, 244 East 163rd Street, 10451, (718) 410-2380, http://www.bxlgj.org, serves 600 students in grades 7–12. Students conduct mock trials in a fully equipped courtroom, conduct DNA analyses of hair or blood in a forensic lab, and take part in internships at the Bronx Supreme Court and in small law firms and community organizations in the neighborhood and throughout the Bronx. The school's new $75 million building is adjacent to the Bronx Supreme Court, down the street from the Criminal Court, and just a few blocks from the new Yankee stadium. Classrooms have large sun-filled windows and a library that overlooks a two-story lobby. The building has four science labs, a weight room, a rooftop terrace, and a library with granite countertops and leather couches. Judges visit the school once a month for a question-and-answer lunch. All 11th-graders take forensic science, which links law and science. For example, students examined the density of broken glass to determine which make of car was involved in an accident—part of an effort to solve a case they were studying in their law class. Test scores, attendance, and graduation rates, while respectable, are lower than ideal; Principal Meisha Ross-Porter told Insideschools.org that the Department of Education sometimes places over-age students with a history of truancy in the school. Admission is open to anyone living in the Bronx. Students must attend an open house, fill out an application, and be interviewed. There are generally 500 applicants for 75 seats in 7th grade.

Bronx Academy of Letters, 339 Morris Avenue, 10451, (718) 401-4891, www.bronxletters.com, is one of the most promising high schools to open in the Bronx in recent years. In 2007 it started as a middle school, beginning with 6th grade. With small classes, passionate teachers, and a dynamic principal, Bronx Academy of Letters is off to a good start. Opened in 2003 in a wing of an undistinguished concrete middle school in the South Bronx, the high school has quickly become a viable, academically challenging school in one of the poorest neighborhoods in the city. Founding principal Joan Sullivan is a Yale graduate who studied history and published a book on her experiences working on Bill Bradley's presidential campaign. She has created a small school in which children are surrounded by great books; are coached in the art of reading and writing by attentive, knowledgeable teachers; and are exposed to professional writers regularly. The school has attracted tens of thousands of dollars in grant money, lots of book donations, and graduate student volunteers who work with children individually on the children's writing. The school is housed in a wing of the former IS 183, a building constructed in the 1970s. Attendance at 94% is well above the citywide average. The school is open to children in District 7.

MS 223, the Laboratory School of Finance and Technology, 360 East 145th Street, 10454, (718) 292-8627, www.ms223.org, is housed on the top floor of the old IS 149. It has low test scores, but does a good job of engaging kids who have poor academic skills and in helping them get excited about school. Students may learn to take apart a computer and put it back together again. Or they may play fun computer games with historical themes, such as Civilization. In one class, a teacher helped children studying ancient Egypt to make a mummy out of a chicken and bury it in the schoolyard. There is a "school economy" in which children earn prizes (such as movie tickets or computer time) for good behavior. Managers from the nearby Banco Popular volunteer to help kids think of the jobs they might have when they grow up.

Principal Ramon Gonzalez—who grew up on welfare, attended public schools in East Harlem, and went on to win a scholarship to Cornell University—is determined to offer the children of the South Bronx the same educational opportunities that allowed him to rise from poverty. He has assembled a young, energetic, and idealistic staff. The school has a cheerful, welcoming feel, and the children seem happy to be there. About 30% of the student body receives either special education services or English classes for English Language Learners. The school is open to children living in District 7.

Brooklyn
Schools

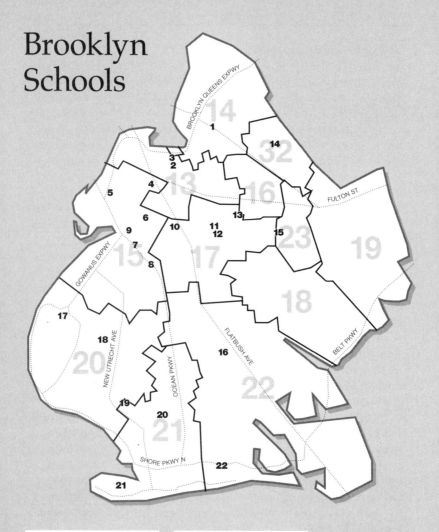

District 11
1 Eugenio Maria De Hostos

District 13
2 Ronald Edmonds
3 Urban Assembly

District 15
4 Math & Science
5 Collaborative Studies
6 William Alexander
7 New Voices
8 MS 88
9 Sunset Park Prep

District 17
10 North Star
11 Medgar Evers
12 Crown School
13 KIPP AMP

District 32
14 Philippa Schuyler

District 23
15 IS 392

District 22
16 Andries Hudde

District 20
17 Mary White Ovington
18 Christa McAuliffe

District 21
19 Brooklyn Studio
20 David A. Boody
21 Mark Twain

District 22
22 Bay Academy

BROOKLYN

There is a pent-up demand for good public middle schools in the city's most populous borough. Sadly, Brooklyn has far more good elementary schools than good middle schools, and most parents face nail-biting anxiety as their children prepare to graduate from 5th grade. Only a handful of neighborhoods (Bay Ridge, for example) have good zoned middle schools; in most of the borough, children are required to fill out an application and rank their choices. The district in which you live must find your child a space, but it may not be in your first-choice school.

Your child may also apply to a handful of middle schools that accept children from across the borough; in addition, you may want to consider schools in Manhattan, or charter schools. Since each of these requires a different application, the process can be daunting. Luckily, the Department of Education (DOE) has made tentative progress in making the application process simpler and fairer, and the options are better than they were even a few years ago.

For many years, each of the 12 districts in Brooklyn operated as its own fiefdom. Each tried to lure the best students from other districts—while making it next to impossible for its own children to find out anything about schools outside its borders. Tours for parents were perfunctory or nonexistent. Each district—and sometimes each school—had its own admissions criteria and its own timetable for admission. One Brooklyn mother had her daughter sit for five different entrance exams on five different Saturdays.

In 2008, the DOE imposed a uniform timetable for middle school admissions, encouraged schools to offer tours to prospective parents, and published middle school directories for each district that clearly outlined children's choices. These directories are available from your elementary school, the borough enrollment offices, or online at http://schools.nyc.gov/enrollment (keep checking—the DOE doesn't keep them up all year). The DOE also limited each district's ability to poach the best out-of-district students while leaving their own children out of the best schools; with a few exceptions, schools must now admit only children living within their district. Encouraging (or forcing) good students to stay in their home district has had the side effect of improving the schools in some districts. In my most recent visits, I particularly saw gains in District 15, which includes Park Slope and Sunset Park.

The neighborhoods of Williamsburg, Carroll Gardens, Brooklyn Heights, Fort Greene, Park Slope, and parts of Sunset Park and Bedford-Stuyvesant (Districts 13, 14, 15, and 16) are served by a borough enrollment office at 131 Livingston Street, Room 309, 11201, (718) 935-4197.

A large swath of Brooklyn, from Crown Heights to the sleepy seaside community of Bergen Beach (Districts 17, 18, and 22), is served by the borough enrollment office at 1780 Ocean Avenue, 11230, (718) 758-7687.

Bushwick, Ocean Hill–Brownsville, and East New York (Districts 19, 23, and 32) are served by a borough enrollment office at 1665 St. Marks Avenue, 11233, (718) 922-4946.

Southern Brooklyn, from Bay Ridge to Coney Island (Districts 20 and 21), are served by the borough enrollment office at 415 89th Street, 11209, (718) 759-4914.

The six gifted-and-talented programs of District 21 are among the few that are permitted to accept children from across the borough and even from Queens. For current information, you should try calling Mark Twain Middle School at (718) 449-6697.

Eugenio Maria De Hostos
Intermediate School, IS 318

101 Walton Street
Brooklyn, NY 11206
(718) 782-0589
www.is318.com

Admissions: District 14 preference
High school choices: Brooklyn Tech, Murrow, Fashion Industries
Grade levels: 6–8   **Test scores:** R ****, M ****
Enrollment: 1,453   **Ethnicity:** 9%W 17%B 66%H 8%A
Class size: 30   **Free lunch:** 70%

A safe, traditional school with a seasoned staff and a dedicated administration, IS 318 offers high school–level math and science to its top students and programs ranging from photography to a marching band. The IS 318 chess team regularly wins national competitions.

The building is immaculate. Desks are in rows, and teachers tend to offer lessons from the front of the class. What distinguishes IS 318 is not its innovative teaching methods (although the school has adopted some progressive techniques), but an *esprit de corps* among the staff and a sense of pride in the school shared by both teachers and students.

"The teachers are dedicated and would do anything for the students, even volunteer to teach on weekends," one student said. "Everyone treats one another with respect," said another.

New teachers are not merely dumped into classrooms, as is the case in many schools, but receive the help and support necessary to become experts. All new teachers attend a weeklong training institute, sponsored by the school, before the school term begins. Each one is paired with not only a senior teacher to act as a mentor, but also with a "buddy" teacher, one with just a little more experience working at the school. The new teachers we met were enthusiastic about the training.

Every child in 6th grade takes chess, a program that owes much to assistant principal John Galvin, who has taught at the school for many years. Expert players, among them a grandmaster, regularly coach the children. The school's team has been a winner in the Junior High National Chess Championship for 9 years in a row. In 2008 the team won the New York City High School Chess Championship—competing against much older students.

The school has a pleasant garden, which is planted by students and teachers, is open to the community, and is also used as an amphitheatre for outdoor classes. About 80 kids take part in an award-winning composting program that recycles 15% of the school's kitchen's scraps.

The school has eight self-contained **special education** classes, including two "life skills" classes for developmentally disabled students.

The Academy of the Arts and Sciences, a program for gifted students, requires participation in early-morning sessions on such subjects as computer illustration and pre-engineering. About 40 of the 160 students in this academy are admitted to highly selective schools such as Brooklyn Tech, Brooklyn Latin, or Townsend Harris in Queens.

A free after-school program offers activities like soccer, academic prep, and Trout in the Classroom—where students raise fish from eggs and then release them to their watery homes.

Eighth-graders may take high school–level algebra, as well as the 9th-grade Earth science Regents course. Some 7th-graders also take the Living Environment Regents exam, generally offered in 9th grade.

The school offers tours every Friday at 9 a.m., or on request. Admission is open to any child in District 14.

Ronald Edmonds Learning Center, IS 113
300 Adelphi Street
Brooklyn, NY 11205
(718) 834-6735
www.relc113.com

Admission: District 13
High school choices: Banneker, Brooklyn HS for the Arts, Murrow
Grade levels: 6–8   **Test scores:** R ****, M ***
Enrollment: 914   **Ethnicity:** 2%W 80%B 16%H 2%A
Class size: 20–30   **Free lunch:** 56%

MS 113 is a popular school that prepares its mostly African American student body for selective public and private high schools. Divided into three programs—performing arts, visual arts, and environmental science/math—MS 113 has far more applicants than seats. Both teachers and students take pride in their African heritage: Many classrooms are decorated with Kente cloth, for example. Students go on trips to historically Black colleges as well as to Ivy League schools. One year, the school band traveled to Howard University to perform with that historically Black college's marching band.

The Academy of Performing Arts offers instruction in dance, drama, chorus, and band, while the Fine Arts and Design program teaches painting and drawing as well as how to develop a portfolio of work. The Environmental Summit and Technology program has advanced science and math courses.

Students wear khaki or dark pants (no blue jeans) and white shirts. Most students take the 9th-grade math Regents exam, and several dozen take the advanced math Regents exam, generally given in 11th grade. To motivate students, teachers offer awards ranging from stars on charts that track grades and attendance to bicycles or iPods for students with the highest grades. In the spring the top prizes go to students who have shown the most improvement. High school choices include Benjamin Banneker, Bedford Academy, and the Brooklyn High School of the Arts. A few students go to the specialized high schools and some attend private schools. An open house is held in January. Students must audition for the arts programs.

Urban Assembly Academy
of Arts and Letters
225 Adelphi Street
Brooklyn, NY 11205
(718) 222-1605
www.uaaal.org

Admissions: Districts 13, 14, 15, and 16
High school choices: NA
Grade levels: 6–8   **Test scores:** R ****, M ****
Enrollment: 300 (projected)   **Ethnicity:** 14%W 70%B 14%H 2%A
Class size: 25   **Free lunch:** 45%

Opened in 2006 with just 83 students in 6th grade, the Urban Assembly Academy of Arts and Letters has quickly become a viable choice for children looking for small classes, thoughtful teaching, and an emphasis on the arts. Housed on the top floor of a 50-year-old elementary school, PS 20, Arts and Letters has attracted a mix of children of different ethnic groups, neighborhoods, and abilities. Children may sample drama, dance, music, cultural studies, fashion, and puppetry.

In the morning, Principal Allison Gaines Pell greets each child at the entrance to the school—a side door, painted purple. Parents say they appreciate the individual attention children receive. "They've created a culture of kids' supporting each other," said one mother. "Kids tell me they know their teachers intimately."

Pell, who studied English and theater at Brown University and education policy at the Harvard School of Education, says that she wants to give children the kind of education she received as a child attending St. Ann's School, a private school in Brooklyn Heights. On my visit, one teacher read aloud from Frederick Douglass's slave narrative. In another class, children read the Greek myth of Persephone. In science, children discussed how the atmosphere gets heated. Children wrote imaginary biographies of themselves at age 40—a clever way to think about their goals and dreams. Students have an advisory period twice a week, a place to get tips on how to organize their notebooks and adjust to middle school life.

Check the school's website or call their office for information about tours. Applicants are interviewed. Children from Districts 13, 14, 15, and 16 may apply.

Math and Science Exploratory School, MS 447

345 Dean Street
Brooklyn, NY 11217
(718) 330-9328
www.ms447.org

Admissions: District 15
High school choices: Murrow, Midwood, Telecom
Grade levels: 6–8   **Test scores:** R ****, M *****
Enrollment: 510 (projected)   **Ethnicity:** 29%W 25%B 39%H 7%A
Class size: 30   **Free lunch:** 26%

The teachers at MS 447 believe that children learn best from projects they can see and touch, not just from textbooks—and that they need to discover their own solutions to problems, not merely absorb knowledge from someone who gives them the answers. Children are encouraged to work at their own pace, and the school accommodates both academic stars and kids who are struggling. About 30% of the students receive special education services, including some high-functioning children with autism.

The science program is especially strong, with imaginative projects and frequent class trips to places like the New York Aquarium and the Brooklyn Botanical Garden. Each year students take part in three interdisciplinary projects called "Expos." They spend each Friday working on them, often taking expeditions outside the school. Teachers from different disciplines plan these Expos together: A unit on plant ecology, for example, might look at the growth of agriculture in ancient Egypt, collect mathematical data on plants growing in Prospect Park, and observe plants in different habitats (from deserts to rain forests) at the Botanical Garden. Each grade takes an overnight trip with an environmental theme: Seventh-graders, for example, go to an environmental camp in the Poconos.

In one class, children learned about convection currents by putting drops of food color in a pan of water placed on a burner: As the water heated, they observed currents move from the center of the bottom of the pan to the top and back down along the sides. They then compared these currents to those in the ocean and learned how currents cause continents to shift. In another project, science students tried to predict whether the vapor from dry ice, dropped into water that was dyed blue, would come out blue or clear. (It was clear.) So many children told their parents about the project that during a curriculum night one year, parents were all asking to see the "dry ice class."

Children are grouped by ability in math, with a regular track, an honors track, and a high honors or Regents track. Students complete 9th-grade algebra in the 8th-grade Regents track. Children of different abilities are placed in classes together for English and social studies, and teachers may offer stronger students more difficult assignments or more challenging books to read.

Everyone has a chance to pursue the arts, including dance, instrumental music, visual arts, drama, and web design. Students select a "talent" area for 3 years and study it for three periods a week. Students may choose another talent area to pursue in the early morning or after school, so they need not feel limited to one area. The music program is particularly strong: There is a full orchestra and even a recording studio, where children may compose their own music using computer programs such as GarageBand. Students take trips to the Whitney Museum of American Art; the Metropolitan Museum of Art; the Museum of Modern Art; the New Victory Theater, in Manhattan; and the Brooklyn Academy of Music, located a few blocks from the school.

Housed on the 3rd and 4th floors of the former Sarah J. Hale High School in Boerum Hill, MS 447 shares a sprawling building, constructed in 1929, with the Brooklyn High School for the Arts. The pale-green floors are shiny, the cream-colored corridors are wide, and the space is well lit, but the layout is awkward: The 6th-grade classrooms are housed in an atticlike space on the 4th floor, with exposed pipes and sloping walls. Seventh- and 8th-grade classes, on the 3rd floor, are cramped. Long corridors connect the main building to an annex called the West Wing.

MS 447 has its own gym. The cafeteria is shared with Brooklyn High School of the Arts, but MS 447 students have lunch together at a time set aside for them. There are three lunch periods, starting at 10:10 a.m. Children have recess in a concrete yard between the main building and the West Wing. There is a well-equipped computer lab and technology is integrated into the curriculum, with extensive use of laptop computers both in the classroom and in the field.

The school integrates **special needs** children in Collaborative Team Teaching (CTT) classes, which have two teachers, one of whom is certified in special education. These classes have 10 special needs students, most of whom are learning disabled, and 20 general education students. In addition, MS 447 is home to a new program for children on the autism spectrum called ASD NEST. In the classes, 5 children with autism spectrum disorder (ASD) are in a class with 20 general education students. The ASD students are assigned their own special education teacher, who travels with them from class to class. Principal Lisa Gioe-Cordi said ASD NEST is the only middle school program of its kind in New York City and that it has been successful in helping high-functioning children with autism develop much needed social skills. For example, a withdrawn child who successfully makes eye contact might be rewarded with "points" that can be used to buy pizza.

There is an extensive after-school program offering activities like basketball, soccer, tennis, school newspaper, crocheting, dance, and instrumental music.

MS 447 opened in 2003 with 120 students in 6th grade in rather cramped quarters on the top floor of PS 58 in Carroll Gardens. It moved to its present location in 2005 and expanded from four classes in each grade to six.

In recent years, between 20% and 30% of 8th-graders have been admitted to specialized schools, including Brooklyn Tech, Stuyvesant, and LaGuardia High School of Music and Art and Performing Arts. Other popular high school choices are Midwood, Murrow, Telcommunications, Bard High School Early College, Beacon, and Millennium.

Open houses are scheduled in the fall and winter. Teachers interview applicants, who also are given a math or science problem to test their analytical abilities (rather than their knowledge). The school seeks to maintain a diverse student population and attracts children from a wide range of ethnic backgrounds and academic abilities.

Brooklyn School for
Collaborative Studies, MS 448

610 Henry Street
Brooklyn, NY 11231
(718) 923-4750
www.bcs448.org

Admissions: District 15
High school choices: NA
Grade levels: 6–12
Enrollment: 601
Class size: 28

Test scores: R ***, M ***
Ethnicity: 19%W 46%B 32%H 3%A
Free lunch: 50%

At Brooklyn School for Collaborative Studies, kids work in groups on nearly all their projects, whether they are making balsa wood towers (and testing their strength with a machine that simulates an earthquake); analyzing the causes of illegal immigration to the United States from Mexico; or producing new shows for WBCS, the students' own radio station that broadcasts to the classrooms. Kids are on a first-name basis with teachers and the principal. BCS is a place where both grown-ups and kids seem to be happy. The school is committed to serving a diverse range of kids—from both different ethnic groups and different academic abilities.

BCS occupies the 4th and 5th floors of a well-kept 100-year-old brick building that takes up a whole city block. Founded in 2001 as a middle school to serve as the continuation of Brooklyn New School (BNS), a popular progressive elementary school housed on the first three floors of the same building, BCS added high school grades in 2005 and became a full 6–12 school in 2008–2009.

Sunlight streams in through tall windows. Wooden coat closets, sofas, rugs, and wooden benches covered with cushions give the school a comfy feel. Children's work covers the walls—such as the authentic-looking imaginary diaries of people living in Salem, Massachusetts, at the time of the witch trials. A cheery library decorated with papier-mâché masks and sculptures serves the whole building.

The school sends home weekly newsletters and long monthly curriculum letters that detail what is happening in every class. Sixth grade is a transition year, and children stay with one teacher for most of their subjects. Every grade has "crew," similar to advisory, where students learn skills like how to organize homework.

"Crew" comes from the slogan: "We're all crew, not passengers," designed to make students think of themselves as active learners.

The school has a good band, led by a conservatory-trained teacher; a photography program in which kids learn to develop their own pictures in a real darkroom; and a dance program that includes visits from the African American troupe Urban Bush Women. Computer technology is integrated into the curriculum. In one geometry class, for example, students plotted polygons on computer screens using a computer program to assist them.

About 30% of the students receive **special education** services. Children with special needs are fully integrated into regular classes, assisted by a teacher certified in special education. Half the middle school classes and one-quarter of the high school classes have Collaborative Team Teaching (CTT), in which two teachers work together in a class that mixes special needs kids with those in general education. There is also one class for blind and visually handicapped children, which is provided by the "district" for severely handicapped children, District 75.

Test scores are not the school's strong suit: About half the children meet state standards for English, and 4 in 10 meet state standards in math. But Principal Alyce Barr is proud of the fact that the weakest readers may make 3 or 4 years' progress in a single year. (The Department of Education gave the school an "A" on its 2007 "progress report," reflecting the students' gains.) There is a wide range of abilities within a class: Some 6th-graders read very easy books more commonly read by 2nd- or 3rd-graders, while others read books written for adults. The school doesn't offer separate honors classes, but high-achieving students are encouraged to do honors-level work by completing more complex projects.

Big kids work with little kids in a building-wide initiative called the Unity Project: High school students may read aloud to elementary school students, or help them build structures from Legos, or supervise their woodworking projects. High school students are trained as babysitters—providing a useful service for elementary school parents and building a sense of community. In the 11th grade, students have interesting internships at local businesses: A boy and a girl worked at the Food Network and showed off their cooking skills on a television show.

BCS is a work in progress. The high school, in particular, had a not-quite-finished feel during my most recent visit. Class changes can be noisy. Some high school students arrive late and ill-prepared for class, and not all are on target to graduate in 4 years.

At the same time, the school has a hyper-educated, passionate teaching staff and dedicated leadership. Barr, a founding parent at BNS, where she also taught, oversees the whole school. Wanda Barbot, a long-time BNS parent and teacher, is assistant principal for the middle school; Scill (short for Priscilla) Chan, who studied environmental science at Harvard and taught at Manhattan Center High School, is assistant principal for the high school. Barbot is bilingual in Spanish and Chan is bilingual in Cantonese.

Unlike some 6–12 schools, which discourage kids from leaving for high school, BCS offers guidance to those who want to transfer to a larger school. About half the 8th-graders decide to stay; those who leave have been accepted at top schools such as LaGuardia High School of Music and Art and Performing Arts, Brooklyn Tech, or Beacon.

Admission is generally limited to District 15. There are five tours in the fall and winter. Prospective students are asked to participate in a sample class. Barr said that she wants to ensure that parents are committed to the values of the school: "If you want a school with tracking [grouping kids by ability], this is not the school for you."

William Alexander School, MS 51

350 5th Avenue
Brooklyn, NY 11215
(718) 369-7603
www.ms51.org

Admissions: District 15
High school choices: Murrow, LaGuardia, Beacon, Brooklyn Tech
Grade levels: 6–8   **Test scores:** R ****, M****
Enrollment: 987   **Ethnicity:** 38%W 19%B 31%H 12%A
Class size: 28–33   **Free lunch:** 29%

Long the highest-scoring middle school in the district, MS 51 is known for its solid academics, as well as its creative "talent" programs in drama and the arts. A selective school, it accepts high-achieving children from across District 15. The school also has an unusual program for gifted children who need special education services.

The physical plant is nothing special: Corridors are long and straight, with low ceilings, institutional-looking cinderblock walls painted light green or gray, and fluorescent lights. But children's work covers the walls and many of the classrooms are cozy, with rugs and sofas. Walk through the halls and you may see kids practicing monologues for a drama class or putting together their notes for a class project.

The school has long been known for its strong teaching in the humanities. English teachers have been trained in the methods of Teachers College's Readers and Writers Workshop, in which children write multiple drafts of their papers and edit one another's work.

On one of our visits, a social studies class in American history was studying the robber barons and the rise of corporations in America. The children had many questions about the buying and selling of stocks and about public versus private corporations. All came alive when they broke up into groups to create their own companies: an ice cream shop, a lip gloss company, and a sausage factory.

In another social studies class, children were doing research on daily life in ancient Egypt, drawing from a variety of sources and discovering interesting tidbits, like the fact that girls didn't attend school. Down the hall children discussed the importance of Ellis

Island in U.S. history and planned a class trip to the port of entry for turn-of-the-century immigrants.

For years parents have complained that math and science classes take a backseat to the arts and humanities. Now a new principal, Lenore DiLeo Berner, a science specialist, is focused on improving math and science instruction. She is expanding the course offerings to encourage advanced students to take Regents (9th-grade) exams in math and biology. Berner, who became principal in early 2007, has asked Brooklyn Tech's Principal Randy Asher for advice on how to strengthen math and science. Science facilities have been improved, with new tables, computers, microscopes, and cameras.

Berner is also putting more emphasis on children's social and emotional development. Monthly assemblies focus on themes like citizenship, respect, and courage. Assistant Principal Nance Speth coordinates an active community service program. For example, 8th-graders work one on one with elementary school children, helping them to master reading.

The talent program has long been the pride of the school. Kids choose a specialty in 6th grade and stick with it for 3 years. The "talents" include photography, drama, dance, fine arts, band, and vocal music. The chorus is renowned and kids willingly come in early and give up their lunch hours to rehearse for frequent performances. The drama program is particularly strong. It has its own "black box theater" classroom, with a platform for performances and stage lights; even the lockers are painted black. Students perform a Shakespeare play every year, such as *Romeo and Juliet* or *Twelfth Night*. Visual arts talents are also offered. The dance program gets high marks from the students, as does the Show Choir, which has traveled to California to perform. Drama students have visited Scotland and have welcomed Scottish exchange students to Brooklyn.

The school offers **special education** services to children who meet the academic qualifications for the school but who have disabilities, like Attention Deficit Disorder. These children are placed in a Collaborative Team Teaching (CTT) class with two teachers, one of whom is certified in special education. The CTT classes have 19 children in general education and 7 in special education; the latter receive services, including speech and occupational therapy. The CTT class I observed, in which kids worked on challenging math problems, seemed unusually focused and engaging. There are also five self-contained special education classes for children with more severe disabilities who do not meet the academic cutoff for admission to the school.

Students are allowed off campus during lunch.

The homework load is heavy: Students typically have a half hour of homework each day in each of their academic classes. The school is faster paced than some of the small, progressive schools in the district, but is less of a pressure cooker than the super-competitive schools like Mark Twain. Depending on your child, that could be too competitive, not competitive enough, or just right. One parent complained that the pace is too slow and that any child who aspires to a specialized high school must have a math tutor. On the other hand, an 8th-grader complained that teachers expect way too much of students and that the school is best suited for a competitive child who can handle numerous projects at one time.

What's missing? The instrumental program is weak. Sports are "hit or miss," one parent said. Physical education is offered three times a week. There is a coed soccer team and girls' and boys' basketball teams.

The administration boasts that 90% of the graduates go to the high school of their choice. Murrow, Midwood, Beacon, and LaGuardia High School of Music and Art and Performing Arts accept many MS 51 graduates. Increasing numbers are admitted to Brooklyn Tech, Stuyvesant, or Bronx Science. Telecommunications offers a lot of support for special needs students, and is the choice for many students in the CTT classes. The school holds its own high school fair in October.

Admission is restricted to children in District 15. Tours are offered twice weekly during the fall and early winter. They fill up fast, so call early to reserve a spot. Students must have test scores of at least 660 on the 4th-grade ELA and math tests. Applicants are also asked to provide a copy of their 4th- and 5th-grade report cards and a writing sample; applicants also undergo a brief interview. There are many more applicants than seats available. Students who have been offered a place may rank their choices for talent classes.

New Voices School of
Academic and Creative Arts, MS 443

330 18th Street
Brooklyn, NY 11215
(718) 965-0390
http://nvoices.org

Admissions: District 15
High school choices: Murrow, Telecommunications, Millennium
Grade levels: 6–8   **Test scores:** R ****, M ****
Enrollment: 418   **Ethnicity:** 19%W 17%B 56%H 8%A
Class size: 27–30   **Free lunch:** 68%

Long known as a school with an unusually good arts program, New Voices for Academic and Creative Arts has strengthened its academic offerings in recent years, particularly in math and science. It still serves kids with a range of academic abilities, but now there is plenty to challenge the top students, as well as those who are struggling.

New Voices has a homey, family feel. Indeed, half a dozen staff members have chosen it for their own children. Principal Frank Giordano prides himself on knowing every child by name: One parent insists that he knows all the 6th-graders' names on the first day of school.

Halfway between Park Slope and Sunset Park, New Voices shares a 100-year-old building with PS 295, a neighborhood school that also specializes in the arts. Located on the top two floors of the H-shaped building, New Visions has high ceilings, big windows, and shiny hardwood floors. The corridors are painted lavender with white trim. Classrooms have hexagonal tables and bins of books, not just novels and biographies but science books on topics like sea life, electricity, wild animals, and insects.

Reading, writing, and social studies are combined into one "humanities" class, in which students have one teacher for two or three periods a day. This means that a humanities teacher has only two classes a day—and a total of just 50 or 60 pupils to get to know, instead of the 180 that would be typical at a traditional junior high school. In one class, children proposed solutions to modern-day problems based on their study of Hamurabi's ancient legal code. For example, may birth parents take back a child after an adoption? (The children decided "No.")

New Voices has replaced the progressive math programs used in many New York City schools with a series published by Glencoe, which teachers described as more "parent friendly." Sixth-graders are have an introduced to algebra, geometry, and probability; by 8th grade the most advanced students may take the 9th-grade Regents-level math exam.

The math and science teachers work together to coordinate their lessons. For example, children might learn to use the metric system, protractors, and line graphs in both subjects. The science lab reports I saw were quite sophisticated: One child tested the hypothesis that kosher salt is more soluble in water than Epson salt because the kosher salt grains are larger. (Wrong: It's because the kosher salt has less density.) Another tested the lowest pH at which mustard seeds could germinate.

Children study Shakespeare with teaching artists from Theatre for a New Audience, a non-profit organization. They see productions of Shakespeare plays at the New Victory Theater, in Manhattan, and act out scenes in class. The day I visited, children were miming a scene from *Antony and Cleopatra*.

"How does Cleopatra feel in the beginning? Powerful!" the teacher said. "One, two, three, freeze!" and the children all tried to look powerful. "How does a queen fall in love?" "Jealous!" and "Angry!" the children said and tried to look jealous and angry. "Remember your body language and facial expression," said the teacher. "What does Cleopatra feel like at the end?" "Heartbroken," and "Scared," the children replied and acted accordingly.

All students have instruction in the arts, taught by working professionals, two or three times a week for 1½ hours. Sixth-graders take classes in all disciplines—visual arts, graphic arts, dance, music, and theater (including musical theater)—and then specialize in 7th and 8th grade, when the arts curriculum becomes more demanding. (To make time in their schedule for all the arts, 6th-graders have no physical education or Spanish classes.)

Children hung papier-mâché sculptures of sneakers in the corridor, part of an art project that began with their making a pencil drawing of their own shoes. In 6th grade, children learn to draw with one-point perspective. By 7th and 8th grade, they work in sculpture. They study art history and make trips to the Museum of Modern Art and the Guggenheim Museum.

On the day of my visit, in a pleasant, mirrored dance studio, students leaped across the floor in a class led by teacher Michael Kerr—a professional dancer trained in both classical ballet and modern dance.

In a graphic arts class, children learned computer programs such as Photoshop and Illustrator. They designed book covers, travel brochures, and bubble gum wrappers.

There are five classes in each grade. One or two are designated as accelerated or honors classes. The school also offers Collaborative Team Teaching (CTT) classes with two teachers, one of whom is certified in **special education**, and a mix of children, some of whom have special needs.

The school helps children prepare high school portfolios and auditions and is fairly successful in gaining admission to art-focused schools such as Murrow, LaGuardia High School of Music and Art and Performing Arts, and Frank Sinatra. A few children have been admitted to the specialized high schools, and that number seems likely to increase as the school attracts more high-achieving students.

Students from District 15 are eligible for admission; students are interviewed. There are regular tours. The school accepts children with a range of abilities.

MS 88

544 7th Avenue
Brooklyn, NY 11215
(718) 788-4482

Admissions: District 15
High school choices: FDR, New Utrecht, Telecommunications
Grade levels: 6–8   **Test scores:** R ***, M ***
Enrollment: 891   **Ethnicity:** 10%W 16%B 60%H 14%A
Class size: 22–28   **Free lunch:** 97%

MS 88 doesn't make a great first impression. The poured-concrete and brick exterior of the building, constructed in 1965, is foreboding. Inside, ceilings are low, and ugly brown tiles line the walls. But stay awhile, and the place begins to grow on you. Some classrooms have rugs and loveseats. Colorful bulletin boards are covered with kids' projects. Most important, there's a sense of shared mission and camaraderie among the staff. (There have been four marriages between faculty members in the past few years.) Teachers seem to relish coming up with imaginative projects and sharing their ideas with one another.

A social studies teacher put together a study of Japan that included origami, a Japanese tea ceremony, and a trip to the Botanical Garden to study bonsai. An English teacher designed a class that combines acrobatics with poetry—and teaches acrobatic salsa dancing after school. (A boy leaped from the shoulders of his teacher when I visited this class, both demonstrating their fine acrobatic form.) A science teacher had kids make larger-than-life-size drawings of the human body, outlining the circulatory system. A math teacher guided students in making bar graphs, analyzing data from a mock presidential election in which the students voted.

MS 88 has made striking progress in recent years. In 2002, it was placed on the state's list of worst schools—Schools Under Registration Review, or SURR. Ailene Altman Mitchell, who became principal in 2004, said she replaced nearly the entire staff, instituted gifted classes for high-achieving students, and put in place a system of "lead teachers" to guide new staff members. The state removed MS 88 from the SURR list the following year. In 2007, the city awarded the school an "A" on its annual progress report, citing a big improvement in test scores.

The school is organized into three academies: the School for Media Arts, Research and Technology; the School for Medical and Health Careers; and the School for Integrated Studies through the Arts. Each academy serves about 300 children in grades 6–8. Each has a mix of high-achieving, average, and struggling students. The strongest students are placed in classes for the gifted, where they take 9th-grade (Regents-level) algebra and biology in 8th grade. There are also classes for average students, for students of English as a Second Language, and for children with **special education** needs. Collaborative Team Teaching (CTT) classes combine general education and special needs children. These classes have two teachers, one of whom is certified in special education.

MS 88 still has a long way to go. In 2007, only 42% of students met state standards (scoring at Level 3 or 4) on the state English Language Arts exam, and 62% met state standards in math. A tiny handful of graduates are admitted to the specialized high schools. But the school is beginning to attract students from highly regarded elementary schools such as PS 130 and PS 154. If MS 88 makes as much progress in the next few years as it has in the past few, it will surely become an increasingly attractive option for District 15 children.

The school offers regular tours during the fall months. No appointment is necessary to attend a tour. Check Insideschools.org or call the school for dates and times.

Sunset Park Prep, MS 821
4004 4th Avenue
Brooklyn, NY 11232
(718) 965-3331
www.prepms821.org

Admissions: District 15
High school choices: Telecommunications, Fort Hamilton, New Utrecht
Grade levels: 6–8   **Test scores:** R****, M****
Enrollment: 474   **Ethnicity:** 6%W 11%B 74%H 9%A
Class size: 24–28   **Free lunch:** 77%

An orderly school with a collegial, cohesive staff and a warm and gentle atmosphere, Sunset Park Prep Academy gives students both the academic skills and the hand-holding they need to succeed in high school and in the wider world. Most of the students are children of immigrants from Latin America, with a few from China and India, and the multilingual staff works hard to connect with parents and kids.

"The teachers know the students extremely well," said Karen Blume, who serves as a reading and writing consultant to the school as part of a program called A.U.S.S.I.E. (Australian and United States Services in Education). "They know their quirks and strengths and weaknesses and they know about their families. They're interested in whether Mum has a new baby. They spend time with the students after class, at lunchtime. School becomes a second home."

Housed on the 3rd and 4th floors of a brick building constructed in 1901, the school is old but spotless, with tall windows that let in lots of light, high ceilings, and oak coat closets. Some of the rooms are painted in soft pastels. The principal's office is painted pink. Some classrooms display the American flag. The classrooms have bins of fun-to-read books. Class changes are smooth, with kids moving quietly through the corridors and settling quickly into their work.

There is plenty of emphasis on basic skills: In a geography class, kids matched cities and capitals around the world. In a math class, they plotted points on graph paper. In science, they completed a worksheet on evaporation and the water cycle. But there are also interesting projects: Children learned prime numbers using the ancient Greek algorithm called the sieve of Eratosthenes. They made dioramas of the gods from Greek myths. In an art class, they watched a PBS documentary on the origins of graffiti art in New York City; and in music, they listened to Led Zeppelin. The ambitious drama program helps kids put on musical productions such as *The Wizard of Oz* and *Grease*. An after-school program offers activities such as chess, music, math club, and crocheting.

While the school is open to anyone in District 15, most of the kids live in the Sunset Park neighborhood. In addition, a number of graduates of the Children's School, the special education inclusion program in Park Slope, have chosen Sunset Park Prep for its Collaborative Team Teaching (CTT) classes, said Principal Lola Padin. CTT classes have two teachers, one of whom is certified in **special education**, and a mix of general education and special needs children. Sunset Park Prep also offers separate special education classes that serve only special needs children, and a special education class for children learning English as a Second Language.

Sunset Park Prep serves children with a range of abilities and attempts to find good high schools for everyone. Although most children stay in the neighborhood and attend schools such as Telecommunications and Fort Hamilton, the guidance counselor encourages them to consider small schools such as Millennium or Brooklyn College Academy. Top students, many of whom have taken the 9th-grade math and Earth science Regents exams, are encouraged to apply to the specialized high schools. Teachers even escort children to the exam at Stuyvesant High School or to the audition at LaGuardia High School of Music and Art and Performing Arts, easing parents' fears about children going to Manhattan. "Parents are reluctant to let them leave Brooklyn," said a teacher.

Sunset Park Prep offers weekly tours. Call the parent coordinator for information.

North Star Academy, MS 340
227 Sterling Place
Brooklyn, NY 11238
(718) 857-5516

Admissions: District 17
High school choices: Science Skills, Westinghouse, Middle College
Grade levels: 6–8   **Test scores:** R ****, M ****
Enrollment: 342   **Ethnicity:** 1%W 92%B 6%H 1%A
Class size: 29   **Free lunch:** 57%

MS 340 is a selective school with a slightly formal tone that matches its red brick century-old building. Students must wear uniforms with white shirts and plaid ties. The school is warm and nurturing and feels like a close-knit community. Geographically separate from the rest of District 17, MS 340 mostly enrolls students from Crown Heights and East Flatbush, and many kids travel to the school by subway.

Students are grouped in classes according to their abilities. "I think there's greater competition that way," Principal Jean Williams told Insideschools.org. To help 6th-graders ease into the middle school routine, each class is assigned a core teacher who stays with them for English, social studies, and math instruction.

Kids don't change classes here. Teachers do. That's because the halls in the old building are so narrow that having students change classes would result in chaos. But the policy has the effect of giving kids a sense of belonging—to their classroom as well as to their school.

Science instruction, a main focus of the school, suffers from the lack of lab space and equipment. Despite the poor facilities, the school manages to push its students. Seventh-graders take the state's 8th-grade science test (almost all pass), so that in 8th grade they take the high school–level Regents course in Living Environment. Construction of a big science lab was slated to begin in the summer of 2008.

MS 340 is not for the claustrophobic. Classrooms are small and stuffy, and though the computer lab is well equipped, students must work in it elbow to elbow. In the low-ceilinged basement that serves as a gym, participants in a dance class have to maneuver around pillars. Yet the school has enthusiastic dance and step teams, as well as a trophy-winning basketball team that practices off campus. The school has a student-run bookstore, which parents say gives students a sense of pride.

"Overall the school was calm, though we did observe some unruly student behavior," Nicole LaRosa wrote on the Inside-schools.org website. "On the day of our visit, five students were in the detention room, where Williams said typical offenses are horseplay, refusing to follow rules, or verbal rudeness. Kids told us there weren't many fights."

There is one self-contained **special education** class for students with special needs. "The class, we observed, was led by a nurturing, confident teacher who encourages the students to participate in the school community by applying for "jobs" helping staff in the technology lab and offices.

District 17 students who score at Level 3 or 4 on 4th-grade standardized tests are eligible for admission. Students must also take the Otis-Lennon School Ability Test (OLSAT).

Medgar Evers Preparatory School at Medgar Evers College

1186 Carroll Street
Brooklyn, NY 11225
(718) 703-5400
www.mecps.org

Admissions: citywide
High school choices: NA
Grade levels: 6–12   **Test scores:** R *****, M *****
Enrollment: 850   **Ethnicity:** 3%W 90%B 5%H 2%A
Class size: 20–25   **Free lunch:** 29%

Formerly called Middle College High School, Medgar Evers Preparatory School at Medgar Evers College added a middle school in 2005 and now serves students in grades 6–12. Students may take the high school Regents exams for math and Living Environment as early as 7th grade. By 8th grade, they may take the chemistry, English, and U.S. history Regents exams. High school students may take college courses—for free. The high school offers 13 Advanced Placement courses.

"We want students to leave the school with a level of confidence that they can do well in college," said the principal, Dr. Michael Wiltshire. In addition, students who accumulate college credits will save considerable money on tuition later. Wiltshire is a traditionalist who insists on discipline—no cellphones or hats allowed—but he also tries to make the school nurturing.

Middle College High School was established in 1993 to give personal attention to all students, so that even alienated kids could learn the math, science, and technology skills needed for college. Class size is small, with 20 to 25 students in each class, and the school has two full-time college placement officers. Nearly all the graduates go on to college, and about three-quarters are admitted to 4-year colleges.

The *New York Daily News* named the school one of the best in Brooklyn in 2007 because of its high test scores. The *News* highlighted an unusual Chinese-language class in which 6th-graders learned a song in Chinese. The school also offers instruction in French and Spanish.

Students from anywhere in the city may apply. An open house is offered in October. Entering 6th-graders must take an entrance exam, usually offered in February.

Crown School for
Law and Journalism at PS 161

330 Crown Street
Brooklyn, NY 11225
(718) 756-3100
www.ps161.com

Admissions: District 17 preference
High school choices: Brooklyn Tech, Murrow
Grade levels: 6–8   **Test scores:** R ****, M ****
Enrollment: 60   **Ethnicity:** 2%W 88%B 8%H 2%A
Class size: 28–30   **Free lunch:** 92%

The Crown School for Law and Journalism is a tiny, highly selective middle school on the top floor of a gigantic elementary school. Children wear navy-blue-and-gray uniforms. Some students have internships with judges, lawyers, or journalists. As part of their journalism curriculum, the students publish an ambitious newsletter, *The Crown Jewel*, featuring the activities of the school. Students typically have 3 to 4 hours of homework a night.

As part of their American history study, 7th-graders went to Boston, where they saw historical sites like the scene of the Salem witch trials. As an adjunct to their law course, in which they studied the Bill of Rights and the Constitution, 6th-graders went to Philadelphia, where they visited the Liberty Bell and other sites related to their social studies curriculum. After reading the Harry Potter books, the students decided to start a house system in their small school. The five or six houses do individual fund-raisers and volunteer projects. House banners hang in the classrooms. Students exhibit pride in their school and their work. Those needing extra help in math work with the principal in a special after-school program.

One mother called the school "traditional, but not oppressive." "There's a lot of class discussion, and children have the opportunity to give their opinions," she added. Many teachers have creative ideas for projects, she said, like the Spanish teacher who had kids write their own comic books in Spanish.

The minischool was founded in 1995 by three PS 161 teachers who, as parents, found that children were lost in large, anonymous junior high schools. With the backing of their principal, they set up their own program for 6th, 7th, and 8th grades in PS 161.

The teachers believed it was important for children to have more contact with teachers than is typical in junior high school. Instead of children changing classes for every subject, they might have math and science with one teacher and English and history with another. Teachers spend time with children outside regular school hours as well. A music teacher, for example, takes kids to the opera.

Children are expected to write multiple drafts of their papers, correcting and improving them each time. One English class combined the rigor of grammar exercises—with sentence diagramming and drills on subject-verb agreement—with a subtle discussion of the use of irony in a book about the introduction of Western customs to an Indian village in the Pacific Northwest. The children were serious and attentive, and the school was very orderly.

In the law classes they visit courts and put on their own mock trials. One teacher said that kids are so wrapped up in the study of the Constitution that when they bump one another in the hall, they say, "Hey! You're violating my Fourth Amendment rights!"

Parents say that the admissions process is competitive, but once children are enrolled they help one another in class and the competition isn't cutthroat. In addition to academics, there are arts and crafts after school and a step-dancing team. Children in the chorus sing classical music, like Handel's *Messiah* and Bach's *Jesu, Joy of Man's Desiring* in four-part harmony.

Eighth-graders may take Regents level (9th-grade) math and science.

The school prides itself on the number of graduates who go to Stuyvesant or to other selective high schools. Some are part of Prep for Prep, an organization that helps kids prepare for admissions to selective private day and boarding schools.

Sixty 5th-graders from PS 161 are accepted by lottery.

KIPP AMP Charter School

1224 Park Place
Brooklyn, NY 11213
(718) 943-3710
www.kippamp.org

Admissions: District 17 priority, citywide
High school choices: NA
Grade levels: 5–8 **Test scores:** R ****, M *****
Enrollment: 192 **Ethnicity:** 1%W 97%B 2%H 0%A
Class size: 35 **Free lunch:** 75%

Part of a national network of charter schools, KIPP AMP has long school days, an extra-long school year, and a strict discipline code. Students have a "silent period" from their arrival at 7:25 a.m. until 8 a.m., part of a routine to help them focus. Classes continue until 5 p.m, Mondays through Thursdays. Dismissal is at 3:30 p.m. on Fridays, and classes resume for 4 hours every other Saturday and for a few weeks in July. Teachers, whose cellphones are paid for by KIPP AMP, take calls from students at night, and Principal Ky Adderley bikes around the neighborhood "to be a presence."

"Children are expected to behave in a civilized manner, and they mostly do," Pamela Wheaton wrote on the Insideschools. org website. "Minor infractions (an untied shoe, an untucked shirt, or even not being polite enough while taking a seat on the rug) are grounds for detention or exclusion from a group activity." The school offers incentives to students to stay on track, however. Fifth-graders who earn enough "KIPP dollars" for good behavior and completed homework may go on a year-end trip to Washington, DC. A highlight of KIPP AMP is instruction in capoeira, a Brazilian martial arts form. This brings music and movement into a curriculum otherwise focused on core academic subjects. KIPP AMP, opened in 2005, shares a building with three other schools. Students are accepted by lottery in April. Priority is given to District 17 residents. Most kids who graduate from KIPP middle schools go on to top private and boarding schools, Adderley said.

Philippa Schuyler School, IS 383
1300 Greene Avenue
Brooklyn, NY 11237
(718) 574-0390
www.philippaschuyler.org

Admissions: citywide
High school choices: Brooklyn Tech, Benjamin Banneker, Midwood
Grade levels: 5–8   **Test scores:** R *****, M *****
Enrollment: 1,229   **Ethnicity:** 1%W 68%B 27%H 4%A
Class size: 29   **Free lunch:** 60%

Philippa Schuyler School for the Gifted and Talented has a proud history of preparing children for demanding high schools, both public and private. It draws from a wide spectrum of social classes—from families in homeless shelters to the children of doctors and lawyers. Children come from as far away as Staten Island and the Bronx to the school, which sits next to the rumbling elevated subway in the Bushwick section of Brooklyn. It has long served African American and Latino children, and in recent years has attracted some Asian children as well.

Philippa Schuyler has challenging academics. In an English class, students wrote essays reflecting on a comment made by poet W. H. Auden about Edgar Allen Poe's *The Raven*. A science fair project investigated whether punk rock or heavy metal music results in larger surface vibrations—using sophisticated computer software called WinDaqLite to measure the vibrations. One student wrote about the history of the French walled city of Carcassonne as part of a study of the Middle Ages. Students in a French class learned why French is spoken in Haiti by reading the accounts of early European explorers. In a legal studies class, children prepared jury selection for a mock criminal trial.

In addition to their regular academic classes, children may take "major electives" 5 days a week. These courses—some of which last a semester, some of which last a year—include art, music, dance, and physical education, as well as unusual courses like finance; legal studies; and steel pan, the Caribbean musical instruments made of metal drums. The steel pan band is the pride of the school.

Students have many experiences outside the classroom. Sixth-graders climb mountains on an overnight trip to the Adirondacks, while 7th-graders spend the night at an environmental camp in the Poconos. Art classes visit the Metropolitan Museum of Art in Manhattan, while drama students write their own play and perform it on Broadway as part of a program called Fidelity Future Stages.

An attentive high school adviser, Keyon Armstead, herself a Philippa Schuyler graduate, gives students advice about all their options—not just well-known schools like Brooklyn Tech, but newer ones like Bard High School Early College, Brooklyn Latin, and a new science program at Murrow High School. She helps prepare them for admission to private schools by telling them about recruitment programs for Black and Hispanic children like Prep for Prep, or informing them about the entrance exam for Catholic schools. Of the graduates, 15% or 20% go on to private day or boarding schools, some on full scholarship. Of a graduating class of about 300, 40 students typically go to Brooklyn Tech, about 10 to LaGuardia High School of Music and Art and Performing Arts, half a dozen to Stuyvesant, and a handful to the other specialized schools. Benjamin Banneker, Clara Barton, Midwood, and Murrow are also popular choices.

Students may attend special Saturday classes at New York University through a program called STEP (Science and Technology Entry Program), designed to encourage youngsters to consider careers in medicine and technology. They receive career counseling, conduct research, and prepare for the specialized high school exam.

Principal Barbara Sanders, a former assistant principal who has led the school since 2003, has sought to maintain the school's tradition of high academic standards, all the while softening what some considered a sink-or-swim attitude toward students who were struggling. In years past, children who couldn't keep up with the fast pace of the school were sometimes asked to leave. Now, Sanders said, teachers work with them to help them succeed.

Homework, while heavy, is not the grueling 4-hour-a-night ordeal it was some years ago. Sanders said some children commute an hour or more to school, and expecting them to do many hours of homework is unrealistic. Nevertheless, children I spoke to said they studied about 2 hours a night. Parents are expected to help children with their homework and with organizing their assignments, for example, buying poster board and foam balls for science projects.

Sanders has worked to make the school more welcoming to boys who, in years past, were more likely than girls to leave. She has hired at least 11 male teachers, a male assistant principal, and a male parent coordinator. (The PTA president, incidentally, is a man.) She has also added more sports and physical education classes; boys often play football in a park near the school before school begins.

In many respects, Philippa Schuyler is a traditional school. Girls wear white shirts and blue plaid skirts; boys wear white shirts and neckties. Children learn old-fashioned (but useful) skills in classes in public speaking and diction. (Sanders is proud that children can "code switch," that is, switch from Brooklynese or African American dialect to Standard English according to the circumstance.) Some of the classrooms have desks in rows, and there is plenty of emphasis on textbooks and worksheets.

Sanders has taken steps to incorporate the progressive methods of teaching that became popular under Chancellor Joel Klein's administration: replacing literature anthologies with paperback novels, encouraging children to select books based on their interests, and creating interdisciplinary projects, for example. One teacher I spoke to lamented the shift away from traditional grammar exercises like diagramming sentences. But other teachers embraced the new approach. In one social studies class, for example, children took part in a "colonial day," in which they dressed in period costumes, churned butter, made soap, made ink from fruit, wrote with a quill, and danced the Virginia reel.

Philippa Schyuler has been undergoing a transition since its founding principal, Mildred Boyce, retired in 2003. At the time, the school had a seasoned staff, many of whom had founded the school with Boyce in 1977; when Boyce retired, many of them retired as well. The current staff has many strong teachers, but not all are successful in striking a balance between structure and creativity: A few classes I visited seemed orderly but dull, and a few seemed lively but unfocused. Nonetheless, the loyalty of the teachers and students for their school is palpable. School spirit is strong. Many of the teachers are Philippa Schuyler alumni, which gives the school a sense of community and continuity.

The four-story, red brick building is a bit drab, with brown tile corridors. Some of the desks are chipped, and some of the paint on the classroom walls is scuffed. On the positive side: An old parking lot has been transformed into a new playground, complete with tennis courts and a baseball diamond.

The school has six **special education** classes, whose pupils are assigned by the borough enrollment office. These children may take electives with pupils from the rest of the school. Philippa

Schuyler is also the site of a regional suspension center for children who are suspended from other schools. The day of my visit, two students were in the suspension center in a wing separated from the rest of the school.

Any child who lives in the city may apply for admission. Applications may be picked up in person between October and January. Students may enter from 5th to 7th grade, with most entering in 6th. Students must take the Otis-Lennon School Abilities Test (OLSAT), usually administered between December and March. Parents are invited to attend an orientation session while children are taking the exam. Some parents hire private vans to bring their children to school.

IS 392

104 Sutter Avenue
Brooklyn, NY 11212
(718) 498-2811

Admissions: District 23
High school choices: NA
Grade levels: 5–8   **Test scores:** R *****, M *****
Enrollment: 295   **Ethnicity:** 1%W 86%B 12%H 1%A
Class size: 25–30   **Free lunch:** 75%

A few years ago, District 23 suffered a brain drain, as many top 5th-graders deserted the district and enrolled at such middle schools as Philippa Schuyler in District 32 and Mark Twain in District 21. To stem the flow, the district created its own middle school for gifted students: IS 392, located on the 4th floor of the popular PS 156 in Brownsville.

A soaring wall of windows overlooks a playground, while a gracious double-wide staircase leads to a gymnasium and dance studio. Well-equipped science labs, a darkroom, kiln-filled art studios, and equipment for a soon-to-be-set-up recording studio complete the picture.

With fewer than 100 students per grade and studious-looking children wearing the required white-and-gray uniforms, IS 392 is pleasant and orderly. The school has stellar rates of attendance. Writing assignments often revolve around subjects of interest to adolescents, like whether the school cafeteria would be a good venue for the 8th-grade prom. (Kids gave an unmistakable thumbs-down to that idea in well-reasoned essays.)

Classes connect art to social studies: Children studying slavery made Popsicle-stick models of slave ships complete with tinfoil "shackles." Eighth-graders studying the Civil War created paper quilts after learning that slaves would display the patchworks to alert others to secrets like the arrival of representatives of the Underground Railroad.

I love this school," a student wrote on the Insideschools.org website. "It is extremely spacious, artistic, and overall amazing to me. My peers are wonderful, and teachers are there to help." One complaint from this student: Discipline is very strict.

Students who score a 3 or 4 on the standardized math and ELA exams are eligible to take an entrance exam. Preference is given to District 23 students and then to those from other districts.

Andries Hudde School, IS 240
2500 Nostrand Avenue
Brooklyn, NY 11210
(718) 253-3700

Admissions: Districts 17, 18, 22
High school choices: Murrow, Madison, Midwood
Grade levels: 6–8   **Test scores:** R ***, M ***
Enrollment: 1,450   **Ethnicity:** 8%W 72%B 9%H 11%A
Class size: 33   **Free lunch:** 73%

A large, traditional neighborhood school, the Andries Hudde School has three gifted programs that attract some of the brightest kids in District 22. The gifted programs offer accelerated classes in math and science, and "majors" in drama, orchestra, band, dance, fine arts, and chorus. About half the children enrolled are in the gifted program; the rest are assigned to Hudde because they live in the school zone.

The school serves children of immigrants from Jamaica, Trinidad, Pakistan, India, Bangladesh, and Egypt, as well as many African American children and "a few red-headed Irish kids," as Principal Elena O'Sullivan calls them. (The surrounding Midwood neighborhood has many Orthodox Jewish families, most of whom send their children to private religious schools.)

The tone of the school is serious. Kids follow a dress code of black or blue trousers and yellow, white, or blue shirts, and they move quietly from class to class. The staff is older, and most teachers rely on traditional methods of instruction; many of the classrooms have desks in rows. On my visit, I saw some lackluster classes. At the same time, some classes have interesting projects: One social studies class made a documentary of the history of their school, weaving in topics like demographic changes in the neighborhood and how students in the 1960s reacted to the civil rights movement and the Vietnam War. In a science class, students made posters and PowerPoint presentations on great natural disasters in history. Other students described how the Greeks and Romans used simple machines in their architecture.

Children in the gifted programs take part in the Johns Hopkins math program, in which students work independently and at their own pace. That means that some students may move ahead of their peers, while those who are struggling get the help they need. Some children finish high school algebra in 8th grade. Advanced students may also take Regents-level Earth science and Living Environment courses.

The school is best known for its arts programs. Children in the gifted programs may choose an art or music "major," which they study once a day for 3 years. On our visit we saw a dance class in which the students choreographed their own hip-hop number, and an art class in which students painted with acrylics and learned perspective. The drama department puts on ambitious musical productions, including *Annie, Oklahoma!* and *Into the Woods*. Students in the music program not only learn to play instruments, they also attend performances at the Brooklyn Academy of Music.

The school isn't as crowded as it was a few years ago, when enrollment approached 2,000. Still, the three-story brick building, constructed in the mid-1950s, shows signs of wear. Desks are scratched and antique lab tables are scarred with graffiti. The cafeteria is crowded and noisy, with four lunch periods starting at 10:30 a.m., and staff members shout through bullhorns to keep order. Bathrooms are locked. Several parents complained to us about bullying and fights.

The school has a "family movie night" to encourage parents to spend a relaxed evening at the school with their children. Other events, such as a high school fair, are well attended—a sign that Hudde parents care a lot about their children's education. The most popular high school choices for graduates are nearby Midwood, Madison, and Murrow, but many students are admitted to the specialized high schools as well.

There are five self-contained **special education** classes and five collaborative team-teaching classes that integrate special needs children and general education pupils.

There are tours in November and January. Children who are zoned for the school are automatically admitted. Children in Districts 17, 18, and 22 may apply to the gifted programs. Students with 4th-grade test scores of 680 in English Language Arts and 700 in math are eligible to take the test for admission, called the Otis-Lennon School Abilities Test (OLSAT). Call the borough enrollment center at 1780 Ocean Avenue, (718) 758-7687, for details. The three gifted programs are the Center for the Intellectually Gifted (CIG), the magnet program, and the NOVA program for children who just miss the cut off for CIG and magnet. (NOVA students don't take courses for high school credit.) For further information, contact the gifted coordinator, Madeline Louison, at (718) 758-1362 or mlouiso@schools.nyc.gov.

Mary White Ovington School, IS 30

415 Ovington Avenue
Brooklyn, NY 11209
(718) 491-5684

Admissions: District 20
High school choices: Brooklyn Tech, Staten Island Tech, Fort Hamilton
Grade levels: 6–8   **Test scores:** R ***, M ***
Enrollment: 340   **Ethnicity:** 59%W 3%B 21%H 17%A
Class size: 33   **Free lunch:** 68%

A neighborhood school in Bay Ridge that also accepts out-of-zone children who qualify for the gifted or "superintendent's" program, IS 30 is a small school with imaginative teachers and a good arts program. Located in an apartment building that once housed a Lutheran day school, the lobby is bright and pleasant, with colorfully painted wooden furniture and mosaics made by the children.

Trips bring the curriculum to life: Students may examine weapons and other artifacts from the Revolutionary War at the nearby Fort Hamilton Army Base, or use mathematical equations to design square-foot plots at the Brooklyn Botanical Garden. After-school activities include the Road Runners Club, in which kids run up to 5 miles twice a week and participate in weekend races in Central Park.

The building has no gymnasium, but children have physical education classes in the cafeteria or outside. Some students play tennis in a nearby park.

At lunchtime, some kids play chess in the lobby. Students may select drama, band, and visual arts as specialties. The school has a "wonderful" art teacher who helps students prepare portfolios for admission to LaGuardia High School of Music and Art and Performing Arts, parent coordinator Donna Borgia said. Honors students may take Regents-level (9th-grade) algebra and Earth science. Technology is integrated into the curriculum and students receive laptops to use at school and at home.

Any child zoned for the school is eligible for admission. The honors class, called the "superintendent's program," is open to high-achieving students from District 20 who take an entrance exam—the Otis-Lennon School Abilities Test (OLSAT)—in the spring. An open house is held in January. Applications are available at the student enrollment office, 415 89th Street, 11209, (718) 759-4914.

Christa McAuliffe School, IS 187
1171 65th Street
Brooklyn, NY 11219
(718) 236-3394
www.is187.com

Admissions: District 20
High school choices: Brooklyn Tech, Stuyvesant, Fort Hamilton
Grade levels: 6–8   **Test scores:** R *****, M *****
Enrollment: 994   **Ethnicity:** 39%W 2%B 10%H 49%A
Class size: 30   **Free lunch:** 47%

Open to gifted students from across District 20, Christa McAuliffe has three minischools, or academies, each with about 350 children, its own personality, its own floor, and its own director. Christa McAuliffe also has an unusually pleasant **special education** program for 36 developmentally delayed children—who run their own café in the school.

The building was constructed in the 1920s as an elementary school, and it has the homey feel of a school for little kids rather than the factory-like feel of so many junior high schools. There are lots of floor-to-ceiling murals in the corridors and colorful bulletin boards covered with the children's work. The school is overcrowded and the halls are jammed during class changes, but kids are serious and attentive—and also seem to be having fun.

The school has a very high rate of acceptance into the specialized high schools. One year, 42 students were admitted to Stuyvesant and 97 to Brooklyn Tech. Other popular choices are the honors program at nearby Fort Hamilton or New Utrecht, to Catholic schools, or to LaGuardia High School of Music and Art and Performing Arts.

There is an extensive music program, and each grade of each academy has its own band. There is an ambitious schoolwide drama program: One year, students made multiple stage sets for a production that included scenes from *Wicked, Hairspray, West Side Story, The Wizard of Oz,* and *The Music Man.* Enrichment classes—including mural painting, Latin dancing, student newspaper, crocheting, and Spanish cooking—are held 3 afternoons a week after school. Each academy has overnight trips to Boston; Washington, DC; and Philadelphia.

On the 1st floor is the coffee shop run by kids in special education who are developmentally disabled. The children prepare lunch—on one of our visits, eggplant parmesan, shrimp, and pizza—for staff and any school visitors who want to eat. They learn arithmetic by making change and reading and writing by making signs. The children are paid $1 a week and open their own bank accounts.

The Academy for Scientific Research, housed on the 2nd and 3rd floors, has wall murals that depict marine life and jungle scenes. Many middle schools mark their success in science by how many high school Regents exams the children can pass before they get to high school. Here, the approach is different: Rather than racing through a textbook so children can a pass a standardized exam in the spring, teachers concentrate on exploring a few topics in depth.

On the 4th floor is the **Academy for Global Communication**. There is a focus on technology, where computers and Smartboards—an electronic white board attached to the Internet—are an integral part of instruction. Sixth-graders study archaeology, taking a trip to the Jewish Museum, for example, to study artifacts from an archaeological dig in Israel. Seventh-graders study law and may watch video clips of trials from Court TV. Eighth-graders study international finance and may compete in the Econ Bowl, sponsored by the New York Federal Reserve Bank. In this competition, students prepare 15-minute oral arguments on topics such as "Is globalization good for the U.S. economy?"

On the 5th floor is the **Academy for Arts and Humanities**, which has the most progressive approach to teaching of the three minischools. Director Albert Catasus has a beard and often wears a black turtleneck and jeans. His favorite word is "cool" and he's as likely to be found sitting on a child's desk and chatting with kids as holed up in his office, where he has posted a sign with a twist on a quote from Dante's *Inferno*: "Abandon all despair ye who enter here."

The walls of the corridor are covered with giant murals painted by the kids on subjects related to their studies: street scenes from Verona to tie in with their reading of *Romeo and Juliet*; a painting of rural China to go along with *The Good Earth*; and scenes from ancient Athens and Egypt to go along with the study of ancient civilizations. Teachers bring history to life with imaginative projects. One year Holocaust survivors visited the school to tell children about life in concentration camps. There are plenty of class trips: The entire academy saw a production of the *Pirates of Penzance* at

City Center in Manhattan, and then analyzed Gilbert and Sullivan's use of irony and parody.

Catasus believes in a collaborative approach with his staff: "I sit with the teachers and say: 'What do you want to do this year?'" And he's not afraid to get down on the floor and paint with the kids. "A little chaos is good once in a while," he says.

Children who live in District 20 may apply. There is an open house in January. Students must have high standardized-test scores and must take the Otis-Lennon School Abilities Test (OLSAT), given in March. Applications are available at the student enrollment office, 415 89th Street, 11209, (718) 759-4914.

Brooklyn Studio Secondary School
8310 21st Avenue
Brooklyn, NY 11214
(718) 266-5032

Admissions: District 21 preference, citywide
High school choices: NA
Grade levels: 6–12   **Test scores:** R ***, M ****
Enrollment: 822   **Ethnicity:** 59%W 15%B 16%H 10%A
Class size: 20–28   **Free lunch:** 48%

Brooklyn Studio Secondary School offers a gentle alternative to large neighborhood middle and high schools. Serving 800 children in grades 6–12, this Bensonhurst school was founded in 1994 as an "inclusion" program, where children with special needs get extra help in regular classes—without being segregated. It's a nurturing place, and adults know most students by name.

A quarter of the students have Individualized Educational Programs (IEPs) and many more benefit from resources usually reserved for students with **special needs**, such as two teachers in most classrooms and the assistance of paraprofessionals. For this reason some children, who would have been referred to special education in other schools, have thrived here without that official label. Principal Martin Fiasconaro calls his three assistant principals "instructional superstars," who carry out the belief that "every kid in the class can learn and it's our job to figure out how."

Middle school students may take special "magnet" classes in creative writing, dance, and math technology. Classes are structured and orderly, and a variety of teaching styles are used.

Priority in admission goes to children who attend PS 128, the elementary school located right next door. However, students from across District 21 and from outside the district may apply to the school through the District 21 magnet program. The district magnet office is located at Mark Twain Intermediate School for the Gifted and Talented, (718) 449-6697 (profiled later in this section). Parents of disabled students may contact the school directly to ask whether it might be an appropriate placement.

David A. Boody School, IS 228

228 Avenue S
Brooklyn, NY 11223
(718) 375-7635
www.freewebs.com/pta228

Admissions: neighborhood school/citywide
High school choices: Murrow, Dewey, Midwood
Grade levels: 6–8   **Test scores:** R ***, M ****
Enrollment: 983   **Ethnicity:** 35%W 24%B 17%H 24%A
Class size: 26–28   **Free lunch:** 63%

A dynamic principal, a stellar music program, and well-regarded "talent classes" attract students from across Brooklyn to David A. Boody, a zoned neighborhood school with a large magnet program that is open to students from outside the zone. Boody seems to be more relaxed and less of a pressure cooker than its rival, Mark Twain. "It's not on steroids about the academics," said a mother who had children at both schools.

The school appears to be emerging from a difficult period: A few years ago there was a revolving door of principals. Discipline was uneven and parents complained of fights. Now, a well-regarded new principal, Dominick A. D'Angelo, who took charge in 2007, seems to be reviving the school. Parents say their kids feel safe and D'Angelo has invigorated some of the "talent" classes for which the school is best known.

The building is one of the oldest junior high schools in the city, built in 1929. It has pleasant big windows and high ceilings, and the walls, once a bit shabby, have been spruced up with fresh paint.

Students may audition for "talent" programs in art, sports, band, creative writing, dance, drama, keyboards, math/computer, chess, legal studies, vocal music, and science. While parents describe the regular academic courses, overall, as "not bad, but not inspiring," the talent courses are uniformly strong.

The music talent includes a jazz band and a symphony orchestra. A popular teacher, Thomas Brennan, is the conductor of the boroughwide middle school orchestra. He has "such a connection with kids. . . . He changed my son's life," said one mother, whose son went on to LaGuardia High School of Music and Art and Performing Arts. Some students in the music talent played at Carnegie Hall.

Science and math-computer talent courses are particularly popular. On one of our visits, kids sat at high-tech-looking computers with translucent cases, learning Photoshop and Illustrator. The school is well equipped with laptops and Smartboards—electronic white boards attached to the Internet. The school also has a Lego robotics program. The science talent includes classes in astronomy, marine biology (at the New York Aquarium in Coney Island), and herpetology (the study of reptiles). Some classrooms have tanks with animals. On our most recent visit, one tank had an iguana and another had a skink (a type of lizard).

One year, a science teacher had children collect live turtles, bullfrogs, and other wildlife from Jamaica Bay and bring the specimens back to the classroom, where they lived in a "pond" made out of a tub. The kids retrieved a drop of water from the bay and looked at the algae in the water under a microscope.

D'Angelo acknowledges he has some work to do to make the regular academic classes as lively as the talent classes. Pamela Wheaton of Insideschools.org wrote: "Some academic classes we visited, alas, lacked the spark of the 'talents' and we saw some bored students, with heads on desks." While some teachers had interesting lessons, they "appeared to rely heavily on worksheets and dry textbook lessons," Wheaton added.

The school has five self-contained **special education** classes. One seemed particularly cozy, with a rattan sofa, chairs, and teddy bears. The school is also adding Collaborative Team Teaching (CTT) classes, which have two teachers, one of whom is certified in special education.

Many students go on to the "three M's"—Midwood, Murrow, and Madison. Leon Goldstein is also a popular choice, as are LaGuardia High School of Music and Art and Performing Arts (14 admitted in 2008) and Brooklyn Tech (30 admitted in 2008). Four students were admitted to Stuyvesant in 2008.

Like Mark Twain and Bay Academy, Boody accepts children from across Brooklyn who take "talent" tests to be admitted to its magnet program. But unlike Twain and Bay, Boody is also a neighborhood school. Children who live within the school zone are automatically admitted. Open houses are held in January. Tours are given throughout the school year. Contact the school for more information. Tests and auditions for the talent programs are held in March. Pick up an application at the District 21 magnet office, housed at Mark Twain, or call (718) 449-6697.

Mark Twain Intermediate School
for the Gifted and Talented, IS 239

2401 Neptune Avenue
Brooklyn, NY 11224
(718) 266-0814
http://is239.schoolwires.com

Admissions: citywide
High school choices: Stuyvesant, Brooklyn Tech, LaGuardia
Grade levels: 6–8   **Test scores:** R *****, M *****
Enrollment: 1,253   **Ethnicity:** 57%W 8%B 6%H 29%A
Class size: 30–32   **Free lunch:** 30%

A beautifully equipped, first-rate school in a desolate corner of Brooklyn, Mark Twain Intermediate School for the Gifted and Talented is one of the most sought after in the city. The school attracts children from all over Brooklyn and even parts of Queens—despite its grim setting on a nearly abandoned spit of land west of Coney Island, amid vacant lots and dirty marshes.

Mark Twain provides a firm foundation for entrance to the city's most selective high schools. The school typically sends 25% of its graduating class to Stuyvesant, an extremely high admissions rate.

The building is one of the oldest junior high schools in the city, built in 1936. The school is spotless and cheerful, with two giant, sunny gymnasiums and a pleasant library filled with plants, colorful murals, and papier-mâché figures made by the kids. The classrooms are big and bright, with wood floors, wood coat closets and cabinets, and large windows.

The school has a drama department that puts on plays and musicals worthy of Broadway. It has a sports department with elaborate gymnastics equipment and tournament-level tennis competitions. It has an extensive music department with an impressive orchestra and a full band and has a vocal department in which children learn both sight-reading and music theory.

Mark Twain has science labs where kids may study microbiology and organic chemistry for 3 years, a television studio, a darkroom equipped with free cameras for kids to study photography, a mirrored dance studio, an art studio, a woodworking lab, and a sewing room.

Children are admitted based on a demonstrated talent in one of ten areas: art, athletics, computer math, creative writing, dance, drama, instrumental music, photo media, science, or vocal music.

Each child takes a test or audition in two talent areas. Once enrolled, a child is assigned to one talent, which becomes a sort of supermajor for his or her 3 years at Mark Twain. In addition to regular academic classes, children take five extra periods a week in their talent area. That means, for example, if your talent is science, you'll take five periods a week of science with your regular classmates plus five periods of science with your talent class.

Principal Carol Moore works hard to foster a sense of school spirit among both the students and the staff. Every day, after the morning announcements, she shouts: "Let's go, team!" over the public address system.

She has given teachers red polo shirts emblazoned with the school's logo, and on "dress-down" Fridays, the whole staff wears them. I visited the school on a Friday; Moore, wearing sneakers, casual pants, and a whistle on a ribbon around her neck, looked like the phys ed teacher and coach she once was. Teamwork is more than a gimmick here. The whole staff pitches in much more than is required by the teachers' contract. It's common to see kids and teachers eating lunch together in classrooms and working on special projects. Teachers also work in teams with the same small group of students, thereby getting to know the students really well.

The drama teacher, Peter DeCaro, helps the kids put on ambitious productions ranging from musicals like *West Side Story* and *Beauty and the Beast* to serious plays by Anton Chekhov and dramatizations of African American poetry.

Unlike most middle school music departments—where one teacher offers lessons in everything from band to chorus—the music department at Mark Twain has enough staff to be specialized in vocal, strings, or wind instruments. All students study general music and piano, and the most advanced students may perform in chamber music quartets at Lincoln Center. The music classes I visited had unusually strong teachers. The department as a whole seems superb.

The science talent is one of the most demanding and one of the most sought after. Teacher Margaret Homsey pushes kids to study material that even bright high school students would consider challenging. Kids in one science research class I visited used their knowledge of organic chemistry to create their own version of Silly Putty from laundry soap—and experimented with different formulas to make it bounce.

In a creative writing talent class, children wrote and illustrated their own books; the quality of writing was excellent. In a dance class, children choreographed their own hip-hop version of a song from *Hairspray*. In a photography class, they studied famous photographers, then took their own pictures in the style of a photographer they chose, such as Jacob Riis.

The workload is heavy. Kids we spoke to said they did about 2 hours of homework a night. "It's an academically intense place," one mother said. "Some kids drown, some are stimulated."

Outside the talent classes, the academic instruction is fairly traditional. Teachers talk more than the kids do, and there isn't a lot of group work. But the lessons are interesting for the most part, and the kids are engaged. A large proportion of students take Regents (9th-grade) math and science exams. "I'm a firm believer that you need to impart knowledge to the youngsters," Moore said, explaining why she prefers traditional teaching methods, based on direct instruction, to progressive ones, based on group work or projects. Moreover, she believes appropriate behavior is key to learning. "I would consider myself a strict disciplinarian. I think it's important that kids have respect for authority and that kids have respect for each other."

The school is safe, orderly, and disciplined. Members of the staff wait outside in the morning and afternoon to make sure kids come and go without incident. Because the school is far from the nearest subway stop and few children live within walking distance, nearly everyone comes by bus. Some parents say that this leaves little opportunity for students to socialize after school.

The school sends an enormous number of graduates to the specialized high schools. According to the school's website, in 2008, 74 children were accepted at Stuyvesant, 114 at Brooklyn Tech, and 61 at LaGuardia High School for Music and Art and Performing Arts. One complaint: One mother said that the guidance department is mostly geared toward sending kids to the specialized high schools and is unfamiliar with other challenging options, such as Bard High School Early College.

There are three self-contained **special education** classes. Students in these classes are placed by the enrollment office and don't audition for admission. These students join the general education kids for certain classes and take advantage of some of the school's facilities.

Mark Twain became a magnet school for the gifted and talented in 1975, as part of a court-ordered desegregation plan. For years, children were admitted according to racial quotas designed to maintain integration. As the years went by, and more non-Whites moved to Brooklyn, the formula effectively served as affirmative action for Whites. In 2008, as the result of a lawsuit brought by a South Asian girl who claimed that the formula discriminated against her, a federal court judge lifted the racial quotas. Children are now admitted without regard to their race.

Any child in the city may apply. An open house is held in January. Children take admissions tests or have auditions in March. Out-of-district children should call the school to request an application, or check out the school's website. Call (718) 449-6697 for audition dates.

Bay Academy for Arts and Sciences, IS 98

1401 Emmons Avenue
Brooklyn, NY 11235
(718) 891-9005

Admissions: citywide
High school choices: Murrow, Midwood, Madison
Grade levels: 6–8   **Test scores:** R *****, M *****
Enrollment: 1,000   **Ethnicity:** 54%W 23%B 8%H 15%A
Class size: 28–34   **Free lunch:** 48%

The Bay Academy for Arts and Sciences was founded in 1995 as a way for the district to build on the enormous success of Mark Twain's gifted and talented program. But it's a more relaxed school than Twain, and the atmosphere is a bit less competitive. Long-time principal Marian Nagler is a serious, hardworking traditionalist whom parents describe as both a "tough cookie" and a "very sweet lady."

Bay Academy faces Sheepshead Bay, a narrow inlet crisscrossed by bridges. A tiny park nearby has a memorial to the Russian Jews who died in World War II—a touch-point for the Jewish community of Manhattan Beach across the bay.

Built in the 1960s, the building has a prisonlike exterior of gray concrete. But it has a cheerful, brightly lit entry hall, and the classrooms are bright and attractive, with plain white plaster walls and lots of children's work displayed. There is an interior courtyard with stone paving and a greenhouse filled with plants. Many classrooms have plants as well.

Much of the teaching is by the book, with an emphasis on textbooks and worksheets to prepare children for standardized tests. One mother said that her son thrived in the structured environment, adding that teachers are good at keeping parents informed if, for example, a child fails to turn in his homework.

Foreign languages and the arts are among the school's strengths. Children display their art in the school's own gallery. There are three music rooms—two choral and one instrumental—a dance studio, and three art rooms. Spanish, Italian, and French are offered. Sixth-graders sample each of the languages offered, then choose one to study in 7th and 8th grade. Sports have long been a big part of the school, and IS 98 has traditionally had a strong tennis team and girls' basketball team.

One mother liked the fact that the school pushed children to excel without fostering unpleasant competition. "You have to try hard, but the kids are nice to each other," she said. The school stresses social development as well as academic achievement, offering, for example, lots of school dances. Principal Nagler believes academics shouldn't crowd out all other aspects of a child's life. "Let children be children," she said, herself the mother of seven grown children. There are some sweet, old-fashioned touches to the school: For example, children who make the honor roll are rewarded with a ceremony and cookies from an Italian bakery.

The "talents" are the most popular feature of the school. Each child is admitted based on his or her talent in art, music, drama, dance, athletics, creative writing, math, or science. Students have four periods a week in their talent area in addition to their regular academic classes, and they stay together with the children in their talent for all 3 years—good or bad depending on the group of kids. One boy complained that students in the athletic talent were rarely allowed to go on field trips because some kids were "goof-offs." Kids in the science talent, on the other hand, have a reputation as more serious and as a result teachers are more likely to take them on class trips.

The school houses two self-contained **special education** classes for children with learning disabilities. Nagler clearly feels she is principal for all the children in the school—not just the gifted—and she is just as proud of the children in special education. "The whole school is Bay Academy," she says. Her formula for success is the same for all children: "A lot of love, a lot of special attention."

Popular high school choices include Midwood, Madison, and Murrow. Some students attend Brooklyn Tech and other specialized high schools.

Prospective parents should attend an open house in January. Applications are available from the district magnet office housed in Mark Twain. Exams and auditions are held at Mark Twain in March. Call (718) 449-6697 for details.

SCHOOLS WORTH WATCHING

New schools are opening every year in Brooklyn, as in the rest of the city. One promising new one is **Achievement First Bushwick Middle School**, 1300 Greene Avenue, 11207, (718) 455-1594, www.achievementfirst.org. Modeled on the successful Amistad Academy in New Haven, Connecticut, the new Bushwick charter school opened with a 5th grade in 2007 and planned to add a grade each year until it serves children in grades 5–8. Like its sister schools, AF Bushwick Middle has highly structured classrooms, a longer school day and school year, and a relentless focus on academics. "Every moment is a learning opportunity," Philissa Cramer wrote on the Insideschools.org website, "even bathroom lineup, when students must recite multiplication facts or answer vocabulary questions before being allowed to enter the bathroom.

The new school is "faithful to the model" of the Achievement First network of schools in Connecticut and New York, while "adding a layer of warmth," Cramer said. Teachers are encouraged to develop engaging lessons, such as having students debate the outcomes of classic fairy tales. Many children enter the school woefully behind in math and reading. As a result, core classes in literature, writing, and math are kept very small. And even though much of the curriculum comes from Achievement First's central office, teachers stay flexible. When teachers realized that students needed more individual attention, they rearranged the schedule to allow for almost a full hour of small-group activity each day. Students are admitted by a lottery in April. Preference is given to children in Districts 23 and 32.

The school opened in temporary space at 84 Schaefer Street, then moved in 2008 to share the Philippa Schuyler building.

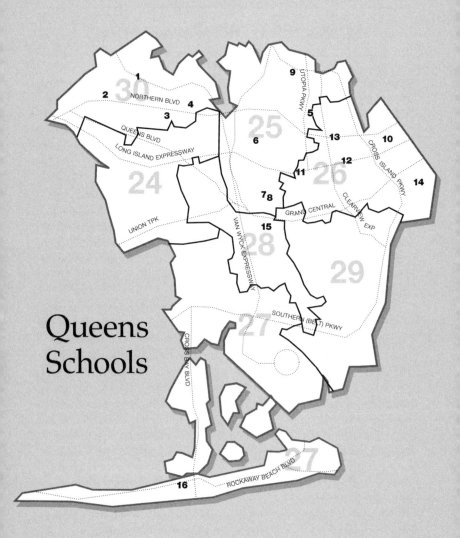

Queens
Schools

District 30
1   Academy at PS 122
2   Baccalaureate
3   Renaissance Charter
4   Louis Armstrong

District 25
5   World Journalism Prep
6   East-West
7   School of Inquiry
8   Robert Francis Kennedy
9   William H. Carr

District 26
10 Louis Pasteur
11 George J. Ryan
12 Nathaniel Hawthorne
13 Marie Curie
14 Irwin Altman

District 28
15 Gateway to Health Sciences

District 27
16 Scholars' Academy

QUEENS

Queens was once a place of scattered villages set amid farmland. Today, the farmland is gone, but the identity of the old villages remains. Ask people where they live, and they're likely to say Richmond Hill or Woodside or Douglaston—rather than just "Queens."

Some neighborhoods have the distinctive feel of one ethnic group. You're just as likely to hear Greek spoken on the busy streets in Astoria, where the music from bouzouki fill the air late in the night, as you are English. In Little India in Jackson Heights, there are more women dressed in saris than in blue jeans, and the perfume of curry spices wafts through the streets. Other neighborhoods are a polyglot, where you'll see newsstands with papers in a dozen different languages. More than 100 languages are spoken in the borough today.

Much of Queens was rural until World War II, and the borough still has many suburban neighborhoods with single-family homes and large lawns. Junior high schools came late to the borough. Children went to small neighborhood K–8 schools until the 1950s, when the population finally was ample enough to justify the construction of large junior high schools still in use today.

The population boomed again in the 1980s and 1990s with newcomers from all over the world, particularly from Asia. Single-family homes were divided into many small apartments, often in violation of zoning regulations. School construction didn't keep pace with immigration, and many of the schools are now badly overcrowded.

District 26, which includes the neighborhoods of Bayside, Floral Park, and Fresh Meadows, has high-performing, zoned middle schools; parents often buy houses in those neighborhoods just so their children can attend these well-regarded schools. The neighborhood schools are not as successful in the rest of the borough (with a few exceptions, such as JHS 194 in Whitestone.)

School choice is limited, partly because of the overcrowding, partly because the bureaucracy discourages shopping around, and partly because it's inconvenient to get from one school to another. The borough is large—almost as large as Manhattan, the Bronx, and Brooklyn combined—and many neighborhoods are not particularly well served by public transportation.

Still, there are an increasing number of options for parents who aren't satisfied with their neighborhood schools. A few schools accept children from across the borough. Many districts have gifted-and-talented programs that accept children from an entire district. Many Queens students try out for Hunter College High School in Manhattan, a highly selective school for the gifted that accepts children citywide in 7th grade. District 25, encompassing Whitestone and Flushing, has recently added a number of "option" schools for children of all ability levels.

There are four borough enrollment offices for Queens. Western Queens, or Districts 24 and 30, are served by the office at 28-11 Queens Plaza N., Long Island City, 11101, (718) 391-8386. Whitestone, Flushing, and Bayside, or Districts 25 and 26, are served by the office at 30-48 Linden Place, 11354, (718) 281-3791. Forest Hills and Jamaica, or Districts 28 and 29, are served by an office at 90-27 Sutphin Boulevard, Jamaica, 11435, (718) 557-2774, and Ozone Park and the Rockaway Peninsula, or District 27, are served by an office at 82-01 Rockaway Boulevard, Ozone Park, 11416, (718) 348-2929.

Academy at PS 122
21-21 Ditmars Boulevard
Long Island City, NY 11105
(718) 721-6410

Admissions: District 30
High school choices: Stuyvesant, Bronx Science, Townsend Harris
Grade levels: 6–8   **Test scores:** R *****, M *****
Enrollment: 200   **Ethnicity:** 33%W 9%B 31%H 27%A
Class size: 25–30   **Free lunch:** 59%

The Academy at PS 122 is a small, selective middle school that attracts many of the top-achievers in District 30 and prepares them well for the entrance exams to the city's specialized high schools. Housed in a pleasant neighborhood elementary school, the Academy is a friendly place, where office secretaries speak to kids in a kindly tone and teachers speak patiently to parents on the telephone.

A traditional school in many respects, PS 122 has recently introduced some new teaching techniques. The school has expanded its classroom libraries and has incorporated more novels, biographies, and nonfiction science discovery books to supplement textbooks. Teachers have adopted the Teachers College Workshop approach to writing, in which students write multiple drafts of each paper and work in small groups, editing one another's work. For math, they use the Impact Math program, which teaches math concepts as well as formulas. The long-time principal, Mary Kojes, teaches an after-school math class that prepares the students for the specialized high school exam. There is still a lot of focus on test scores and test preparation, but there are also some creative lessons.

One 6th-grade math teacher (who also teaches social studies) takes an unusual, interdisciplinary approach. The teacher arranged for the captain of a merchant marine ship to write letters to the class with math problems that relate to navigation. The students write letters in response, answer the problems, and pose their own math problems to the captain. The students then chart locations of the ship on a map posted on the board. They also conduct research on tankers and the merchant marines on the Internet.

All 8th-graders take the Regents exams in math (high school algebra) and Earth science (usually offered in 9th grade). The principal credits the school's success to the strong teaching staff and a collegial atmosphere—as well as to the bright, eager-beaver student body. "You have to give a lot of credit to the kids," she says. "We have a good natural resource."

PS 122 is located in a trendy neighborhood where many young people have flocked in recent years. The school's pretty red brick building is immaculate. There is a nice, small library staffed by a full-time librarian, and the building has two computer labs—one for the middle schoolers and the other for the elementary grades. There are also two gymnasiums, again one for the older kids and one for the younger ones. There is a nice art room, with a friendly teacher—who teaches Pre-K kids about balance by letting them play with wooden shapes, and instructs older students about colors and blending and how to paint shapes that look three-dimensional. There is a good music program.

The school has several classes in which students receiving **special education** services are integrated into general education classrooms.

Students living in District 30 are eligible for admission. Students must take the Otis-Lennon School Abilities Test (OLSAT) to be considered. Call (718) 391-8386 for more information.

Baccalaureate School for Global Education

34-12 36th Avenue
Astoria, NY 11106
(718) 361-5275
http://www.bsge.org/

Admissions: Queens residents
High school choices: NA
Grade levels: 7–12   **Test scores:** R *****, M *****
Enrollment: 431   **Ethnicity:** 30%W 19%B 26%H 25%A
Class size: 12–25   **Free lunch:** 30%

The Baccalaureate School for Global Education is the first public school in New York City in which all students prepare for the International Baccalaureate (IB), a degree widely accepted at universities in 124 countries outside the United States. The school, opened in 2002, strives to combine the spirit of inquiry and discovery that characterizes a good progressive school with the broad curriculum for which good traditional schools are known.

It's an intimate school, where students and teachers get to know one another well. The administration and staff think deeply about their teaching methods. They are eager to chat with visitors and one another about what they believe works best, and they are willing to adapt their lessons from year to year. "We're a close-knit faculty," said one teacher. "We meet every morning. It's fantastic, because they [the administration] really encourage you to be creative."

Teachers encourage collaboration and cooperation among the students—not competition. "They are very respectful of each other," a mother said. "The thing you can't buy is that sense of community that you have here."

Housed in a renovated factory in an industrial neighborhood, the school has brightly recessed lights, sparkling white walls, and gleaming blue tile floors. The principal's door is always open, and kids feel free to wander in for an informal chat. The guidance counselor's office has wicker chairs with colorful cushions. The classrooms have tables—not desks. The facilities are basic but comfortable. Lots of classrooms are windowless. There is no gym, but there is a fitness center and a nice dance studio. The school hopes to build a gym and an auditorium on the roof of the building. The atmosphere is relaxed. There are no bells, and classes last

70 minutes, with 5 minutes between classes—slightly longer than the typical 3 minutes. The longer passing time is based on the notion that informal learning goes on between classes, when kids talk to each other, kids talk to teachers, or teachers talk to one another.

Kelly Johnson, former assistant principal, was named principal in early 2007, replacing founding principal William Stroud, who left midyear to work for the central office of the Department of Education.

Most students enter in 7th grade, although there are some spots available for students entering in 9th grade. Baccalaureate has attracted 7th- and 8th-grade teachers who are passionate about teaching young adolescents. "I love this age," said one teacher. "They are so curious about the world; it's fun to help them explore."

The lessons are kid-friendly: In an art class, kids made up their own coats of arms. In music, they drummed rhythmically on rubber pans. In a science class, they invented their own elements for an imaginary periodic table, including "elementism" and "videogamism." In another science class, children had to predict which would produce more carbon dioxide: baking soda or baking powder, mixed with water, lemon juice, orange juice, or vinegar. In a French class, kids spoke the language much more than is typical in middle school foreign-language classes.

Many of the projects are interdisciplinary. Students learning to speak and write in Mandarin Chinese made decorative wall hangings, drawings, and posters in celebration of the Chinese New Year. Beginning in 7th grade, students take electives like human rights, journalism, music, technology, or SAT test prep, though Johnson said that the school changes the available electives every year based on teachers' availability, interests, and schedules, and on student need.

Although there are lots of projects, high school students say they have many hours of traditional homework each night, because they must study to pass both New York State Regents exams and to earn the IB diploma. "It's a lot of hard work, but most of the teachers are great," said a student.

In 2005, the Baccalaureate School received accreditation with the International Baccalaureate Organization, a nonprofit group that includes 1,395 IB schools in 114 countries, and the school is working with the organization to implement the IB curriculum. One benefit of the IB: Because the curriculum is standardized, students who move from one country to another may transfer easily from one IB school to another.

Three private schools in New York—United Nations International School and the Dwight School in Manhattan and the Xavier School in Brooklyn—offer an IB, as do programs within Washington Irving High School, a public school in Manhattan, and Curtis High School, a public school on Staten Island. The Queens school is the only public school in New York City to offer an IB diploma program to all students, not just those in a small honors program.

Baccalaureate graduated its first class in 2006, and students were admitted to highly regarded colleges like Yale, Mount Holyoke, Colby, Hampshire, and Barnard, as well as SUNY and CUNY schools. "The IB accreditation is really a plus when you are applying to college," said PTA co-president Julie Levine Schwartz. "We have a wonderful college advisor."

The school has an open house in November. Applicants take on-site reading, writing, and math exams. Students and parents are interviewed by the staff. The school is open only to Queens residents.

Renaissance Charter School

35-59 81st Street
Jackson Heights, NY 11372
(718) 803-0060
www.renaissancecharter.org

Admissions: citywide
High school choices: NA
Grade levels: K–12   **Test scores:** R ****, M ****
Enrollment: 525   **Ethnicity:** 29%W 27%B 31%H 13%A
Class size: 25   **Free lunch:** 40%

The Renaissance School was founded in 1993 by a group of teachers with a grand vision: to build a progressive and democratically run school that would spark a revival of the city itself—a New York City Renaissance. It quickly became one of the most sought-after schools in the neighborhood and attracts students from across the borough. If you are interested in having your child attend for middle school, 5th grade is the best year to apply.

The school, which serves children in kindergarten through 12th grade, has one class in each grade in kindergarten through 4th grade. In 5th grade it expands to include two classes in each grade, and 25 new children are admitted. Children are admitted in other grades only if a seat becomes available when someone leaves.

Children concentrate their studies on the history, people, and culture of New York, with traditional disciplines of math and English woven in to this overall theme. They may spend months designing and constructing a scale model of an ideal city, and then use what they've learned to think of ways to improve the real place they live in.

The school is committed to enrolling children of all races, income levels, and abilities. The school is particularly successful at integrating students who receive **special education** services in regular classes.

Housed in a former department store, the school has an unusual architectural design that gives the building a homey feel and encourages children of different ages to mix. Kindergarten and 1st-grade classrooms on the ground floor open on a central indoor playroom equipped with playground equipment. It serves as a gathering place for parents at the end of the day and for teachers to meet informally between classes. Upstairs, classrooms open on a central lounge with computers and work tables—places for students to work and chat with teachers or one another.

Classrooms have sofas and tables, not desks. Tables are moved around according to whether children are working in small groups or meeting together as a class. The cafeteria has round tables, which encourages children to talk to one another rather than to scream across the long institutional tables so common in other schools. The noise level is actually low enough to permit carrying on a regular conversation.

Half a dozen parents work at the school; others volunteer on a regular basis. Children call grown-ups by their first names. The school can be noisy and a bit disorganized, and the teachers spend a fair amount of time cajoling children to settle down and behave. But Renaissance has a joyous, liberating atmosphere; tests scores are respectable; and parents are enthusiastic.

On one of our visits, 8th-graders were building bridges out of toothpicks and a 3-by-5 index card. Some efforts were quite basic; others were extremely sophisticated. Teacher Richard Doherty introduced the lesson in "static force" by arm wrestling with the kids. "That's zero force—nothing is moving," he said. "Ideally, when you cross a bridge, you want nothing to move."

Then he held up an index card and showed how easily it bends. Children experimented with ways to make it stronger—for example, by folding up edges of the card. With a box of toothpicks and a bottle of glue, they set to work making their own suspension bridges. Doherty tested each bridge for strength, piling it with pebbles until it broke.

In a 5th-grade math/science class, children studied the reaction times of astronauts and learned to calculate a "mean" by dropping strips of paper and calculating how long it took them to catch the paper with either hand. Sixth-graders studying China made Chinese robes from brown paper and learned to write Chinese characters. Kids are grouped in different ways. For example, in a 6th-grade math class, kids were divided into groups on the basis of how many baskets they made, tossing wadded up papers into wastebaskets; on another day their shoe size might be the criterion.

The Renaissance School is particularly welcoming to **special needs** kids who don't fit the mold, and teachers are skilled at using students' strengths to help compensate for their weakness. For example, one student who suffered from "disgraphia"—the inability to write—was able nonetheless to design a beautiful website. A handful of children with more severe disabilities, such as autism, seem to flourish here, integrated into regular classes.

About 80–90% of middle school children stay for high school. Those who leave tend to go to selective high schools such as Townsend Harris or Bronx Science. Children are admitted by lottery in April. Siblings of current students have priority. Children from anywhere in New York City may apply, but priority is given to children living in District 30. One year, there were 200 applicants for 25 seats in 5th grade. The middle school open houses are held in January and February.

Louis Armstrong Middle School, IS 227

32-02 Junction Boulevard
East Elmhurst, NY 11369
(718) 335-7500
www.armstrong227q.com

Admissions: Queens
High school choices: Townsend Harris, LaGuardia, Francis Lewis
Grade levels: 5–8   **Test scores:** R ****, M *****
Enrollment: 1,480   **Ethnicity:** 31%W 17%B 35%H 17%A
Class size: 32   **Free lunch:** 50%

An experienced, enthusiastic staff, a well-equipped building, and a top-notch special education program have made the Louis Armstrong Middle School one of the most sought-after schools in Queens. The school is open to all children in the borough—from the most disabled to high-achievers who do high school–level work while still in middle school. Unfortunately, there are far more applicants than seats available.

Founded in 1979 as a court-ordered experiment in racial integration, Louis Armstrong embodies the philosophy that children learn best when they have classmates from different ethnic groups, neighborhoods, and academic abilities. The administration prides itself on giving all children the chance to try all subjects. At IS 227 you don't need to audition to play in the band. Teachers try to draw on children's interests, and it's not a supercompetitive school. "We don't push kids," said one administrator. "We invite them, we motivate them."

Large schools have gone out of fashion in recent years, but visit IS 227 and you'll see why large schools were built in the first place. The school has equipment and labs that would be too expensive for a small school to provide: three computers labs, an arts-technology shop, and a ceramics lab. One science teacher runs a gardening club. Three full-time music teachers offer classes in music appreciation, as well as band, orchestra, and chorus. Children may take part in a robotics program, video productions, the school musical, dance, and theater.

The school librarian, who calls herself a "school library media specialist," boasts that the IS 227 library is the best middle school library in New York City. A full-time librarian, a library aide, high-speed Internet connections, and access to the Queens

Public Library database give children the ability to do sophisticated research projects. Children can even dial into the school library—and the Queens public libraries—from their home if they have their own computer and Internet access.

The school was one of the first in the city to recognize that children in early adolescence often need more individual attention than a traditional junior high school provides. Accordingly, IS 227 is divided into three "houses" of about 500 pupils—each with its own assistant principal. Children spend 3 years in a house and get to know the assistant principal and the guidance counselor. "If you mention a kid's name, the teacher knows it," said parent coordinator Deborah Cataldo.

Each house is divided into "clusters" of four or five classes. Teachers in each cluster work as a team, plan lessons together, and talk about each child's progress. A common hall connects each cluster of classrooms. When classes change, kids mostly stay within their cluster: It doesn't feel like Grand Central Terminal at rush hour.

Teachers within a cluster meet frequently. On one of our visits, we saw teachers having lunch together in a classroom, chatting informally about how best to help a bright girl who was goofing off in class. In another classroom, a math teacher gave a special education teacher tips on how to use computers—also during their lunch breaks. IS 227 is unusual in that most teachers have their own offices, a sign, teachers say, that they are considered professionals.

The **special education** program is a model for the city. The building is wheelchair accessible. Children with disabilities are integrated into regular classes whenever possible, sometimes with full-time assistants, called paraprofessionals, helping them. On one of our visits, a boy with cerebral palsy was seated in his wheelchair in a regular English class, listening intently while a paraprofessional took notes for him. She said the boy learned best by listening and had a phenomenal memory, but he had trouble writing. With her help, he was able to keep up with a regular class.

Children receiving special education services are assigned to "clusters" with three or four regular classes and one special education class. That means children in special education have the same teachers as other children. If a child needs a segregated special education class for one subject—say, reading—but can cope in a regular class for other subjects, the cluster can accommodate him or her.

A paraprofessional who works with Down syndrome kids at the school said she appreciated the "cooperation, unity, and respect" she receives from her colleagues. A parent whose son has a disability called pervasive developmental disorder called the school "the best," and another parent of a special needs child said: "My son has skyrocketed academically and socially."

For many years, parents complained the school had no "special progress" or "honors" track with accelerated courses for advanced students. Now, 8th-graders may take the Regents (9th-grade) math and biology courses. The school has a good record of sending its graduates to selective schools such as the super-selective Townsend Harris. Stuyvesant, Bronx Science, LaGuardia High School of Music and Art and Performing Arts, Frank Sinatra, and the music program at Bayside High School are also popular choices.

The school has a cheerful, relaxed atmosphere. Students lounge on the floor of some hallways, working together in groups. The school is safe. Bathrooms are unlocked and children are allowed to use them as needed. Race relations seem to be good. "My kids had very diverse groups of friends," said the mother of seven children, all of whom attended Louis Armstrong. "The school offered an opportunity for my kids to interact with kids from so many different backgrounds, to share cultures."

Fifth-graders use Everyday Math, a hands-on math curriculum. Teachers have been trained in the Workshop model for writing, in which children work together in groups, writing and editing multiple drafts of their papers. In one 6th-grade classroom, students were rewriting fairy tales from the perspective of unlikely characters: *Snow White* from the perspective of the seven dwarfs, or *Cinderella* from the perspective of the evil stepsisters.

Teaching techniques are a mixture of traditional and progressive. The lower grades look more like an elementary school than a traditional junior high school. Desks are in groups. There are lots of colorful bulletin boards. Teachers help children with individual projects. By 8th grade, the school has more the feel of a traditional high school.

Science is particularly strong. Science labs are filled with lots of interesting stuff, including Madagascar giant hissing roaches and horny toads. Greg Grambo, a popular science teacher who looks like an aging punk rocker, wears a T-shirt with a big red *A* (for *Anarchy*), red boots and laces, and a goatee with rubber bands. No textbooks are used in the class, and kids seem unusually excited by experiments designed by the teacher. They compile notebooks about the experiments over the course of the year. "By the time they are done with the class, they will have written their own textbook," he said.

Louis Armstrong has a complicated admissions process—the result of the stormy history that preceded its opening in 1979. Officials in two adjoining districts, District 30 and District 24, each claimed they needed the new school the most.

District 30, which includes Astoria and Long Island City in western Queens, was the most overcrowded district, and mostly White at the time; District 24, which includes Corona, Elmhurst, and Middle Village, had several overcrowded schools that were mostly non-White.

The NAACP filed suit saying that the new building should be part of District 24 and should be racially integrated. A court decided that the school should attempt to both relieve overcrowding and achieve racial integration, and that it shouldn't be part of either district, but instead report directly to the chancellor.

The admissions formula is a result of that court order. A certain number of seats are reserved for children from District 30 and District 24, but children from all over Queens may apply. Bus transportation is provided for children from outside the neighborhood.

Children are admitted according to an extremely complex lottery designed to maintain the school's racial balance without upsetting the racial balance in neighboring schools. The lottery also ensures that the school has a mix of children of different abilities: Twenty-five percent of the seats are reserved for children who score below average on standardized tests, 50% are for average scorers, and 25% are for children above average. The racial quotas were determined by the 1980 census for the borough, at a time when Queens had a higher proportion of Whites than it does today.

According to the formula, the school is supposed to maintain a racial balance of 45% White and 55% non-White. It is also supposed to give preference to children who would otherwise attend schools where most children are of their own race—rather than children whose presence in their neighborhood school serves what the bureaucrats call an "integrative function."

Interested parents should attend an open house at the school in December or January. Usually one open house is on a Saturday morning, and one is on a weekday evening; some 800 parents attend. In November, parents can pick up an application from their child's elementary school.

If your heart is set on Louis Armstrong, send a letter explaining why you believe the school would be the best for your child. If your child is placed on a waiting list, there's still a possibility he or she will be admitted over the summer. For those willing to wait, some children are even accepted in September.

World Journalism Preparatory:
A College Board School

34-65 192nd Street
Flushing, NY 11358
(718) 461-2219
www.wjps.org

Admissions: District 25
High school choices: NA
Grade levels: 6–12
Enrollment: 560 (projected)
Class size: 28–30

Test scores: R *****, M *****
Ethnicity: 43%W 8%B 31%H 18%A
Free lunch: 23%

At World Journalism Preparatory School, students publish a newspaper, edit videos, and develop websites. Located on the top floor of IS 25, the school has a computer lab equipped with both PCs and Macs, plenty of laptop computers, and sophisticated video equipment. It opened in 2006 with a 7th grade and a 9th grade, and plans to add grades each year until it serves 560 students in grades 6–12.

Kids seem to get a lot of attention. Students attend daily "advisory" sessions, small discussion groups led by a teacher. Online progress reports allow parents to review their child's homework assignments, teacher comments, and student blogs.

"There aren't a lot of electives, but the emphasis on journalism allows for interesting projects," Laura Zingmond wrote on the Insideschools.org website. "Students create mock news reports in the school's film studio, a classroom equipped with a floor to ceiling backdrop of a cityscape, the kind one usually finds on morning television shows."

Student work posted on the school's website includes a social studies class's "interviews" with key figures from the American Revolution and animated instructional videos on such tasks as baking cookies and repairing Internet modems. Latin and Spanish are offered, and advanced 8th-graders may take Regents (9th-grade) math and science. Students are required to wear a shirt with the school emblem and pants other than jeans. World Journalism shares the building's library, gym, auditorium, and cafeteria with IS 25.

The middle school, which limits admission to students from District 25, has attracted high-achieving students seeking an alternative to their large, zoned schools. Admission to the high school is unscreened, with applicants randomly selected by computer, which means that there is a broader range of students enrolled in the upper grades. Contact the school for tour dates.

East-West School of International Studies
46-21 Colden Street
Flushing, NY 11355
(718) 353-0009
www.ewsis.org

Admissions: District 25
High school choices: NA
Grade level: 6–12 (projected)
Enrollment: 525 (projected)
Class size: 28

Test scores: R ****, M ****
Ethnicity: 6%W 16%B 24%H 54%A
Free lunch: 75%

East-West School of International Studies is a new, promising school designed to make students proficient in an Asian language—Japanese, Korean, or Mandarin Chinese—while teaching them about technology, Asian history, and Asian culture. The school offers Asian arts like calligraphy, anime (Japanese animation), and film, as well as sports like judo and other martial arts.

Opened in 2006 with just 143 students in grades 7 and 9, East-West will add a grade each year until it serves students in grades 6–12. Housed in a wing of a junior high school, JHS 237, also known at the Rachel Carson School, across the street from Kissena Park, East-West has its own entrance, arrival, and dismissal times, and class schedules. Student wear uniforms of pullovers, collared shirts (royal blue, light blue, or white) emblazoned with the school insignia, and dark pants other than jeans. Attendance is high, and test scores are good.

East-West was founded with support from New Visions for Public Schools, an education reform group, and the Asia Society, which received a grant from the Bill and Melinda Gates Foundation to set up a nationwide network of small schools focusing on international studies. Founding principal Ben Sherman and assistant principal Josh Solomon said they were inspired by reading *The World Is Flat*, Thomas Friedman's book about how globalization and technology have fueled Asian economies. "We don't know what the future will look like, but we do know that employers will want to hire college-educated people who speak different languages, know how to use technology, and have a good background in science," said Sherman. "This is going to be the Asian century."

East-West accepts students with a range of abilities. Some have good command of the material, while others struggle to keep up.

Nonetheless, throughout the school, students seem engaged, and there is a nice rapport between faculty and students. And the courses seem challenging. Students in a 9th-grade Japanese class were able to understand and say simple sentences just a few weeks into the school year. Eighth-graders may take 9th-grade-level (Regents) math and science.

The school hopes to enlist research departments at nearby New York Hospital to help students prepare for participation in competitions such as the Intel Science Talent Search.

The middle school is open to students from District 25. Students are selected at random. The school will consider students from outside District 25, but only if there are open seats after the main round of selections and acceptances has been completed. It's a little hard to get to by public transportation. Students may take the number 7 train to Main Street Flushing and a bus from there. Contact the school for open house information.

Queens School of Inquiry

158-40 76th Road
Flushing, NY 11366
(718) 380-6929
http://qcpages.qc.cuny.edu/provost/QSI/

Admissions: District 25
High school choices: NA
Grade levels: 6–12
Enrollment: 560 (projected)
Class size: 27

Test scores: R ★★★★, M ★★★★★
Ethnicity: 23%W 12%B 27%H 38%A
Free lunch: 40%

Queens School of Inquiry, opened in the fall of 2005 with a small 6th-grade class, has a seasoned principal, engaged kids, energetic teachers, and close ties to Queens College just a mile away. Housed in the former JHS 168, Parsons Junior High School, the Queens School of Inquiry plans to add a grade each year until it serves students in grades 6–12.

Schoolwork is based on projects. For example, humanities and math classes collaborated on an architecture project when students studied ancient Greece and Rome, Philissa Cramer wrote on the Insideschools.org website. A student recalled a project in which students were charged with devising games that would favor the house—and then played the games at an end-of-year party. "We get to be creative," a student told Insideschools.org.

Principal Elizabeth Ophals, former principal of the well-regarded Louis Armstrong Middle School in Queens, encourages students to "make up their own questions and learn to answer them." Students are given a great deal of decision-making power, sitting on the committee that evaluates prospective teachers and debating whether to adopt uniforms. (They chose not to.) The students we met were self-assured, articulate, and eager to talk about what they were learning.

There are at least two adults in each classroom. In a 7th-grade math class, we saw four adults: a lead teacher, another teacher helping during her free period, and two student teachers from Queens College. Students and professors from Queens College work in classrooms, and high school students will be permitted to take college courses. A summer academy program each year helps integrate new students into the school.

The School of Inquiry selects students by lottery and is open to students living in District 25. Priority goes to students zoned for JHS 168, to English Language Learners, and to children with special needs.

Robert Francis Kennedy
Community Middle School, IS 250
158-40 76th Road
Flushing, NY 11366
(718) 591-9000

Admissions: District 25
High school choices: RFK
Grade levels: 6–8
Enrollment: 445
Class size: 30

Test scores: R ****, M *****
Ethnicity: 37%W 22%B 23%H 18%A
Free lunch: 42%

Long a successful school serving grades 6–12, Robert F. Kennedy divided into separate middle and high schools in 2007 so it could expand to serve more children. The middle school moved into the former Parsons Junior High School building, which it shares with Queens School of Inquiry, and more than doubled its enrollment. There has been some grumbling about the move, and the school has had some growing pains as enrollment has increased, but the leadership remains strong.

The long-time middle school principal, Marc Rosenberg, continued as principal. RFK was one of the first in the city to integrate children receiving **special education** services into regular classes. The school has Collaborative Team Teaching (CTT) classes, with two teachers, one of whom is certified in special education.

Teachers try to weave different disciplines together in their lessons, and we saw lots of lessons that encouraged kids to be creative and think independently. In a technology class, 7th-graders were designing PowerPoint presentations about fiction stories they had written. In a science class, 8th-graders read an article about atomic tests in the 1950s, and the classroom discussion was part science class, part history lesson, and part social debate. The lesson touched on Geiger counters (devices used to measure radioactivity) and the effects of radioactivity on the human body, the ethics of atomic tests, and the Chernobyl disaster. A teacher gave a lesson to 6th-graders about patterns and the Fibonacci sequence.

In recent years, about 60% of the kids go on to RFK high school. Many others go on to specialized high schools. Others go on to Francis Lewis, Cardozo, or parochial schools. Admission is open to children living in District 25, but preference is given to children zoned for the Parsons Educational Complex, also known as JHS 168. Call the school for open house dates.

William H. Carr School, JHS 194
154-60 17th Avenue
Whitestone, NY 11357
(718) 746-0818
www.jhs194.com

Admission: neighborhood school
High school choices: Bayside, Cardozo, Bronx Science
Grade levels: 6–8   **Test scores:** R ****, M ****
Enrollment: 1,076   **Ethnicity:** 44%W 3%B 26%H 27%A
Class size: 33   **Free lunch:** 32%

A large middle school on a quiet residential street, JHS 194 has strong teaching, focused students, and a calm and relaxed atmosphere.

Impressive student artwork lines the hallway of the main floor. In addition to visual arts, students study dance and may participate in the school's jazz and orchestral bands. The school has art and dance studios, a library, an auditorium, a renovated gymnasium, and a band room. At recess, students play basketball and handball in a large yard maintained by the New York City Parks Department.

"JHS 194's suspension rate is high, which we found to be the product of strictly enforced rules rather than an unruly environment," Laura Zingmond wrote on the Insideschools.org website. "Students earn detention for offenses such as chewing gum or not waiting their turn to buy lunch. The payoff, we observed, is good behavior and order."

In an 8th-grade math class, students solved complex equations displayed on a Smartboard (a whiteboard connected to a computer monitor). Elsewhere, 7th-graders were busy editing their classmates' work while their English teacher went from desk to desk offering comments. We listened to an 8th-grader lead a book discussion from a podium at the front of her classroom. The teacher had asked for the podium to encourage public speaking, Principal Anne Marie Iannizzi said.

Each floor is a kind of minischool, with its own assistant principal; guidance counselor; lunch period; mix of grades; and group of math, science, and English teachers. JHS 194 is a zoned neighborhood school in District 25.

Louis Pasteur Middle School, MS 67
51-60 Marathon Parkway
Little Neck, NY 11362
(718) 423-8138

Admissions: neighborhood school
High school choices: Cardozo, Stuyvesant, Bronx Science
Grade levels: 6–8   **Test scores:** R *****, M *****
Enrollment: 943   **Ethnicity:** 35%W 9%B 9%H 47%A
Class size: 28–33   **Free lunch:** 10%

Louis Pasteur has a lush campus complete with tennis courts, a track, handball courts, a pleasant auditorium, science labs, room for a full band and orchestra, a well-equipped library, and even a mock courtroom (complete with paneled judge and jury boxes) for its law class. It has hardworking, serious, high-achieving kids; an involved parent body; and teachers who seem to love their jobs. Even among the sought-after schools of District 26, MS 67 stands out.

It's easy to see why people buy houses in Little Neck just to send their kids to MS 67—and on to one of the best neighborhood high schools in the city, Benjamin Cardozo. For those who want to send their kids to specialized high schools, MS 67 paves the way: The school sends large numbers of its graduates to Bronx Science; Stuyvesant; and the selective school for humanities, Townsend Harris.

The school is spotless and brightly lit, with cheerful yellow tiled walls, wide corridors, and floors so clean they shine. It's an orderly place. Rules of conduct are clearly outlined in a student handbook given to all entering students.

Classical music plays in the hallways during class changes, which are smooth and quiet, and most children settle down quickly to study at the beginning of lessons. Discipline is strict—which parents appreciate even if some of the kids may chafe a bit. Consistent rules (such as no hats or coats inside) help keep the school safe.

The children seem well behaved and a large number are active participants in class. The school uses math and science textbooks published by the Glencoe group, a well-regarded series that some teachers consider more challenging than those used in many New York City middle schools.

Students read a mix of books, some that teachers choose for them and some that they choose for themselves. One 6th-grade boy, for example, read *Flowers for Algernon*—Daniel Keyes's short story about the friendship between a developmentally disabled man and a mouse—as part of his class, and biographies of baseball players for himself. Students put together fun projects, like a study of hurricanes and tornadoes that included a written report and an oral presentation.

"We watched students in a robotics class maneuvering computerized machines that they had designed and built out of Lego pieces and motorized parts," Laura Zingmond wrote on the Insideschools.org website. "There we saw enthralled students hunched over tables, some maneuvering their robots, others revising commands on laptop computers. All kept logs of their work and wrapped up the period by grading their effort."

"I could've talked a little less and listened a little more today," one girl told Insideschools.org, explaining why she gave herself a "B" in the category of "following instructions." She did, however, give herself an "A" for "preparedness."

More than half the students, or six classes per grade, are placed in the accelerated SP (special progress) program. A smaller group, one class per grade, enters a gifted magnet program, mostly graduates of a gifted program at PS 18. Three classes in each grade are dedicated to students who are in regular classes that are not accelerated. There are also self-contained **special education** classes for children with special needs.

In addition to the core academics, students take drama, art, band, dance, robotics, and law. There are sports teams in tennis, softball, and basketball. Both French and Spanish are taught. Seventh-graders take a class trip to Philadelphia, and 8th-graders go to Washington, DC. Parents praise the parent coordinator, Rhonda Bogaty, who puts together useful parent workshops on topics like controlling bullying. She also sends out regular newsletters via e-mail and telephones all parents with a weekly recorded announcement about coming events. The school has had stable leadership: Zoi P. McGrath, who became principal in 2005, had been an assistant principal at the school.

The school has an excellent record of sending children to specialized high schools. In 2008, 207 students in 8th grade took the exams for the specialized high schools, for the selective DaVinci program at Cardozo, and for Townsend Harris; some 80% were offered seats.

Alas, even a well-oiled machine like MS 67 has problems: Although it is better equipped than most New York City schools, students complain that classes are too large. Budget slashing has forced the school to eliminate a popular ballroom dancing program.

MS 67 is open to any child who lives in the zone.

George J. Ryan Middle School, MS 216
64-20 175th Street
Fresh Meadows, NY 11365
(718) 358-2005
www.ryan216.org

Admissions: neighborhood school
High school choices: Francis Lewis, Cardozo, Jamaica
Grade levels: 6–8   **Test scores:** R ****, M *****
Enrollment: 1,247   **Ethnicity:** 16%W 13%B 14%H 57%A
Class size: 33   **Free lunch:** 37%

The largest middle school in District 26, George J. Ryan Middle School serves a wide range of students: high-achievers who need grief counseling if they don't get into Stuyvesant, less motivated kids, and immigrant children who arrive with little English. Yet somehow Ryan works, scoring well on standardized tests and serving as a lab for the college education majors who regularly come to observe it.

The building is divided into three academies—Science, Communications, and Law and Justice. The academies bring children into closer contact with adults. And, as at Harry Potter's Hogwarts, students identify with "their" academy, which has its own lunch period, assistant principal, dean, and guidance counselor.

Sixth-graders rotate through four art electives, including art, chorus, instrumental music, and computers. Seventh-graders choose one of the art electives to study for the next 2 years.

Up to 20 students in 8th grade compete in the citywide Science Olympiad, working on experiments that include building towers, bridges, catapults, and a protective case for an egg so that it can be dropped without breaking. Workshops for parents include talks on topics like "How to talk so kids will listen and how to listen so kids will talk."

The school has a nice-sized gym and auditorium and a large renovated schoolyard, equipped with a track encircling an astro-turf field, basketball and handball courts, chin-up bars, and tables with chessboard surfaces. Despite a new paint job and lighting, some classrooms are still depressing, but adventurous student artwork brightens the hallways.

Ryan is a neighborhood school. Open houses for parents are held several times a year; call the school for more information.

Nathaniel Hawthorne School, MS 74

61-15 Oceania Street
Bayside, NY 11364
(718) 631-6800
www.ms74.com

Admissions: neighborhood school
High school choices: Cardozo, Stuyvesant, Bronx Science
Grade levels: 6–8   **Test scores:** R *****, M *****
Enrollment: 1,022   **Ethnicity:** 22%W 12%B 9%H 57%A
Class size: 30   **Free lunch:** 25%

MS 74 is a neighborhood school with serious, high-achieving kids; a solid and experienced teaching staff; and a hyper-involved principal, Andrea Dapolito. Many MS 74 graduates go on to Cardozo High School—widely considered one of the best neighborhood schools in the city; a substantial number go on to Stuyvesant, Bronx Science, and Townsend Harris. The exterior of the building has pleasant landscaping and plants, and the custodial staff keeps the interior clean.

The arts are integrated into the curriculum. Children studying Spanish, for example, might learn a Latin dance and prepare food from a Spanish-speaking country. A full-time drama teacher helps students put on ambitious productions like *Fiddler on the Roof.* There is a jazz band and a "chamber society" of young string musicians.

Teachers come up with imaginative research projects. One 8th-grade class compared how the U.S. military recruited soldiers during World War I, World War II, and now. "They encourage discussion and feedback and dissent," Dapolito said, referring to her teachers.

All 8th-graders must complete a social studies "exit project," including an oral presentation, on a subject of their choosing. One student researched the music and political climate of the 1960s, including "oral histories"—interviews with grandparents.

Students may participate in ThinkQuest, a statewide competition in which students work in groups on interdisciplinary projects that might research anything from Roman aqueducts to fuel alternatives to gasoline.

A large proportion of the students are of Korean or Chinese ancestry. Parents may participate in an orientation held for new students in May.

Marie Curie Middle School, MS 158
46-35 Oceania Street
Bayside, NY 11361
(718) 423-8100

Admissions: neighborhood school
High school choices: Bayside, Cardozo, Francis Lewis
Grade levels: 6–8   **Test scores:** R ****, M *****
Enrollment: 1,146   **Ethnicity:** 22%W 12%B 16%H 50%A
Class size: 33   **Free lunch:** 34%

A large neighborhood school, MS 158 serves a wide range of children, with accelerated classes for the gifted, special education for kids with special needs, and English as a Second Language for new immigrants. About 10% of the students are new immigrants from China and Korea.

Students participate in art, band, chorus, graphic arts, computers, and dance. Boys' and girls' basketball teams, bridge, and the yearbook are popular extracurricular activities.

An SP (Special Progress) program accepts students on the basis of standardized test scores, grades, and teacher recommendations. A small gifted magnet program is open only to graduates of a similar program at PS 188. For high-achievers not in the gifted program, MS 158 offers a separate program that begins in 7th grade. The academics in these classes are basically the same.

MS 158 uses of mix of teaching techniques, both traditional and progressive: In one traditional 8th-grade math class, students worked quietly at their desks, neatly arranged in rows, while a few stood at the blackboard solving equations. In a more progressive social studies class, students learning about Reconstruction assumed the roles of ex-slaves, crafting "advertisements" to search for lost family members. Some classes are as large as 35 students. Still, the school maintains a calm tone.

The school has both self-contained classes for children with **special needs**, and Collaborative Team Teaching classes, where two teachers work in the same classroom with both general education students and those needing special services. A program for hearing-impaired students run by District 75, the citywide district for students wih severe disabilities, is housed on the premises. The parent coordinator offers parent workshops on issues like how to communicate with adolescents and how to build self-confidence and a sense of identity.

The school regularly sends graduates to Stuyvesant, Bronx Science, and other elite high schools. Deaf students continue in a program for the deaf at Van Buren High School.

Irwin Altman School, MS 172
81-14 257th Street
Floral Park, NY 11004
(718) 831-4000

Admissions: neighborhood school
High school choices: Bayside; Cardozo; High School of Teaching, Liberal Arts, and Sciences
Grade levels: 6–8   **Test scores:** R ****, M *****
Enrollment: 1,082   **Ethnicity:** 22%W 13%B 14%H 51%A
Class size: 31–32   **Free lunch:** 27%

MS 172 is a cheerful place, with an engaging curriculum and innovative teaching. The building, constructed in the 1950s, is a bit drab, with gray tiles, beige walls, and just-adequate lighting. But some of the classrooms have fish tanks and plants. There's a digital studio where kids make videos and an art studio where kids splatter paint in the style of Jackson Pollock. The school has outdoor athletic courts and a playground that students can enjoy during lunch.

Close to the Nassau County border, Floral Park is a sleepy residential community with big trees and modest single-family homes. Once made up primarily of families of Irish and Italian descent, it now has a large number of recent immigrants from India and Pakistan. In an exploratory language course, which introduces 6th-graders to Latin, French, and Japanese, children eagerly answered questions about Latin conjugations.

Many teachers integrate English and history. For example, children studying ancient civilizations might read a mystery story set in ancient Egypt. Children studying the American Revolution might read a historical novel about a young man who joined the Minutemen although his father was loyal to England. One year, Tanuja Desai Hidier, author of *Born Confused*, a novel about growing up Indian in New Jersey, gave a reading at the school.

One science teacher taught students about vacuums by lighting a candle inside an overturned beaker placed in a dish of water. when the oxygen was gone, the candle went out and the water rose in the beaker. One year, as part of the school's space science program, 200 students in 6th grade launched minirockets—made of cardboard tubes and fueled by gun-powder—around the Unisphere in Flushing Meadows–Corona Park.

Admission is limited to children living in the zone.

Queens Gateway to Health Sciences Secondary School, JHS/HS 680

150-91 87th Road
Jamaica, NY 11432
(718) 739-8080

Admissions: District 28
High school choices: NA
Grade levels: 7–12
Enrollment: 613
Class size: 30

Test scores: R *****, M *****
Ethnicity: 3%W 52%B 16%H 29%A
Free lunch: 41%

Queens Gateway to Health Sciences School is designed to encourage students, particularly children of color, to consider careers in medicine or other hospital-related jobs, by giving them challenging science courses and hospital internships starting in middle school. Opened in 1995 with the backing of Mt. Sinai School of Medicine, the school has a high attendance rate (96%), a high graduation rate (94%), and a stellar record of college admission: According to the school's profile in the high school directory, 6% of graduates were admitted to Ivy League schools.

During the school day, students take part in sessions held at nearby Queens Hospital, visiting departments ranging from radiology to administration and offering oral presentations on what they've learned about each. The hope is that students exposed to a variety of departments will develop interests in different kinds of jobs—not just those of doctor and nurse.

The school has a new, well-kept building, a formal, no-nonsense tone, and a traditional approach to classroom teaching. "It doesn't have the facilities of a big school, such as an auditorium or a traditional gym," said Principal Cynthia Edwards. "Yet the sense of home and family is greater here." Parent involvement is high, with standing-room-only PTA meetings. Advanced Placement courses are offered in biology, calculus, English, and U.S. history. Priority in admission is given to students in District 28. Students are asked to write an essay saying why they want to attend and why they would be a good student at Gateway. Most successful candidates have grades averaging 80 or above and score at least at Level 2 on their standardized tests. There are weekly school tours. Call to make an appointment.

Scholars' Academy

320 Beach 104th Street
Rockaway Park, NY 11694
(718) 474-6918

Admission: District 27
High school choices: NA
Grade levels: 6–12
Enrollment: 600 (projected)
Class size: 25

Test scores: R *****, M *****
Ethnicity: 47%W 29%B 10%H 14%A
Free lunch: 32%

The Scholars' Academy is a promising new school with strong leadership, imaginative teachers, and smart kids. Founded in 2004 as a middle school for gifted and talented students, the Scholars' Academy added a 9th grade in 2007 and will add a grade each year until it serves students in grades 6–12.

Designed to end the brain drain of District 27's brightest kids to schools in other districts, such as Mark Twain in Brooklyn, the Scholars' Academy has attracted a racially mixed group of students who are inquisitive and eager to learn. Both teachers and students seem excited to be here. The hallways are lined with ambitious student projects, and students work together seated at round tables. Teachers coordinate their lessons, too, so that, for example, when students are studying ancient Egypt in social studies, they might find their art class devoted to making models of sacred scarab beetles and their science class structured around an exploration of mummification.

Principal Brian O'Connell ("Mr. O") is a native of the Rockaways and most recently was principal at the nearby and popular PS 114. He has resuscitated the dormant television studio in the Scholars' Academy building so students can make documentary films.

The school is open to students in District 27. Students must submit an application by the beginning of February. Admission to the gifted-and-talented programs is based on a test given in March. For information, contact the borough enrollment office at 82-01 Rockaway Boulevard, Ozone Park, 11416, (718) 348-2929. The location on the Rockaway Peninsula is remote, but that hasn't deterred some of the district's best middle school students from attending.

SCHOOLS WORTH WATCHING

Young Women's Leadership School, Queens, 109-20 Union Hall Street, Jamaica, 11433, (718) 725-0402, http://tywlsqueens. blogspot.com, is designed to replicate the success of the all-girls school of the same name in East Harlem. It opened in September 2005 with three classes of 25 students in 7th grade in portable buildings in the school yard of PS 40. The school moved into the PS 40 building a year later. It will add a grade each year, to become a 7–12 (or possibly a 6–12) school. Principal Avionne Gumbs became an enthusiastic convert to single-sex education after a 3-year stint as assistant principal at the original Young Women's Leadership School. Girls wear uniforms—crisp white collared blouses and blue vests—and the school emphasizes good manners, but it also has a relaxed feel. Classes offer an unusual degree of discussion and debate, and students feel free to interrupt a teacher if they don't grasp a lesson or concept. In a social studies class, students learning about the tenements of New York City early in the last century looked to one another for help in deciphering unfamiliar words such as "muckrakers," and then made connections between tenement living 100 years ago and their lives today. Working in pairs is common at the school, which frequently matches high-achievers with low-achievers.

The Young Women's Leadership Foundation, a private non-profit group that offers additional funding to the school, pays for important extras like trips to college campuses and performances. Students seem to share a warm relationship with the teachers and the principal, whom they greet with hugs. Space is a problem, because PS 40, an elementary school, does not have science labs or lockers that are appropriate for older students. The middle school is open to students living in Districts 28 and 29. The high school is open to students citywide, with preference given to continuing 8th-graders. All applicants must take a school tour with their families.

The fourth school to replicate the all girls' school in East Harlem, **Young Women's Leadership School of Astoria**, 23-15 Newtown Avenue, Astoria, 11102, (718) 267-2839, opened in September 2006 with 80 students in 6th grade and plans to add a grade each year until it serves students in grades 6–12. Principal Laura Mitchell's drive to start a new school stems from her 2-year stint as assistant principal at the original Young Women's Leadership School, where she was inspired by its solid record of preparing and sending almost all their girls to college. Students at the Astoria school have a serious college-prep curriculum and must wear uniforms. They also have an advisory period every day.

"Girls are not separated by ability, and we noticed a wide range in the quality of student work, from polished four-page essays to papers riddled with grammatical and spelling errors," Pamela Wheaton wrote on the Insideschools.org website. "The school accepts students of all achievement levels and there are no plans to add an honors track at the school, so YWLS might not suit girls looking for an accelerated curriculum," Wheaton continued. "But class participation was strong in every class we saw, with girls' hands flying up in response to teachers' questions." The school gives priority to District 30 residents. Prospective students are asked to write short essays and must attend the school's open house.

Staten Island
Schools

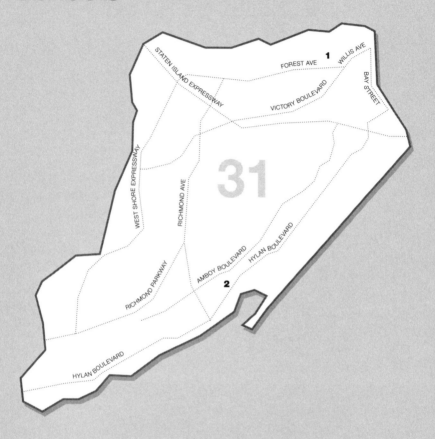

District 31
1 William Morris
2 Myra S. Barnes

STATEN ISLAND

The magnolias are in bloom, and you drive by houses with swing sets and above-ground pools in backyards, patio furniture on decks, and minivans in driveways. Can this really be New York City?

Well, yes and no. New York City police patrol the streets and your Metrocard works on the buses, but Staten Island is culturally and psychologically a world apart. Sleepy, suburban, even rural in parts, Staten Island attracts people who are looking for quiet neighborhoods and (relatively) reasonably priced housing. Many people both live and work on Staten Island and refer to their infrequent jaunts to Manhattan as excursions to "the city." They refer to people who live elsewhere as "off-islanders."

Politically conservative, Staten Island has long been a Republican stronghold in a predominantly Democratic city. For many years, the borough was mostly White, attracting blue-collar Italian American and Irish American families with stay-at-home moms and dads who worked in construction or who were firefighters or police officers. Those families still make up a large part of the population, but they have been joined in recent years by African Americans and immigrants from the Caribbean, Central America, India, and Korea and other Asian countries. An artists' colony has sprung up on the north shore.

Children usually go to their neighborhood schools, and the district serving the island, District 31, has long discouraged shopping around. Two exceptions: **IS 61**, a magnet school profiled here, and the **Michael Petrides School**, 715 Ocean Terrace, Building B, 10301, (718) 815-0186, a K–12 school open to all children in Staten Island by lottery. The Petrides School has few vacancies in the middle school, however. For profiles of neighborhood schools not listed here, visit Insideschools.org.

The borough enrollment office for Staten Island is at 715 Ocean Terrace, Building A, 10301, (718) 420-5629.

William Morris School, IS 61

445 Castleton Avenue
Staten Island, NY 10301
(718) 727-8481

Admissions: Staten Island
High school choices: Curtis, Susan Wagner, McKee, Port Richmond
Grade levels: 6–8   **Test scores:** R ***, M ***
Enrollment: 1,359   **Ethnicity:** 29%W 40%B 25%H 6%A
Class size: 30   **Free lunch:** 52%

IS 61, a zoned neighborhood school, attracts children from across Staten Island to a special "magnet" program, offering classes in visual arts, drama, vocal music, instrumental music, dance, and journalism. A drama class puts on elaborate plays. Journalism students write their own literary magazine, put on their own television show, and publish the yearbook. Children may study violin, flute, or clarinet. There's a jazz band, a regular band, and an orchestra and classes in sculpture and drawing.

IS 61, with a well-clipped lawn shaded by pink flowering trees, looks more like a suburban school than what you'd expect in an urban neighborhood like New Brighton. On one side there are large Victorian and Tudor houses with mature shade trees. On the other there are public housing projects and a homeless shelter. The school draws students from both sides: the professional families and the working poor and unemployed.

In 2007, the school won a 3-year, $1.5 million federal magnet grant to enhance the arts programs and strengthen the three "academies" within the school. Principal Richard Gallo said that between 100 and 150 children from outside the zone enter 6th grade each year.

The school is divided into three academies, each serving about 450 children in grades 6–8. There are 14 classes in each grade, 3 of which are designated as honors. The school is not perfect: Several parents complained to us about fights and bullying. Gallo said the administration takes a tough stance on misbehavior, reflected in the school's high suspension rate. He points to the high attendance rate as a sign that children are happy to be in school.

Myra S. Barnes School, IS 24

225 Cleveland Avenue
Staten Island, NY 10308
(718) 356-4200
www.barnes-is24.com

Admissions: neighborhood school
High school choices: Tottenville, Wagner, New Dorp, Staten Island Tech
Grade levels: 6–8   **Test scores:** R ****, M ****
Enrollment: 1,557   **Ethnicity:** 83%W 3%B 10%H 4%A
Class size: 32   **Free lunch:** 20%

A gigantic neighborhood school in the mid-island community of Great Kills, IS 24 has a strong teaching staff, creative lessons, and an extensive program in the arts. Student projects are challenging, but they also offer some of the fun you might find in an elementary school. A 7th-grade science class re-created a dinosaur dig, beginning by assembling dinosaur models. In an 8th-grade Math A class (generally taught in high school), there was playful give-and-take between the teacher and the students at the same time serious work was being accomplished, graphing algebraic equations. In a 7th-grade social studies class, the students were studying the American Revolution from both the side of the colonists and the side of the British.

Each entering student chooses a "talent"—art, band, computers, media, performing arts, or stagecraft. The performing arts culminate in a spring musical, in which hundreds of students participate. In a stagecraft class, the students were busy poring over scripts of that year's production, *Grease*, as they prepared a list of required props. The school has an after-school robotics team that competes in citywide contests. There is a marching band, and students put out a number of publications, including a yearbook, a newspaper, and a literary journal.

In order to make the large school seem more personal, each grade is housed on a different floor, with its own assistant principal, guidance counselor, and dean. The school has an active PTA that organizes activities like a drive to collect toiletries, socks, and candies to send to soldiers in Iraq to thank them for their service.

Admission is limited to children living in the zone.

QUICK-REFERENCE GUIDE

Top Zoned Neighborhood Middle Schools

Manhattan

Simon Baruch Middle School, MS 104
Robert F. Wagner Middle School
PS/IS 187, Hudson Cliffs School

Bronx

David A. Stein Riverdale/Kingsbridge Academy, MS/HS 141
William Niles School, MS 118
City Island School, PS/IS 175

Brooklyn

Mary White Ovington School, IS 30

Queens

William H. Carr School, JHS 194
George J. Ryan Middle School, MS 216
Nathaniel Hawthorne School, MS 74
Marie Curie Middle School, MS 158
Louis Pasteur Middle School, MS 67
Irwin Altman School, MS 172

Staten Island

William Morris School, IS 61
Myra S. Barnes School, IS 24

CITYWIDE ADMISSIONS

Manhattan

New Explorations Into Science, Technology and Math
Institute for Collaborative Education
Professional Performing Arts School
Hunter College High School
Manhattan East School for Arts and Academics, MS 224
Young Women's Leadership School
Anderson School
Special Music School of America
Talented and Gifted School

Bronx

KIPP Academy Charter School

Brooklyn

Philippa Schuyler School, IS 383
David A. Boody School, IS 228

Mark Twain Intermediate School for the Gifted and Talented, IS 239
Bay Academy for Arts and Sciences, IS 98

Queens

Baccalaureate School for Global Education (Queens only)
Renaissance Charter School
Louis Armstrong Middle School, IS 227 (Queens only)

SINGLE-SEX PROGRAMS

Young Women's Leadership Schools, in Manhattan, Bronx, and Queens

ACCELERATED MATH PROGRAMS

New Explorations Into Science, Technology and Math
Hunter College High School
Delta Honors Program at Booker T. Washington School
Mark Twain Intermediate School for the Gifted and Talented, IS 239
Anderson School

SCIENCE OR TECHNOLOGY FOCUS

Salk School of Science
Computer School
Columbia Secondary School for Math, Science and Engineering
Urban Assembly School for Applied Math and Science
Math and Science Exploratory School, MS 447
David A. Boody School, IS 228
Mark Twain Intermediate School for the Gifted and Talented, IS 239

HUMANITIES FOCUS

Lab School for Collaborative Studies
Hunter College High School
Clinton School for Writers and Artists
William Alexander School, MS 51

DRAMA OR DANCE FOCUS

Professional Performing Arts School
Hunter College High School
Theatre Arts Production Company (TAPCO)
New Voices School for Academic and Creative Arts, MS 443
Mark Twain Intermediate School for the Gifted and Talented, IS 239

MUSIC FOCUS

Robert F. Wagner Middle School, MS 167
Hunter College High School
Manhattan East School for Arts and Academics, MS 224
Special Music School of America
David A. Boody School, IS 228
Mark Twain Intermediate School for the Gifted and Talented, IS 239

Fine Arts Focus

Clinton School for Writers and Artists
Manhattan East School for Arts and Academics, MS 224
New Voices School for Academic and Creative Arts, MS 443

Noteworthy Sports Programs

Simon Baruch Middle School, MS 104
Robert F. Wagner Middle School, MS 167
Frederick Douglass Academy
David A. Boody School, IS 228
Mark Twain Intermediate School for the Gifted and Talented, IS 239
Bay Academy for Arts and Sciences, IS 98
Louis Pasteur Middle School, MS 67
Irwin Altman Middle School, MS 172

Noteworthy Special Education

Manhattan

East Side Community High School
School of the Future
Lab School for Collaborative Studies

Brooklyn

Math and Science Exploratory School, MS 447
Brooklyn Secondary School for Collaborative Studies, MS 448
William Alexander School, MS 51
Brooklyn Studio Secondary School, IS 280
Christa McAuliffe School, IS 187

Queens

Renaissance Charter School
Louis Armstrong Middle School, IS 227
Robert Francis Kennedy Community Middle School, IS 250

K–8 Schools

Hudson Cliffs School, PS/IS 187
Special Music School of America
Future Leaders Institute Charter School
Harbor Science and Arts Charter School
City Island School, PS/IS 175

6–12 Schools

Manhattan

East Side Community High School (grades 7–12)
Institute for Collaborative Education
School of the Future
Lab School for Collaborative Studies

Professional Performing Arts School
Columbia Secondary School for Math, Science and Engineering
Frederick Douglass Academy

Bronx

David A. Stein Riverdale/Kingsbridge Academy, MS/HS 141
Bronx Preparatory Charter School (grades 5–12)
Theater Arts Production Company (TAPCO)
Bronx School for Law, Government and Justice (grades 7–12)
Bronx Academy of Letters

Brooklyn

Brooklyn Secondary School for Collaborative Studies, MS 448
Medgar Evers Preparatory School at Medgar Evers College
Brooklyn Studio Secondary School, IS 280

Queens

Baccalaureate School for Global Education (grades 7–12)
Queens School of Inquiry
East-West School of International Studies
Queens Gateway to Health Sciences Secondary School,
    JHS/HS 680 (grades 7–12)
World Journalism Preparatory: A College Board School

K–12 Schools

New Explorations Into Science, Technology and Math
Renaissance Charter School
Michael Petrides School

Charter Schools

Achievement First Bushwick Middle School
Bronx Preparatory Charter School
Future Leaders Institute Charter School
KIPP Academy Charter School
KIPP AMP Charter School
KIPP S.T.A.R. College Prep Charter School
Renaissance Charter School
Harbor Science and Arts Charter School

INDEX

ABOUT THE AUTHOR

Clara Hemphill, the founding editor of Insideschools.org at Advocates for Children, is a freelance writer, editor, and consultant. She is the author of *New York City's Best Public Elementary Schools* and *New York City's Best Public High Schools*. *New York* magazine called her one of the city's 200 most influential people for her work "empowering parents." She serves on the Public Advocate's Commission on School Governance, which is charged with making recommendations to the state legislature on the future of mayoral control of the schools.

She was a foreign correspondent for the Associated Press, a producer for CBS News in Rome, and a reporter and editorial writer for *New York Newsday*, where she shared the 1991 Pulitzer Prize for local reporting. Her work has appeared in *The New York Times*, *The New York Daily News*, and *Newsday*. She lives in Manhattan with her husband and two children, who both attend public school.

If you would like her to speak at your school or business, contact her through her website, http://clarahemphill.net

The Insideschools.org staff is made up of committed public school parents (and one grandparent), children's advocates, and journalists dedicating to improving the New York City public schools. Insideschools.org is a project of Advocates for Children. Contributors to this book include Judith Baum, Philissa Cramer, Nicole LaRosa, Catherine Man, Jacquie Wayans, Pamela Wheaton, Vanessa Witenko, Helen Zelon, and Laura Zingmond.